Garry Wills

SIMON & SCHUSTER
New York London Toronto Sydney Tokyo Singapore

Lincoln at Gettysburg

THE WORDS THAT REMADE AMERICA

SIMON & SCHUSTER
Simon & Schuster Building
Rockefeller Center
1230 Avenue of the Americas
New York, New York 10020

Designed by Carla Weise/Levavi & Levavi
Manufactured in the United States of America

1 3 5 7 9 10 8 6 4 2

Library of Congress Cataloging-in-Publication Data
Wills, Garry, date.
Lincoln at Gettysburg : the words that remade America / Garry
Wills.
p. cm.
Includes bibliographical references and indexes.
1. Lincoln, Abraham, 1809–1865. Gettysburg address. 2. Lincoln,
Abraham, 1809–1865—Oratory. I. Title.
E475.55.W54 1992
973.7′092—dc20   92–3546
CIP

ISBN: 0-671-76956-1

TO
GREAT EXPECTATIONS BOOKSTORE
SECOND HOME

Contents

Theodore Parker (c. 1852).
Transcendentalist, abolitionist,
celebrant of the Declaration of
Independence.

Daniel Webster
(c. 1825). Theorist
of constitutional
Union based on the
Declaration of
Independence.

Edward Everett (c. 1830). President of Harvard, founder of Mount Auburn, leader of the Greek Revival, and principal speaker at Gettysburg.

Greek funeral column (the Ilissos Stele), c. 330 B.C.E. The dead hero in a world of grieving men.

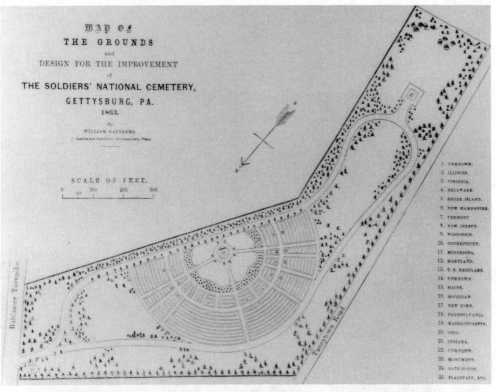

William Saunders, plan of Gettysburg Cemetery. The dead formed in ideal and equal ranks.

Mount Auburn. The living and the dead commune through Nature.

Lincoln with his young secretaries, John Nicolay and John Hay, who accompanied him to Gettysburg.

Key to Brief Citations

SW Abraham Lincoln, *Speeches and Writings*, edited by Don E. Fehrenbacher (Library of America, 1989), 2 volumes.

CW *The Collected Works of Abraham Lincoln*, edited by Roy P. Basler (Rutgers, 1955), 9 volumes.

Hay *Lincoln and the Civil War in the Diaries and Letters of John Hay*, edited by Tyler Bennett (Dodd, Mead, 1939).

Herndon-Weik *Herndon's Lincoln: The True Story of a Great Life*, by William H. Herndon and Jesse W. Weik (1889), in the Paul M. Angle edition for Da Capo (1942).

Hertz Emanuel Hertz, *The Hidden Lincoln: From the Letters and Papers of William H. Herndon* (Viking, 1938).

Parker Centenary edition *Works of Theodore Parker* (American Association, 1907), 15 volumes.

Cobbe edition *The Collected Works of Theodore Parker*, edited by Frances Power Cobbe (Tübner, 1863, 1864, 1865, 1867, 1871, 1875, 1876), 14 volumes.

TEXTS USED

SW is preferred to CW where the same text is in both, for Fehrenbacher's more up-to-date editing. I occasionally (lightly) modernize punctuation, for two reasons: (1) Many Lincoln texts—e.g., those of the Douglas debates—come only from newspapers, whose punctuation has no authority. (2) Even in Lincoln holographs, punctuation is for speaking purposes and/or nineteenth-century convention (e.g., commas before and after clauses), which is sometimes more confusing than clarifying. No other changes are made in the texts—which, however, are sometimes printed colometrically to bring out Lincoln's effort to balance rhetorical members *(cola)*. The text of the Gettysburg Address used here is Lincoln's final one, called the Bliss Text, printed as Appendix III D 2. For other versions, see Appendix I and the Little, Brown text at Appendix III D 1.

Prologue

BUSINESS IN GETTYSBURG

Not all the gallantry of General Lee can redeem, quite, his foolhardiness at Gettysburg. When in doubt, he charged into the cannon's mouth—by proxy. Ordered afterward to assemble the remains of that doomed assault, George Pickett told Lee that he *had* no force to reassemble. Lee offered Jefferson Davis his resignation.[1]

Nor did General Meade, Lee's opposite number, leave Gettysburg in glory. Though he lost as many troops as Lee, he still had men and ammunition to pursue a foe who was running, at the moment, out of both. For a week, while Lincoln urged him on in an agony of obliterative hope, Meade let the desperate Lee lie trapped by a flooded Potomac. When, at last, Lee ghosted himself over the river, Lincoln feared the North would not persevere with the war through the next year's election. Meade, too, offered his resignation.

Neither general's commander-in-chief could afford to accept these offers. Jefferson Davis had little but Lee's magic to rely on for repairing the effects of Lee's folly. (Romantic Southern fools cheered Lee wherever he rode on the day after his human sacrifice at Gettysburg.)[2] Lincoln, on the other side, could not even vent his feelings by sending Meade the anguished letter he wrote him (SW 2.478–79). A reprimand would ravel out the North's morale in long trains of recrimination. Both sides, leaving fifty thousand dead or wounded or missing behind them, had reason to maintain a large pattern of pretense about this battle—Lee pretending that he was not taking back to the South a broken cause, Meade that he not let the broken pieces fall through his fingers. It would have been hard to predict that Gettysburg, out of all this muddle, these missed chances, all the senseless deaths, would become a symbol of national purpose, pride, and ideals. Abraham Lincoln transformed the ugly reality into something rich and strange—and he did it with 272 words. The power of words has rarely been given a more compelling demonstration.

The residents of Gettysburg had little reason to feel satisfaction with the war machine that had churned up their lives. General Meade may have pursued Lee in slow motion; but he wired headquarters that "I cannot delay to pick up the debris of the battlefield."[3] That debris was mainly a matter of rotting horseflesh and manflesh—thousands of fermenting bodies, with gas-distended bellies, deliquescing in the July heat. For hygienic reasons, the five thousand horses (or mules) had to be consumed by fire, trading the smell of burning flesh for that of decaying flesh. Eight thousand human bodies were scattered over, or (barely) under, the ground.[4] Suffocating teams of soldiers, Confederate prisoners, and dragooned civilians slid the bodies beneath a minimal covering, as fast as possible—crudely posting the names of the Union dead with sketchy information on boards, not stopping to figure out what units the Confederate bodies had belonged to. It was work to be done hugger-mugger or not at all, fighting clustered bluebottle flies black on the earth, shoveling and retching by turns. The buzzards themselves had not stayed to share in this labor—days of incessant shelling had scattered them far off.[5]

Even after most bodies were lightly blanketed, the scene was repellent. A nurse shuddered at the all-too-visible "rise and swell of human bodies" in these furrows war had plowed. A soldier noticed how earth "gave" as he walked over the shallow trenches.[6] Householders had to plant around the bodies in their fields and gardens, or brace themselves to move the rotting corpses to another place. Soon these uneasy graves were being rifled by relatives looking for their dead—reburying other bodies they turned up, even more hastily (and less adequately) than had the first disposal crews. Three weeks after the battle, a prosperous Gettysburg banker, David Wills, reported to Pennsylvania's Governor Curtin: "In many instances arms and legs and sometimes heads protrude and my attention has been directed to several places where the hogs were actually rooting out the bodies and devouring them."[7]

Someone had to halt the unauthorized rummaging to identify the dead, had to deal with states preparing to send commissioners to reclaim their units' fallen men. An entrepreneur had bought land, foreseeing that demand for reburial would exceed space in the local cemetery. In the meanwhile, the whole area of Gettysburg—a town of only 2,500 inhabitants—was one makeshift burial ground, fetid and steaming. Andrew Curtin, the Republican governor of Pennsylvania, was facing a difficult reelection campaign. He must placate local feeling, deal with other states diplomatically, and raise the funds to deal with corpses that could go on killing by means of fouled streams or contaminating exhumations.

Curtin made the thirty-two-year-old David Wills his agent on the scene. Wills had studied law with Gettysburg's most prominent former citizen, Thaddeus Stevens, the radical Republican now representing Lancaster in Congress. Wills was a civic leader, and he owned the largest house on the town square.[8] He put an end to land speculation for the burial, and formed an interstate commission to collect funds for the cleansing of Gettysburg's bloodied fields. The states were to be assessed according to their representation in Congress. To charge them by the actual

21

number of each state's dead would be a time-consuming and complicated process, waiting on identification of each corpse, on the division of costs for those who could not be identified, and on the fixing of per-body rates for exhumation, identification, and reinterment.

Wills put up for bids the contract to rebury the bodies—out of thirty-four competitors, the high bid was eight dollars per corpse, the winning bid was $1.59. The federal government was asked to ship in the thousands of caskets needed, courtesy of the War Department. All other costs were handled by the interstate commission. Wills took title to seventeen acres for the new cemetery in the name of Pennsylvania.[9]

The first meeting of the interstate commission was held in Altoona, where Wills learned that a "rural architect" named William Saunders was the perfect man to create the cemetery's layout. Saunders, trained in Scotland and employed by the Department of Agriculture, was steeped in the ideals of the "rural cemetery" movement, which he adapted to military and political ideals. By considerable ingenuity in grading the cemetery's incline, and by arranging the graves in great curving ranks, he avoided preferential treatment of states or inequality in the ranks of the fallen.

Burial by states posed a problem. Saunders did not know how many bodies would be found for each state. His allocation of spaces had to be provisional, shifting as the bodies were processed. That processing was supposed to be pushed forward at the rate of a hundred bodies a day—a rate that would allow safe reburial between the first frost and the ground's freezing. But it was hard to keep up that pace (the task would not be completed till the next spring). First, the Confederate bodies turned up had to be identified as such and reburied deeper down. It was not always easy to make even this identification, since some needy Confederate troops were wearing lost or captured Union pants, blankets, or other equipment when they died. Wills's agent in the matter swore that no enemy tainted the ground where martyrs to the Union lay, but it is now recognized that some Southern bodies were mistakenly included.

Even Northern soldiers were hard to sort into their proper units. Those whose states could not be ascertained—even though their names could—were buried with the "unknown." Some bodies had been stripped of belongings before their first hasty burial. The possessions that survived—mainly Bibles, but also dental bridges and other personal effects—had to be catalogued and labeled for safekeeping, in case relatives sought them. Separated body parts were often hard to assign in the mass-burial trenches. Loose clothing and blankets were reburied to prevent attempts to use contaminated goods. Then the caskets were filled, loaded on carts, taken to the new site, and distributed by state according to Saunders's allotment of space. Finally these bodies—tumbled about in the confusion of war, already buried once or several times, pawed over by foraging humans or beasts, unearthed again and ticketed—rejoined their ranks to lie in the deceptively calm order prepared for them.

Wills meant to dedicate the ground that would hold them even before the corpses were moved. He felt the need for artful words to sweeten the poisoned air of Gettysburg. He asked the principal wordsmiths of his time to join this effort—Longfellow, Whittier, Bryant.[10] All three poets, each for his own reason, found their muse unbiddable. But Wills was not terribly disappointed. The normal purgative for such occasions was a large-scale solemn act of oratory, a kind of performance art with great power over audiences in the middle of the nineteenth century. Some later accounts would emphasize the length of the main speech at the Gettysburg dedication, as if that were an ordeal or an imposition on the audience. But a talk of several hours was customary and expected then—much like the length and pacing

of a modern rock concert. The crowds that heard Lincoln debate
Stephen Douglas in 1858, through three-hour engagements, were
delighted to hear Daniel Webster and other orators of the day
recite carefully composed paragraphs that filled two hours at the
least.

The champion at such declamatory occasions, after the
death of Webster, was Webster's friend Edward Everett. Everett
was that rare thing, a scholar and Ivy-League diplomat who could
hold mass audiences in thrall. His voice, diction, and gestures
were successfully dramatic, and he always performed his carefully written text, no matter how long, from memory. Everett was
the inevitable choice for Wills, the indispensable component in
his scheme for the cemetery's consecration. Battlefields were
something of a specialty with Everett—he had augmented the
fame of Lexington and Concord and Bunker Hill by his oratory
at those revolutionary sites. Simply to have him speak Gettysburg would add this field to the sacred roll of names from the
founders' battles.

Everett was invited, on September 23, to appear October 23.
That would leave all of November for filling the graves. But a
month was not sufficient time for Everett to spend on his customary preparation for a major speech. He did careful research on
the battles he was commemorating—a task made difficult, in this
case, by the fact that official accounts of the engagement were just
appearing. Everett would have to make his own inquiries. He
could not be ready before November 19. Wills seized on that
earliest moment, though it destroyed the reburial schedule that
had been arranged to follow on the October dedication. He decided to move up the reburial, beginning it in October, hoping
to finish by November 19.

The careful negotiations with Everett form a contrast, more
surprising to us than to contemporaries, with the casual invitation to President Lincoln, issued two months later as part of a

general call for the federal Cabinet and other celebrities to join
in what was essentially a ceremony of the participating states.
Frank Klement has argued that Lincoln must have been infor-
mally asked to attend, through his friend and bodyguard, Ward
Lamon, by October 30, when he told a correspondent he meant
to be present.[11] But even that looks to us like a rather late and
lukewarm way of including the commander-in-chief of the men
being memorialized.

No insult was intended. Federal responsibility or participation was not assumed, then, in state activities. And Lincoln took
no offense. Though specifically invited to deliver only "a few
appropriate remarks" to open the cemetery, he meant to use this
opportunity. The partly mythical victory of Gettysburg was important to his administration's war propaganda. (There were,
even now, few enough victories to boast of.) Beyond that, the
impending election in Pennsylvania could vitally affect his own
re-election, and he was working to unite the rival Republican
factions of Governor Curtin and Simon Cameron. He knew, as
well, that most of the state governors would be attending or
sending important aides—his own bodyguard, Lamon, who was
acting as chief marshal organizing the affair, had alerted him to
the scale the event had assumed, with "tremendous crowds"
expected. This was a classical situation for political fence-mend-
ing and intelligence-gathering. Lincoln would take with him
aides who circulated on the scene and brought back their find-
ings. Lamon himself had been invited to police the event because
he had a cluster of friends in Pennsylvania politics, including
some close to Governor Curtin, a man infuriated when Lincoln
overrode his opposition to Cameron's earlier appointment as
secretary of war.

Lincoln also knew the power of his rhetoric to define war
aims. He was seeking occasions to use his words outside the
normal round of proclamations and reports to Congress. His

determination not only to be present but to speak is seen in the way he overrode staff scheduling for the trip. Secretary of War Stanton had arranged for a 6:00 A.M. train to take him eighty miles to the noontime affair in Gettysburg. But Lincoln was familiar enough, by now, with military movement to appreciate what Clausewitz calls "friction" in the disposal of forces—the margin for error that must always be built into planning. Lamon would have informed Lincoln about the prospect for muddle on the nineteenth. State delegations, civic organizations, military bands and units, were planning to charter trains and clog the roads, bringing at least ten thousand people to a town with poor resources for feeding and sheltering crowds (especially if the weather turned bad). So Lincoln countermanded Stanton's plan:

> I do not like this arrangement. I do not wish to so go that by the slightest accident we fail entirely, and, at the best, the whole to be a mere breathless running of the gauntlet. . . . [CW 7.16]

If Lincoln had not changed the schedule, he would very likely not have given his talk. Even on the day before, his trip to Gettysburg took six hours, with transfers in Baltimore and at Hanover Junction. Governor Curtin, starting from Harrisburg (thirty miles away) with seven other governors as his guests, was embarrassed by breakdowns and delays that made them miss the dinner at David Wills's house. They had gathered at two o'clock in the afternoon, started at five, and arrived at eleven. Governor Ramsey of Minnesota started a week before the dedication and was stranded, at 4:00 A.M. on the day of delivery, in Hanover Junction with "no means of getting up to Gettysburg."[12] Lincoln kept his resolution to leave a day early even when he realized that his wife was hysterical over one son's illness soon after the death of another son. The President had important business in Gettysburg.

For a man so determined to get there (and so ready to invite others to attend), Lincoln seems—in familiar accounts—rather cavalier about preparing what he would say in Gettysburg. The silly but persistent myth is that he jotted his brief remarks on the back of an envelope. Better-attested accounts have him considering it on the way to a photographer's shop in Washington, writing it on a piece of cardboard as the train took him on the eighty-mile trip, penciling it in David Wills's house on the night before the dedication, writing it in that house on the morning of the day he had to deliver it, or even composing it in his head as Everett spoke, before Lincoln rose to follow him.

These recollections, recorded at various times after the speech was delivered and won fame, reflect two concerns on the part of those expressing them. They reveal an understandable pride in participation at the historic occasion. It was not enough for those who treasured their day at Gettysburg to have heard Lincoln speak—a privilege they shared with anywhere from ten to twenty thousand other people, and an experience that lasted no more than three minutes. They wanted to be intimate with the gestation of that extraordinary speech, watching the pen or pencil move under the inspiration of the moment.

That is the other emphasis in these accounts—that it *was* a product of the moment, struck off as Lincoln moved under destiny's guidance. Inspiration was shed on him in the presence of others. The contrast with Everett's long labors of preparation is always implied. Research, learning, the student's lamp—none of these were needed by Lincoln, whose unsummoned muse was prompting him, a democratic muse unacquainted with the library. Lightning struck, and each of our informants was there when it struck.

The trouble with these accounts is that the lightning strikes too often, as if it could not get the work done on its first attempt. It hits Lincoln on the train, in his room, at night, in the morning.

If the persistent inspiration was treating him this way, he should have been short-circuited, not inspired, by the time he spoke.

These mythical accounts are badly out of character for Lincoln, who composed his speeches thoughtfully. His law partner, William Herndon, observing Lincoln's careful preparation of cases, records that he was a slow writer, who liked to sort out his points and tighten his logic and his phrasing. That is the process vouched for in every other case of Lincoln's memorable public statements.[13] It is impossible to imagine him leaving his speech at Gettysburg to the last moment. He knew he would be busy on the train and at the site—important political guests were with him from his departure, and more joined him at Baltimore, full of talk about the war, elections, and policy. In Gettysburg he would be entertained at David Wills's house, with Everett and other important guests. State delegations would want a word with him. He hoped for a quick tour of the battle site (a hope fulfilled early on the nineteenth). He could not count on any time for the concentration he required when weighing his words.

In fact, two people testified that Lincoln's speech was mainly composed in Washington, before he left for Gettysburg— though these reports, like all later ones describing this speech's composition, are themselves suspect. Lamon claims that Lincoln read him substantially the text that was given "a day or two before the dedication." But Lamon's remarks are notoriously imaginative, and he was busy in Gettysburg from November 13 to 16. He made a swift trip back to Washington on the sixteenth to collect his marshals, instruct them, and depart again the next morning. His testimony here, as elsewhere, does not have much weight.[14]

Noah Brooks, Lincoln's journalist friend, claims he talked with Lincoln on November 15, when Lincoln told him he had written his speech "over two or three times"—but Brooks also said that Lincoln was carrying galleys of Everett's speech set in type for later printing by the Boston *Journal*. In fact, the Everett speech was not set until November 14, and then by the Boston *Daily Advertiser*, too far away for Lincoln to get such an early copy.[15]

A more reliable indication of Lincoln's preparation in Washington is provided by his consultation with the cemetery's landscaper. The President knew (presumably from talks with Lamon) that William Saunders of the Agriculture Department had conceived the grounds' plan and he called Saunders to the White House.

> A few days before the dedication of the grounds, President Lincoln sent word to me that he desired me to call at his office on the evening of the 17th [Tuesday], and take with me the plan of the cemetery. I was on hand at the appointed time, and spread the plan on his office table. He took much interest in it, asked about its surroundings, about Culp's Hill, Round Top, etc., and seemed familiar with the topography of the place although he had never been there. He was much pleased with the method of the graves, said it differed from the ordinary cemetery, and, after I had explained the reasons, said it was an advisable and benefitting arrangement.[16]

Lincoln no doubt retained some knowledge of the battle places from following reports during and after the three days of fighting there. Lamon, too, may have sketched the general scene as part of his "advancing" preparations over several weeks. But Lincoln's desire to have specific knowledge of the cemetery's features proves that he was not relying solely on a lightning stroke of genius to tell him what to say when he arrived on the spot.

Saunders's pride in his plan may color his reporting of Lincoln's reaction to it. But it is not unlikely that Lincoln approved of the careful way the graves were arranged so that (in

Saunders's words) "the position of each [state] lot, and indeed of each interment, is relatively of equal importance." Lincoln would soon claim that these men died to vindicate "the proposition that all men are created equal." He would not, in his own speech, name a single individual, or distinguish officers from enlisted men (as Everett did in his tribute). In all this, his speech and Saunders's artifact are in aesthetic harmony. Each expressed the values of the other.

Lincoln's train arrived toward dusk in Gettysburg. There were still coffins stacked at the station for completing the reburials. Wills and Everett met him and escorted him the two blocks to the Wills home, where dinner was waiting, along with several dozen other distinguished guests. Lincoln's black servant, William Slade, took his luggage to the second-story room where he would stay that night.[17] It looked out on the square and the courthouse, with Thaddeus Stevens's old law office across the way.

Everett was already in residence at the Wills house, and Governor Curtin's late arrival led Wills to suggest that the two men share a bed. The governor thought he could find another house to receive him, though lodgings were so overcrowded that Everett said in his diary that "the fear of having the Executive of Pennsylvania tumble in upon me kept me awake until one." Everett's daughter was sleeping with two other women, whose bed broke under their weight.[18] William Saunders, who would have an honored place on the platform the next day, could find no bed and had to sleep sitting up in a crowded parlor.

It is likely that Everett, who had the galleys of his speech with him, showed them to Lincoln that night—Emerson, Everett's former student, said he liked for others to know his texts beforehand, so fresh did he make them by the magic of his delivery. Noah Brooks, who mistook the *time* when Everett showed Lincoln his speech, probably gave the right *reason*—so

that Lincoln would not be embarrassed by any inadvertent correspondences or unintended differences.[19]

Lincoln greeted Curtin after his late arrival, and was otherwise interrupted during the night. Bands and serenades were
going through the crowded square under his window. One group
asked him to speak, and the newspaper reports his words:

> I appear before you, fellow citizens, merely to thank you for this
> compliment. The inference is a very fair one that you would hear
> me, for a little while at least, were I to commence to make a
> speech. I do not appear before you for the purpose of doing so,
> and for several substantial reasons. The most substantial of these
> is that I have no speech to make. [Laughter.] In my position it is
> somewhat important that I should not say foolish things. [Inter-
> ruption: If you can help it!] It very often happens that the only
> way to help it is to say nothing at all. [Laughter.] Believing that
> is my present condition this evening, I must beg of you to excuse
> me from addressing you further. [CW 7.16–17]

This displays Lincoln's normal reluctance to improvise words as
president. John Hay, watching the scene in the crowd, noted in
his diary: "The President appeared at the door and said half a
dozen words meaning nothing & went in" (p. 120).

Serenaders got a lengthier and carefully written speech from
Lincoln's secretary of state, William Seward, staying next door at
Mr. Harper's house—Seward later asked that his evening speech
be printed along with those spoken the next day on the platform.
After Seward's own effort, Lincoln went to visit him, carrying
papers. It is assumed that Lincoln wanted to go over his talk with
Seward, who had helped him polish the First Inaugural. But even
that is not certain. Lincoln had received several telegrams since
his arrival, and there are always things for a president to discuss
with his secretary of state, especially when the two have just been

traveling and dining with politicians of their party whom they have not seen in some time.

Lincoln's personal secretaries, John Hay and John Nicolay, were busy sounding out the politicians around town from one drinking spot to another. Hay heard the Pennsylvania party chairman give an account of the conversation he had held with the President on the train—it was very different from the one Hay had listened to at the time. The next day he would wonder at "the intimate, jovial relations that exist between men that hate and despise each other as cordially as do these Pennsylvania politicians" (p. 122).

Early in the morning, Lincoln and Seward took a carriage ride to the battle sites. By eleven, Ward Lamon and his specially uniformed marshals were assigning horses to the various dignitaries (carriages would have clogged the site too much). The march was less than a mile, but Lamon had brought thirty horses into town, to join the hundred Wills supplied, for honoring the officials present.

Lincoln sat his horse gracefully (to the surprise of some), and looked meditative during the long wait while marshals tried to coax into line important people more concerned with their dignity than the President was with his. Lincoln was still wearing a mourning band on his hat for his dead son. He also wore white gauntlets, which made his large hands on the reins dramatic by contrast with his otherwise black attire. David Wills had gambled on the weather when he let Everett delay this outdoor ceremony; but the pumpkin time, good for moving corpses, turned out to be just as good for listening to long speeches under a bright November sky.

Everett had gone out earlier, by carriage, to prepare himself in the special tent he asked for near the platform. At sixty-nine, he had kidney trouble and needed to relieve himself just before and after the three-hour ceremony. (He had put his problem so

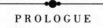

delicately that his hosts did not realize that he meant to be left alone in the tent; but he finally coaxed them out.) Everett mounted the platform at the last moment, after most of the others had arrived.

Those on the raised platform were hemmed close in by standing crowds. When it became clear that the numbers might approach twenty thousand, the platform was set at some distance from the burial operations. Only a third of the expected bodies had been buried, and those under fresh mounds. Other graves were readied for the bodies that arrived in irregular order (some from this state, some from that), making it impossible to complete one section at a time. The whole burial site was incomplete. Marshals tried to keep the milling thousands out of the work in progress.[20]

Everett, as usual, had neatly placed his thick text on a little table before him—and then ostentatiously refused to look at it. He was able to indicate with gestures the sites of the battle's progress visible from where he stood. He excoriated the rebels for their atrocities, implicitly justifying the fact that some Confederate skeletons were still unburied, lying in the clefts of Devil's Den under rocks and autumn leaves. Two days earlier, Everett had been shown around the field, and places were pointed out where the bodies lay. His speech, for good or ill, would pick its way through the carnage.[21]

As a former secretary of state, Everett had many sources, in and outside government, for the information he had gathered so diligently. Lincoln no doubt watched closely how the audience responded to passages that absolved Meade of blame for letting Lee escape. The setting of the battle in a larger logic of campaigns had an immediacy for those on the scene that we cannot recover. Everett's familiarity with the details was flattering to the local audience, which nonetheless had things to learn from this shapely presentation of the whole three days' action. This was like a modern "docudrama" on television, telling the story of recent events on the basis of investigative reporting. We badly misread the evidence if we think Everett failed to work his customary magic. The best witnesses on the scene—Nicolay and Hay, with their professional interest in good prose and good theater—praised Everett at the time and ever after. He received more attention in their biography's chapter on Gettysburg than did their own boss.

Lincoln had no trouble appreciating Everett's brand of rhetoric. It was the kind he had grown up admiring and had imitated himself. He always held that Webster's flowery reply to Hayne was "the grandest specimen of American oratory"—though he probably did not realize that Everett had helped Webster revise that speech's famous conclusion.[22] Nonetheless, Lincoln recognized Webster's constitutional views in Everett's speech, and rightly said, afterward, that Everett had added a deft new argument of his own (SW 2.537).

When Lincoln rose, it was with a sheet or two, from which he read—as had the minister who offered the invocation.[23] Lincoln's three minutes would, ever after, be obsessively contrasted with Everett's two hours in accounts of this day. It is even claimed that Lincoln disconcerted the crowd with his abrupt performance, so that people did not know how to respond ("Was that *all?*"). Myth tells of a poor photographer making leisurely arrangements to take Lincoln's picture, expecting him to be there for some time. But it is useful to look at the relevant part of the program as Wills's committee printed it:

Music, by BIRGFIELD's Band.
Prayer, by REV. T. H. STOCKTON, D.D.
Music, by the Marine Band.
Oration, by Hon. EDWARD EVERETT.
Music, Hymn composed by B. B. FRENCH, Esq.

Dedicatory Remarks, by the PRESIDENT OF THE UNITED STATES.
Dirge, sung by Choir selected for the occasion.
Benediction, by REV. H. L. BAUGHER, D.D.

There was only one "oration" announced or desired here. Though we call Lincoln's text *the* Gettysburg Address, that title clearly belongs to Everett. Lincoln's contribution, labeled "remarks," was intended to make the dedication formal (somewhat like ribbon-cutting at modern "openings"). Lincoln was not expected to speak at length, any more than Reverend Stockton was (though Stockton's prayer *is* four times the length of the President's remarks). In fact, Lincoln's contribution was as ancillary to Everett's as were those of Reverend Baugher and B. B. French (Lamon's friend, who rushed in where Longfellow, Bryant, and Whittier feared to tread). Lincoln's text had about the same number of words as French's, and twice the number of Dr. Baugher's. It is instructive to look at *The New York Times'* coverage of the events in Gettysburg. It ranked Lincoln's talk, about which it had good things to say, with two given the night before in response to roving serenaders, rather than with Everett's, which was kept in a category of its own.[24] The headline reads:

IMMENSE NUMBERS OF VISITORS
ORATION BY HON. EDWARD EVERETT—SPEECHES OF
PRESIDENT LINCOLN, MR. SEWARD AND
GOVERNOR SEYMOUR

Lincoln was briefer, even, than New York's Governor Seymour had been the night before; but comparison with him was more natural at the time than with the designated orator of the day. A contrast of length with Everett's talk raises a false issue. Lincoln's text *is* startlingly brief for what it accomplished, but that would be equally true if Everett had spoken for a shorter time or had not spoken at all.

The contrast in other ways was strong. Everett's voice was sweet and expertly modulated; Lincoln's was high to the point of shrillness, and his Kentucky accent offended some Eastern sensibilities. But Lincoln derived an advantage from his high tenor voice—carrying power. If there is agreement on any one aspect of Lincoln's delivery, at Gettysburg and elsewhere, it is his audibility.[25] Modern impersonators of Lincoln, like Walter Huston, Raymond Massey, Henry Fonda, and the various actors who give voice to Disneyland animations of the President, bring him before us as a baritone, which is considered a more manly or heroic voice—though both the Roosevelt presidents of our century were tenors. What should not be forgotten is that Lincoln was himself an actor, an expert raconteur and mimic, and one who spent hours reading speeches out of Shakespeare to any willing (and some unwilling) audiences.[26] He knew a good deal about rhythmic delivery and meaningful inflections. John Hay, who had submitted to many of those Shakespeare readings, gave high marks to his boss's performance at Gettysburg. He put in his diary at the time that "the President, in a fine, free way, with more grace than is his wont, said his half dozen words of consecration" (p. 121). Lincoln's text was polished, his delivery emphatic, he was interrupted by applause five times. Read in a slow, clear way to the farthest listeners, the speech would take about three minutes. It is quite true that the audience did not take in all that happened in that short time—we are still trying to weigh the consequences of that amazing performance. But the myth that Lincoln was disappointed in the result—that he told the unreliable Lamon that his speech, like a bad plow, "won't scour"—has no basis.[27] He had done what he wanted to do, and Hay shared the pride his superior took in an important occasion put to good use.

At the least, Lincoln had far surpassed David Wills's hope for words to disinfect the air of Gettysburg. The tragedy of macerated bodies, the many bloody and ignoble aspects of this inconclusive encounter, are transfigured in Lincoln's rhetoric, where the physical residue of battle is volatilized as the product of an experiment *testing* whether a government can maintain the *proposition* of equality. The stakes of the three days' butchery are made intellectual, with abstract truths being vindicated. Despite verbal gestures to "that" battle and the men who died "here," there are no particulars mentioned by Lincoln—no names of men or sites or units, or even of sides (the Southerners are part of the "experiment," not foes mentioned in anger or rebuke). Everett succeeded with his audience by being thoroughly immersed in the details of the event he was celebrating. Lincoln eschews all local emphasis. His speech hovers far above the carnage. He lifts the battle to a level of abstraction that purges it of grosser matter—even "earth" is mentioned as the thing from which the tested form of government shall not perish. More than William Saunders himself, Lincoln has aligned the dead in ranks of an ideal order. The nightmare realities have been etherealized in the crucible of his language.

But that was just the beginning of this complex transformation. Lincoln did for the whole Civil War what he accomplished for the single battlefield. He has prescinded from messy squabbles over constitutionality, sectionalism, property, states. Slavery is not mentioned, any more than Gettysburg is. The discussion is driven back and back, beyond the historical particulars, to great ideals that are made to grapple naked in an airy battle of the mind. Lincoln derives a new, a transcendental, significance from this bloody episode. Both North and South strove to win the battle for *interpreting* Gettysburg as soon as the physical battle had ended. Lincoln is after even larger game—he means to "win" the whole Civil War in ideological terms as well as military ones.

And he will succeed: the Civil War *is*, to most Americans, what Lincoln wanted it to *mean*. Words had to complete the work of the guns.

Lincoln is here not only to sweeten the air of Gettysburg, but to clear the infected atmosphere of American history itself, tainted with official sins and inherited guilt. He would cleanse the Constitution—not, as William Lloyd Garrison had, by burning an instrument that countenanced slavery. He altered the document from within, by appeal from its letter to the spirit, subtly changing the recalcitrant stuff of that legal compromise, bringing it to its own indictment. By implicitly doing this, he performed one of the most daring acts of open-air sleight-of-hand ever witnessed by the unsuspecting. Everyone in that vast throng of thousands was having his or her intellectual pocket picked. The crowd departed with a new thing in its ideological luggage, that new constitution Lincoln had substituted for the one they brought there with them. They walked off, from those curving graves on the hillside, under a changed sky, into a different America. Lincoln had revolutionized the Revolution, giving people a new past to live with that would change their future indefinitely.

Some people, looking on from a distance, saw that a giant (if benign) swindle had been performed. The Chicago *Times* quoted the letter of the Constitution to Lincoln—noting its lack of reference to equality, its tolerance of slavery—and said that Lincoln was betraying the instrument he was on oath to defend, traducing the men who *died* for the letter of that fundamental law:

> It was to uphold this constitution, and the Union created by it, that our officers and soldiers gave their lives at Gettysburg. How dare he, then, standing on their graves, misstate the cause for which they died, and libel the statesmen who founded the govern-

ment? They were men possessing too much self-respect to declare that negroes were their equals, or were entitled to equal privileges.[28]

Heirs to this outrage still attack Lincoln for subverting the Constitution at Gettysburg—suicidally frank conservatives like M. E. Bradford or the late Willmoore Kendall.[29] But most conservatives are understandably unwilling to challenge a statement now so hallowed, so literally sacrosanct, as Lincoln's clever assault on the constitutional past.[30] They would rather hope or pretend, with some literary critics, that Lincoln's emotionally moving address had no discernible intellectual content, that "the sequence of ideas is commonplace to the point of banality, the ordinary coin of funereal oratory."[31]

People like Kendall and the Chicago *Times* editors might have wished this were true, but they knew better. They recognized the audacity of Lincoln's undertaking. Kendall rightly says Lincoln undertook a new founding of the nation, to correct things felt to be imperfect in the founders' own achievement.

> Abraham Lincoln and, in considerable degree, the authors of the post-civil-war amendments, attempted a new act of founding, involving concretely a startling new interpretation of that principle of the founders which declared that "all men are created equal."[32]

Edwin Meese and other "original intent" conservatives also want to go back before the Civil War amendments (particularly the Fourteenth) to the original founders. Their job would be comparatively easy if they did not have to work against the values created by the Gettysburg Address. Its deceptively simple-sounding phrases appeal to Americans in ways that Lincoln had perfected in his debates over the Constitution during the 1850s.

During that time Lincoln found the language, the imagery, the myths that are given their best and briefest embodiment at Gettysburg. In order to penetrate the mystery of his "refounding" act, we must study all the elements of that stunning verbal coup. Without Lincoln's knowing it himself, all his prior literary, intellectual, and political labors had prepared him for the intellectual revolution contained in those fateful 272 words.[33]

Oratory of the
Greek Revival

James Hurt says that Lincoln used "the ordinary coin of funeral oratory" at Gettysburg.[1] Insofar as there was a standard coinage of funeral tribute, Pericles struck the master coin 2,394 years before Lincoln spoke. At the end of the first year of Athens' war with Sparta, Pericles gave a speech over the ashes of the Athenians who had fallen in that year. Thucydides put a version of that speech in his history of the Peloponnesian War, and it became the most famous oration of its kind, a model endlessly copied, praised, and cited—especially in the early nineteenth century, during America's Greek Revival.

Edward Everett lost no time referring to that speech at Gettysburg. He opened his talk with a detailed description of the annual funeral rite at which Pericles had spoken, comparing it point for point with the ceremony for the Union dead. Both rites involved *reburial*. Athenian soldiers or sailors were cremated where they fell, then their ashes were returned to Athens and buried, together, on the annual day of military tribute. They were buried by tribe, with a special place for those whose tribes could not be identified—as the Union dead were buried by states, except for those "unknown soldiers" who had their own special place.

But at Gettysburg the reburial was still at the battle site. The ancient parallel for this, Everett was learned enough to know, was the Battle of Marathon (490 B.C.E.), after which the Athenians were buried on the spot where they had saved Hellas from the Persians.

These references, common enough at the time, all had a special meaning for Everett, considered by some the new Pericles for a young democracy of the Western world. Ralph Waldo Emerson, who studied Greek at Harvard in Everett's classroom, was emphatic in his teacher's praise: "There was an influence on the young from the genius of Everett which was almost comparable to that of Pericles in Athens."[2]

America as a second Athens was an idea whose moment had come in the nineteenth century. This nation's founders first looked to Rome, not to Greece, for their model. Like most men of the eighteenth century, they thought of Athens as ruled by mobs. If any Greek city was admired, it was Sparta, whose discipline inspired the severe moralists of the early Roman republic. The "mixed government" of Rome—not Athens' direct democracy—was the model invoked in debates over the proper constitution for the United States.[3] The great republican of the new era, George Washington, was regularly referred to as a modern Cincinnatus, after the Roman who left the plow to serve the republic and then returned to his fields, relinquishing power.[4] When Jefferson laid out the plan for his University of Virginia, he fashioned everything to Roman architectural standards.

All this changed very rapidly as the eighteenth turned to the nineteenth century. Archaeology in Greece brought the ancient democracy to mind just as modern Greece began its struggle for freedom from the Turks. Greece would prove as important to the romantic movement as Rome had been to the Augustan age.[5] Byron died as a military participant in the war for Greek liberty. Shelley wrote a *Prometheus*. Keats rhapsodized on a Grecian urn. Hölderlin and the German romantics composed plays and poems on Greek themes.[6] Architects looked to the Parthenon now, not the Pantheon. (The Elgin Marbles, taken from the Parthenon, had been moved to London by 1806.) It is significant of this changed taste that Washington completed his inherited home (as Jefferson conceived his own house) in the form of a Roman villa, while Lincoln's additions to the house he purchased were in the Greek Revival style. This was a "democratic" style in the eyes of Lincoln's contemporaries:

> Thomas Jefferson's brief and highly personal Roman Revival was the product of an individual mind; the Greek Revival was the product of a popular sentiment. The fact that it became expressive for the whole of American society, from the erudite to the untutored, from the capital to the village, from the city house to the farm, gave it a national independence and set it apart from the architecture of Europe in a way and to a degree that American builders had never before achieved. Indeed, at no time in the history of Western man had a single stylistic form, however sentimentally conceived, been so spontaneously accepted by a total society. It is in this sense that the Greek Revival must be understood as America's first national style of architecture.[7]

Everett played a key role in America's Greek Revival. Harvard established its new chair of ancient Greek studies for him. He had sped through Harvard at the top of his class, completed his divinity studies, and been appointed to the prestigious Brattle

Street pulpit before he was twenty. His promise as a scholar made Harvard call him back from the pulpit to the classroom. But first the university subsidized his studies in Germany, where he was the first American to earn his doctorate at a center of the new philology (in 1817, from Göttingen). While Everett was abroad, he traveled widely and met the leaders of the romantic age, from Goethe to Byron.[8] He went to Greece, to walk over the battlefields where the first democracy of the West won its freedom. He returned to America convinced that a new Athens was rising here.

This was a vision he found it hard to keep alive while teaching teenagers their Greek verb forms.[9] His earlier success in the pulpit made him think he could accomplish in the secular sphere what the ancient orators had in the Greek marketplace, groves, and public cemetery (Agora, Akademy, and Kerameikos). He was confirmed in this sense of vocation in 1825, the year of Lafayette's visit to America. That return occasioned one of this country's great outpourings of romantic feeling. Here was a warrior from the age of General Washington surviving into the age of Byron. His appearances prompted rallies for Greek independence—a favorite cause of Everett.[10] At Cambridge, Lafayette was treated to a long oration by Everett, devoted to the role of literature in America. The response was almost as great as the response to the speech Daniel Webster addressed to Lafayette, across the Charles River, in Boston. Everett's own talk propelled him into the political arena—as congressman, Massachusetts governor, minister to the Court of St. James's in London, senator (after an interval as president of Harvard), and secretary of state. But, all along, his public lecturing remained the most satisfying part of what he considered an essentially pedagogic career. Webster's orations were an offshoot of his role as statesman and legislator; but Everett, in effect, ran for and held office in order to attract an audience for his speeches.

He was always a teacher. He had merely traded the class-room for the stump. And his students followed him out into this wider world. Emerson made the public lecture his own main art form, launching his career with the 1837 address on the modern scholar as Everett had launched himself in the 1825 talk on American letters. Everett was a model to Emerson and the other Transcendentalists because he was so clearly a scholar before he became a popularizer of democratic ideals. Emerson's experience in Everett's classroom gave an entirely new direction to his life:

> Germany had created [literary] criticism in vain for us until 1820, when Edward Everett returned from his five years in Europe, and brought to Cambridge his rich results, which no one was so fitted by natural grace and the splendor of his rhetoric to introduce and recommend. He made us for the first time acquainted with [Friedrich August] Wolf's theory of the Homeric writings, with the criticism of [Heinrich] Heine. The novelty of the learning lost nothing in the skill and genius of its interpreter, and the rudest undergraduate found a new morning opening to him in the lecture room at Harvard.[11]

Emerson's mention of the philologist Wolf struck an ominous note for orthodox Calvinists of New England. By tracing multiple authorship in Homer, Wolf had encouraged a similar approach to the other main text of a "heroic age," calling into question Moses's authorship of the Pentateuch.[12] Transcendentalists like Emerson and Theodore Parker would abandon or alter Christian tenets to accommodate this "higher criticism."[13] The other name Emerson mentioned, that of the lyric poet Heine, suggests a different side of Homer, one that would also be important in the romantic period. Homer, who was thought of as wild and natural, held a relation to the polished Roman poets, like Virgil, roughly resembling that of Wordsworth to Alexander Pope.[14]

Everett's immense prestige sent others to Göttingen for German learning, including the historian George Bancroft, whose lecture on progress Lincoln would later imitate. Bancroft intended to study ancient languages at Göttingen, for interpreting the Bible, but he feared no pulpit would welcome a "higher critic." He moved on to Berlin, where he acquired his personal Transcendentalism from the philosopher Friedrich Schleiermacher.[15] But his main interest was Greek history. After his return to America, he set up a preparatory school to imitate on our soil the methods of educational reformer J. H. Pestalozzi, which he had observed in the German Gymnasium. During his teaching years, he translated from German some works of his Göttingen professor Arnold H. L. Heeren. These included *Ancient Greece*, a history that Harvard accepted as a textbook.[16]

Heeren's book, which glorified the Periclean age, shows how far romantic historiography had moved from the picture of Athens as anarchical. Bancroft was ahead of the wave of histories that would glorify Periclean Athens in Victorian England. Direct democracy, a flawed system in republican theory, was rehabilitated, for its usefulness in the parliamentary reform movement, by British historians like George Grote.[17] In America, a similar motion toward government *by* the people, not just *for* the republic, was signaled by an enthusiasm for Greek symbols. Bancroft became a Jacksonian Democrat when he began to apply the historical skills formed on the Attic democracy to America's development. Walter Savage Landor recognized what was happening in America when he dedicated the second volume of his *Pericles and Aspasia* to President Andrew Jackson.[18]

It was as the voice of a fashionably romantic Hellenism that Everett became famous. This is what led people to turn naturally toward him when the Gettysburg cemetery was to be dedicated— as it had, earlier, led New England orators to imitate the Greek idea of popular debate and instruction. Perry Miller describes

46

Everett's impact on the most influential philosophical school of his period:

> No account of Transcendentalism is ever comprehensible unless it includes a consideration of what seemed, during the 1820s, the unearthly magic of his [Everett's] eloquence. If the whole group, and especially Emerson, were committed to the belief that oratory is among the supreme manifestations of art, they were persuaded not only by such forensic giants as Webster and Clay, but more particularly by Everett, who was one of their own kind. Here at last was a New England scholar who appeared the master of all that European culture could offer, who in native terms made articulate, in a style that could compete with Burke and Pitt and Sheridan, everything that America held precious.[19]

Emerson, who was always ready to pay his debt to the influence of Everett, learned to tighten his own public speeches toward a knottier classicism than Everett's diffuse speeches exhibited. Emerson represented the next step in the modern use of classical rhetoric—and it was a step in the direction of the Gettysburg Address itself. Emerson uses antithesis, aphorism, the nervous rhythms of a quickening time. It is no wonder that Emerson admired Lincoln's speech at Gettysburg more than that of his old master: "His brief speech at Gettysburg will not easily be surpassed by words on any recorded occasion."[20] But, in forming the ideal of modern democratic speech that gave us Emerson, Everett had helped create the very conditions that brought forth Lincoln's demotic oratory. Everett's classicism was as much the forerunner of Lincoln's talk as its foil or contrast.

The classicism of Everett's opening references at Gettysburg should not be taken as mere antiquarian reverence for the past. Everett had always opposed any fetishism of the classics. In his speech on the Battle of Concord (1825), he said:

Are we to be eternally ringing the changes upon Marathon and Thermopylae; and going back to find in obscure texts of Greek and Latin the great exemplars of patriotic virtue? . . . We feel a glow of admiration at the heroism displayed at Marathon, by the ten thousand champions of invaded Greece; but we cannot forget that the tenth part of the number were slaves, unchained from the workshops and doorposts of their masters, to go and fight the battles of freedom. I do not mean that these examples are to destroy the interest with which we read the history of ancient times; they possibly increase that interest, by the singular *contrast* they exhibit. But they do warn us, if we need the warning, to seek our great practical lessons of patriotism at *home;* out of the exploits and sacrifices of which our *own* country is the theatre; out of the character of our *own* fathers. [Italics added.][21]

But, like a good student of Germany's "higher critics," Everett held that certain large themes are only traceable in history's *process*, and a vision of long stretches of time is needed to grasp and advance those themes. Transcendentalism looked to the progressive realization of ideals implicit in ancient art. Everett felt that popular awareness of these ideals could be kept alive by a reverence for the "holy places" of freedom, democracy, and eloquence. Speaking in 1833 to commemorate the Battle of Bunker Hill, Everett urged the citizens of Boston to raise the funds for completing their monument, not trusting to time for the preservation of a site sacred to liberty. He described how "I have searched in vain for the narrow pass [Thermopylae] between the foot of the mountain and the sea. It is gone."[22] He compares, at Gettysburg, his tracing of the battle's course on Pennsylvania fields to his student days at Marathon. That is what made him celebrate the "birthplace" of American democracy at revolutionary-war sites. These, he said, were America's classic places, "the battlefields, the infant settlements," that became our "matter of history, of poetry, of eloquence."[23] He campaigned in the 1850s for the restoration of Mount Vernon as a shrine, raising $90,000 by delivering his eulogy to Washington before many audiences.

As a Greek scholar, Everett knew that the state Funeral Oration (Epitaphios Lōgos, normally shortened to Epitaphios— Epitaphioi in the plural) was a genre established before Pericles spoke, one whose formulae can be traced in the six surviving examples of the genre.[24] As the earliest known prose performance mandated by the democratic polis, it set the tone and style for most later public rhetoric.[25] By the continuity of its themes and values, it established a sense of Athenian identity. Nicole Loraux, in her influential study of the rite, even claims that Athens was "invented" in this communal act:

> Indeed it may well be that from the end of the fifth century right up to Cleidemus [in the second half of the fourth century] the Athenians were officially content with the "Athenian history of Athens" repeated in every Funeral Oration, in which the series of warlike deeds performed by the *polis* was interchangeable with and symbolic of the perennial nature of civic aretē [heroism]. This repetitive oral history had to serve as archive and document.[26]

Everett had such historical ideals in mind as he completed his celebration of modern political deaths. He lived in the pre-professional era of historians like Francis Parkman, William Prescott, and George Bancroft, who meant to create a historical memory in the American public. This made Everett scrupulous in compiling his accounts. In his speeches at Lexington and Concord, for instance, he corrected popular versions of Paul Revere's ride. When he published his amplified text from Gettysburg, he appended a note to show how carefully he had studied this recent event:

Besides the sources of information mentioned in the text, I have
been kindly favored with a memorandum of the operations of the
three days drawn up for me by direction of Major-General Meade
(anticipating the promulgation of his official report), by one of his
aides, Colonel Theodore Lyman, from whom also I have received
other important communications relative to the campaign. I have
received very valuable documents relative to the battle from
Major-General Halleck, Commander-in-Chief of the army, and
have been much assisted in drawing up the sketch of the campaign, by the detailed reports, kindly transmitted to me in manuscript from the Adjutant-General's office, of the movements of
every corps of the army, for each day, after the breaking up from
Fredericksburg commenced. I have derived much assistance from
Colonel John B. Bachelder's oral explanations of his beautiful and
minute drawing (about to be engraved) of the field of the three
days' struggle. With the information derived from these sources
I have compared the statements of General Lee's official report of
the campaign, dated 31st July, 1863, a well-written article, pur-
porting to be an account of the three days' battle, in the *Richmond Enquirer* of the 22d of July, and the article on "The Battle
of Gettysburg and the Campaign of Pennsylvania," by an officer,
apparently a colonel in the British army, in *Blackwood's Magazine* for September.

It was this scrupulousness and dedication to the largest tasks that
Nicolay and Hay admired in the Gettysburg Address:

Edward Everett made an address worthy alike of his fame and the
extraordinary occasion. . . . It is not too much to say that for the
space of two hours he held his listeners spell-bound by the rare
power of his art. . . . If there was an American who was qualified
by moral training, by literary culture, by political study, by official experience, by party affiliation, by long practice in historical
criticism, and ripe experience in public utterance, to sit in calm
judicial inquiry on the causes, theories, and possible results of the

civil war, that man was Edward Everett. . . . [His speech] embodies the calm reflection of the thinker in his study, pronounced with the grave authority of the statesman on his tribune.[27]

The Boston *Journal* understood Everett's historical aspirations when it wrote (on November 20, 1863):

> The detailed narrative of the campaign ending in the battle of Gettysburg reads like the most brilliant pages of Macaulay or Prescott. As Mr. Everett has taken great pains in collecting the data for the narrative, having access to official authorities, it is probably the best history of the campaign which this generation shall have the privilege of reading.[28]

But Everett aspired to more than mere accuracy. Along with Bancroft and other romantic historians of his time, he meant to create a tradition that would inspire as well as inform. Like the Attic orators—and dramatists—he knew the power of symbols to create a people's political identity. By a favoring coincidence, the best estimate of the crowd at Gettysburg is fifteen thousand people—the same number that attended the theater of Dionysos at Athens. In the *Eumenides* of Aeschylus, the heroic myths were altered to explain the historical development of Athens:

> It is thus likely that when Aeschylus identified the Semnai of the [Athenian] Areopagus with the Erinyes who had pursued Orestes, he was making a startling innovation. To the extent that his audience accepted the idea, it would revolutionize their understanding. . . .[29]

It does not overstate Everett's ambition, in this crowning effort of his oratory, to say that he hoped to accomplish something like the impact of Greek drama as well as of the Greek Epitaphios. As

Aeschylus had used the gods to explain Athenian ideals to the Athenians, he would use Greek ideals to explain America to Americans. That he failed is no disgrace, given the height of his aspiration. What is amazing, and can seem almost like a joke of the gods themselves, is that where he failed Lincoln succeeded.

Lincoln brought nothing of Everett's superb background to this charged event. True, his sense of style in words was far greater than his feel for the ornaments on his Greek Revival house; but he was not aiming at Periclean effect. Yet his speech is now at least as famous as the Athenian's. That is because Lincoln was an artist, not just a scholar. Classicism of Everett's sort looks backward; but the classic *artifact* sets standards for the future—for a whole rank *(classis)* of efforts it makes possible.[30] Pericles' speech in Thucydides established a norm, a benchmark—but no more than Lincoln's Address created a political prose for America, to rank with the vernacular excellence of Twain. Lincoln does not, like Everett, archaize—but neither did Pericles. Pericles rejected the notion that his predecessors had done more than his own generation.[31] It was the challenge of *the moment* that both Pericles and Lincoln addressed.

Lincoln sensed, from his own developed artistry, the demands that bring forth classic art—compression, grasp of the essential, balance, ideality, an awareness of the deepest polarities in the situation (life for the city coming from the death of its citizens). Take, first, the matter of compression. Everett addresses many different tasks in his diffuse oration—historical narrative, constitutional argumentation, excoriation of the foe, comparison with the Greeks, etc. This means that, in praising the Greeks, he fails to imitate them. His speech is far longer than any Epitaphios from Athens. Even the Greek orations embedded in literary works (and embroidered there) can be recited comfortably in under twenty minutes. The Gorgias model is actually no longer than Lincoln's Address.[32] The standard recital time seems to have been under fifteen minutes—five times the length of Lincoln's "remarks" but only one-eighth of Everett's sprawling oration.

The compactness is not merely a matter of length. There is a suppression of particulars in the idealizing art of Lincoln, as in the Greek orations. This restraint produces the aesthetic paradox that makes these works oddly moving despite their impersonal air. The Greek orator does not refer to himself except as answering the city's ordinance. Most often, he uses the plural "we" *(hēmeis)* of all the citizenry—as Lincoln does.[33] Nor are the Greek dead referred to by name (except in one late example).[34] The fallen are usually just "these (men)" *(hoide)*—as Lincoln speaks of "what they did here" or of "these dead."[35] The Epitaphios, as Loraux puts it, is "an oration that ignores individuals."[36] Restraint deepens passion by refusing to give it easy vent.

The *prose* form of the Greek orations was meant to be bracing after the sung lament *(thrēnos)* of the burial rite—as Lincoln's astringent speech stood in contrast to B. B. French's preceding hymn and the following "dirge."[37] Plato says the Epitaphios used bald *(psilos)* language, stripped of the poets' ornaments.[38] The prose form is itself a return to political life, a transition from family mourning to the larger community's sense of purpose. There is an air almost of rebuke in the dismissal of mourners at the end of the speech: "Your individual lamenting done, depart."[39] The task left by the dead must be taken up—what Lincoln calls "the great task remaining before us." Milton caught the discipline of this attitude toward death in his imitation Greek chorus:

> *Nothing is here for tears, nothing to wail*
> *Or knock the breast, no weakness, no contempt,*
> *Dispraise or blame, nothing but well and fair,*
> *And what may quiet us in a death so noble.*[40]

The struggle to contain individual sorrow in a larger meaning is pronounced "well and fair" by each orator. Lincoln unconsciously echoes this when he says, "It is altogether fitting and proper that we should do this"—*dignum et justum est,* as the old Latin Mass put it.[41]

No proper names are used in Lincoln's Address—not even the name of the battle, or of the cemetery he is dedicating with his speech. "This ground" is only a testing place where "the proposition" is to be vindicated by "these dead" *(hoide):*

> Now we are engaged in a great civil war, testing whether that nation, or any nation so conceived and so dedicated, can long endure. We are met on a great battle-field of that war. We have come to dedicate a portion of that field. . . .

The general or generalizing articles—*a* great civil war, *a* great battlefield, *a* portion, *any* nation—make this military engagement part of a larger process. There is an almost hygienic air about the *experiment* in liberty. The process can be observed on the broadest scale because its parts are so interchangeable—this portion of a field is of interest only because it is testing what *any* nation of the same condition may expect. The "unfinished work," the "task remaining before us," will affect liberty's prospects over the whole *earth,* as the last word puts it. The draining of particulars from the scene raises it to the ideality of a type.

Everett, despite his training as a Hellenist, is not really classical in spirit. He speaks unabashedly for the romantic age. His earlier speeches are highly colored and full of movement— even Warren's statue is felt to be on the verge of stepping off its pedestal.[42] The dead themselves are still restless under a soil that throbs with their emotions.[43] Looking to the battles, Everett calls up smoke-filled scenes of "the boiling veins, the burning nerves, the almost maddened brain, which alone could have encountered the terrors of that day."[44] Everett liked to name particular heroes, like Henry V looking to future celebration of the fight on Crispin's day. As Everett said at Lexington, echoing Shakespeare's very words:

> Its sacred memories must be transmitted by your citizens, from father to son, till all its thrilling incidents are as familiar as household words, and till the names of the brave men who reaped the bloody horrors of the nineteenth of April, 1775, are as well known to us as the names of those who form the circle of our friends.[45]

And then Everett ends his speech with a call of names: "Parker, Munroe, Hadley, the Harringtons, Muzzy, Brown."[46] Bedford and Exeter, Warwick and Talbot.

By contrast with any of Everett's battle orations, Lincoln's has the chaste and graven quality of an Attic frieze. An ability to balance the particular against the type marks Lincoln's thought, as it did that of the Athenian masters. Lincoln had a logical mind, furthermore, that regularly showed itself in the act of *distinguishing* alternatives. His thought leaned toward antitheses, as classical rhetoricians have noticed.[47] He regularly underlined contrast-words in the texts he prepared for delivery.

> Either the *opponents* of slavery will arrest the further spread of it, and place it where the public mind shall rest in the belief that it is in course of ultimate extinction; or its *advocates* will push it forward, till it shall become alike lawful in *all* the States, *old* as well as *new*—*North* as well as *South*. [SW 1.426]

Nothing marked Greek literature more than its use, in almost every sentence, of the polarizing particles *men* and *de*. These do not crudely spell out "on the one hand" and "on the other." Rather, a first glance (as it were) of the mind *(men)* "serves to prepare for a [following] contrast of greater or less sharpness"—which the second particle *(de)* provides as "a balancing adversative" to the first.[48] President Truman used to ask for "a one-handed economist," to avoid on-the-other-handedness. He would have been a frustrated leader in Athens, where, linguistically, there were no one-handed Greeks. The characteristic organization of Greek prose by polarities is evident in all the surviving Epitaphioi, not only in the use of those omnipresent particles but in the broad contrasts Athenians used to sort out their reactions. For instance:

1. The one and the many. Pericles chafes at the fact that so many dead must rely on one speaker's skill.[49] On the other hand, the many living are blessed by the few who died for them.[50]

2. Light and dark. The dead go into the dark; but the living need the splendor of the departed, as they do the sun.[51]

3. Mortal and immortal. The life of the soldiers was short and is ended, but their fame will live forever.[52]

4. Athenians and others. Athenians differ from all others in their death because they live in a different way, with a characteristic regimen *(politeia)*.[53]

5. Word and deed. It is hard to fit poor words to the heroes' great deeds. On the other hand, the fame of what they did depends on the words people will speak of them.[54]

6. Teachers and taught. The intellectual aspirations of the Greeks made them think of experience as an education *(paideia)* by which the pupil *(mathētēs)* eventually becomes a teacher *(didaskalos)*. So the fallen heroes in the Kerameikos advanced their nobility *(eugeneia)* by going to school to the polis and its values *(politeia)*. Thus, by their death, they teach others to live, making their city a training *(paideia)* for the whole civilized world.[55]

7. Age and youth. Both old and young look toward men in their prime *(akmē)*, who die when life is at its peak. The parent who buries a child reverses the order of nature, but is consoled by the almost supernatural deeds of those who win life for the next generation.[56] The mystery of death in these circumstances is pondered in the sculpture of the "Ilissos stele" of c. 330 B.C.E. In its frieze, a dead man of godlike build is mourned by a cloaked and mysterious father, a dwarfed and helpless son. The approximation of the dead man to the Herakles type suggests his transcendence of the dimmer lives of the old man and young boy. He is more vivid in death than they are in life.[57]

8. Male and female. Though Pericles addresses the heroes' wives, most of the orations refer only to parents and sons. (On the "Ilissos stele" there are no women.) This accentuates not only the male world of battle, but the pre-eminence of *the* mother—the city, the nurturing land. Athenians were, in patriotic myth, "born of the land itself" *(autochthones)*.[58]

9. Choice and determination. The necessity of death for the life of the city is poised against an emphasis on the heroes' free *choice* of death.[59]

10. Past and present. The mythical exploits of the founders and fathers are poised against those of the present heroes in a dialectic that draws strength from the past.[60]

11. Life and death. This is the great contrast underlying all the rest. Life-out-of-death is the mystery by which the polis lives while her finest die. Everything in the oration moves toward an exploration of this claim, an explanation of it to the survivors.[61]

Lincoln, of course, did not think in all these polarities, or have time to include most of them, even if he had thought in them. But Lane Cooper rightly remarked of the Gettysburg Address:

The balance in thought and phrase is easily detected by both eye and ear, and the use of antithesis is obvious, as in the contrast between then and now, birth and death, the living and the dead.[62]

Lincoln's thought does approach several of the points mentioned above. On the third one, for instance, playing mortality off against immortality, Lincoln contrasts "those who here gave their lives" with the system of government that will live on ("shall not perish from the earth"). On the fourth point, Lincoln separates America from other nations by its birth from a proposition. On the fifth, Lincoln opposes word to deed, *logos* to *ergon,* in a way even Gorgias might admire:

> *The world will little note,*
> *nor long remember*
> *what we say here,*
> *but it can never forget*
> *what they did here.*

Lincoln's self-deprecating contrast of his (and Everett's) words with the soldiers' deaths seems to neglect the second aspect of the Attic orators' contrast—the necessity, nonetheless, for words to insure undying fame. But that is implied in the notion of the world's *remembering:* reports will multiply beyond the few words said at any one time, in tribute to a deed that makes words as necessary as they are inadequate.

On the sixth point, of political life and death as an *education,* Lincoln offers his interpretation of the battle at Gettysburg as an experiment testing whether a nation dedicated to a proposition can maintain itself. On the eighth point, Lincoln maintains his dry experimental air by making no reference to women, despite his admiration for Everett's passage on the nurses present at the battle (SW 2.537). He is doing something different, soberer, almost hard in its dedication to the *issues* being tested. On the ninth point, of free choice, Lincoln tells us that the dead "*gave* their lives," they did not simply lose them, and they did so for a single purpose, "that that nation might live."

On the tenth point, Lincoln poises the present against the past, the dead and living at Gettysburg against the fathers, the new birth against the fathers' "bringing forth," without admitting any exclusion of the descendants *(epigoni)* from the nation's epic work. "The great task remaining," the "unfinished work," is what will complete the experiment and keep freedom from perishing.

The principal contrast in Lincoln's speech, as in the Attic ones, is between life and death. Plato says that the twin tasks of the Epitaphios are to extol the dead and to exhort the living—he uses a jingle on the same root word to say something like "laud the dead and lead survivors."[63] The Funeral Orations have two major sections—*epainesis*, or praise for the fallen, and *parainesis*, or advice for the living. The various themes can occur in different places within this large massing of two units, but they have "favored" positions traced in great detail by John Ziolkowski.[64] A sketch of the common shape for an Epitaphios is therefore possible:

epainesis of the dead

logos/ergon:	The spoken word is fitted to heroes' deeds, perpetuating the fame of the dead in the words of the living.
dikaion:	The rite is a good thing despite the sadness of the occasion.
progonoi:	The heroes have the nobility *(eugeneia)* of great ancestors.
autochthones:	All the heroes share an ancestry from the Attic earth itself.

arете: The exploits of the fathers have been matched by the valor *(arете)* shown by the heroes in their exploit *(aristeia).*

parainesis of the living

paramythētikon: The living should be comforted that the dead have won honor.

protreptikon: The living should prove worthy of the fallen.

The Greek authors develop these themes in different detail, expanding, contracting, omitting one or another. But most of the elements show up in most of the speeches, however altered the order or emphasis. They reflect a coordinated vision rather than mechanical formulae. What is astonishing about Lincoln's speech is that he arrived at so similar a vision. Analogues of his themes can be traced in the classical works—in Plato's "these men fathered our freedom as well as our bodies," as in Demosthenes' "the valor of these men in death is the principle of life for all Hellas," or Hyperides' "is it not right to think that in leaving this life they have undergone a new birth, better than the first?"[65]

epainesis

progonoi Four score and seven years ago, our fathers
autochthones brought forth on this continent a new nation,
politeia conceived in liberty
and dedicated to the proposition
that all men are created equal.
paideia Now we are engaged in a great civil war,
testing whether that nation,
or any nation so conceived and so dedicated,
can long endure.
We are met on a great battle-field of that war.
We have come to dedicate a portion of that
field,

as a final resting place for those
arete who here gave their lives that that nation might
live.
dikaion It is altogether fitting and proper
that we should do this.
But, in a larger sense, we cannot dedicate—
we cannot consecrate—we cannot hallow—this
ground.
The brave men, living and dead,
who struggled here,
have consecrated it,
far above our poor power to add or detract.
logos/ergon The world will little note,
nor long remember, what we do here,
but it can never forget what they did here.

parainesis

protreptikon It is for the living, rather,
to be dedicated to the unfinished work
which they who fought here
have thus far so nobly advanced.
It is rather for us to be here dedicated
to the great task remaining before us—
paramythētikon that from these honored dead
we take increased devotion
to that cause for which they gave
the last full measure of devotion—

that we here highly resolve that these dead
shall not have died in vain—

that this nation, under God,
shall have a new birth of freedom—
and that government of the people,
by the people, for the people
shall not perish from the earth.

The basic elements at work in the whole speech are life and death. Commentators from widely different backgrounds all agree on that. The poet Robert Lowell noticed a "curious, insistent use of birth images: 'brought forth,' 'conceived,' 'created,' and finally 'a new birth of freedom.' "[66] The classicist Lane Cooper wrote: "Proem, body, and epilogue are naturally bound together by the successive concepts of birth, death, and rebirth."[67] Literary critic James Hurt finds a "broad structural pattern in the Address [of] imagery of birth-death-rebirth."[68] The survivors at Gettysburg draw life from death, as their forefathers had sown life in the earth of this continent. The survivors take *"increased* devotion,*"* even though the fallen men gave "the last *full* measure of devotion." The increase is not only over what the survivors felt before; it is something that goes *beyond* the ultimate of what the fallen gave. They left a "remaining" task that only the living can complete. The dead not only saved a nation but advanced it on the course it must complete. Their dying was an education for the task ahead, one derived from those

> *who here gave their lives*
> *that that nation might live*

—and not only might live for itself, but might complete the test of government by and for and of the people for others spread around the globe. Life-*in*-death is made a life-*through*-death, so that the miraculous birth from this continent leads to a miraculous not-quite-death in the prehallowed ground where the heroes rest. The largest contrasts of existence are focused on one moment of history, with an implicit suggestion that death and life would give up their ultimate meaning if we could just decipher the inner reality of this event on a testing-field at Gettysburg. The Address does what all great art accomplishes. Like Keats's Grecian urn, it "tease[s] us out of thought / As doth eternity."

Gettysburg and
the Culture of Death

$\mathbf{E}$dward Everett was not only a celebrant of American battlefields; he was also a connoisseur of American cemeteries. He had participated in the creation of Mount Auburn, the Cambridge cemetery that became one of the principal cultural institutions of the nineteenth century.

Everett's interest in battles and burial had a common element—the fad for ancient Greece. The "rural cemetery" movement initiated at Mount Auburn took Athens' Kerameikos as its model, since that ancient burying ground existed outside the city proper, near the groves of the Akademy, in what was still countryside. As Justice Story, of the United States Supreme Court, put it at Mount Auburn's dedication:

The Greeks exhausted the resources of their exquisite art in adorning the habitations of the dead. They discouraged interments within the limits of their cities; and consigned their reliques to shady groves, in the neighborhood of murmuring streams and merry fountains, close by the favorite resorts of those who were engaged in the study of philosophy and nature, and called them, with the elegant expressiveness of their own beautiful language, *cemeteries* or "places of repose."[1]

David Charles Sloane notes that the rural-cemetery movement, launched by Mount Auburn in 1831, brought into widespread use the Greek-derived term "cemetery," from *koimētērion* ("sleeping place").[2]

The removal of the burial ground to places outside the city limits used to be attributed entirely to hygienic considerations—the churchyard and urban gravesites interfered with enlightened city planning. But followers of Philippe Ariès, who study the nineteenth-century culture of death, find that ideological factors were even more powerful.[3] The Greek emphasis is one clue to the attitudes being expressed—an escape from the theological gloom of churchyards, a return to nature, a pantheistic identification of dissolution with initiation. The Transcendentalists played an important role in the cult of cemeteries as "schools of life": Ralph Waldo Emerson delivered the dedication speech at New England's other important rural cemetery, Sleepy Hollow in Concord.

Justice Story's dedication speech contains all these elements. There is, first, the escape from puritan New England's narrow theology:

Why should we deposit the remains of our friends in loathsome vaults, or beneath the gloomy crypts and cells of our churches, where the human foot is never heard, save when the sickly taper lights some new guest to his appointed apartment, and "lets fall a supernumerary horror" on the passing procession?[4]

The old graveyard was set apart from life, a narrow confine cut off from communication with its surroundings, "walled in only to preserve them from violation." The new cemetery would be a place of frequent resort for the living, who would commune with nature as a way of finding life in death. The romantic theory of association made people see death in a new way:

> We know that man is the creature of associations and excitements. . . . The truth which strikes home must have not only the approbation of his reason but it must be embodied in a visible, tangible, practical form. It must be felt as well as seen. It must warm as well as convince.[5]

The associations of a picturesque rural site would instill healing truths, of natural death and rebirth, in the cycle of seasons:

> Here are the lofty oak, the beech that "wreaths its old fantastic roofs so high," the rustling pine, and the drooping willow (the tree that sheds its pale leaves with every autumn, a fit emblem of our own transitory bloom), and the evergreen, with its perennial shoots, instructing us that "the wintry blast of death kills not the buds of virtue."[6]

The place of the dead must be made a school for the living—a *paideia*, as Pericles might have said:

> Our cemeteries, rightly selected and properly arranged, may be made subservient to some of the highest purposes of religion and human duty. They may preach lessons to which none may refuse to listen and which all that live must hear. Truths may be there felt and taught, in the silence of our own meditations, more persuasive and more enduring than ever flowed from human lips.[7]

True to Story's prediction, Mount Auburn became a place of fashionable resort and cultural indoctrination, a school outside Boston to rank with the neighboring Harvard campus (much as the Kerameikos was linked to the Akademy outside Athens). When Edward Everett was Harvard's president, he took important guests out to contemplate Mount Auburn. In 1849, he escorted Lady Emmeline Wortley there even before showing her around the college grounds, and she was more detailed and enthusiastic in her description of the cemetery than of the campus:

> The finely diversified grounds occupy about one hundred acres, in general profusely adorned with a rich variety of trees, and in some places planted with ornamental shrubbery: there are some tombs graced with charming flower-beds. There are also some pretty sheets of water there: it is divided into different avenues and paths, which have various names. Generally they are called after the trees or flowers that abound there, such as lily, poplar, cypress, violet, woodbine, and others. It is, indeed, a beauteous city for the dead. The birds were singing most mellifluously and merrily—it was quite a din of music that they kept up in these solemn but lovely shades. The views from Mount Auburn are fine and extensive. There are some graceful and well-executed monuments within its precincts.[8]

Dickens was also exposed to this national treasure, which received thirty thousand visitors a year.[9] James Russell Lowell said that Bostonians had only two ways of entertaining important guests, with a public dinner and with a drive to Mount Auburn.[10]

As a center of attention in what was still widely considered the nation's cultural capital, Mount Auburn was widely admired and imitated, first in the East and then in the Midwest. In 1859, the year before Lincoln's election, his native state opened the

Chicago rural cemetery, Rose Hill, designed by William Saunders. The next year it opened Graceland, organized by a Harvard graduate.[11] More important, Springfield, Lincoln's hometown, joined the rural-cemetery movement in a highly conscious and organized way. City fathers, friends of Lincoln, were engaged in this civic enterprise. When it came time to dedicate Oak Ridge Cemetery on May 24, 1860, schools were closed and the whole town was urged to attend. Papers carried the message released by the cemetery board:

> It is desired that the places of business be closed on the afternoon of the 24th and that household cares be laid aside, that all may devote the afternoon to the solemnities of the occasion. Free carriages will be found on the north and west side of the public square for the accommodation of ladies and gentlemen as far as practicable free.

The formal speech was delivered by ex-Mayor James C. Conkling, a friend and neighbor of Lincoln who was actively engaged in his campaign for president at the time of the dedication. Conkling struck all the notes expected of such a speech after Story established the model.

> How solemn, how impressive the scene! Far away from the haunts of busy life . . . Here, with naught but the pure arch of heaven above us, and nature in all her silent beauty and loveliness around us, we dedicate the City of the Dead. . . . How appropriate then that this sacred enclosure should harmonize with the subdued and hallowed feelings of the soul, that it should possess all those symbols and emblems which are calculated to inspire the mind with devotion and lead the thoughts from earth to heaven; that all its surroundings and embellishments be of such a character as to

elevate the affections, and purify the heart, and prepare it for a higher and holier state of existence.

Conkling expressly linked Oak Ridge to its predecessors in the rural-cemetery movement, since it exhibited "the surroundings of nature combined with art as exhibited in the cemeteries of Père Lachaise and Mt. Auburn and Greenwood and Laurel Hill and other celebrated burial places of the dead."

Lincoln, it is safe to assume, attended this expression of pride in his hometown. His correspondence shows that he was in Springfield. Not only was Conkling a friend and campaign ally of the moment; Conkling's wife was an old and very close friend of Mary Lincoln. These ties explain the strong, almost ferocious, resistance Mrs. Lincoln put up when the city of Springfield planned a separate memorial vault for Lincoln after his assassination. She threatened to bury her husband in Washington unless he was placed in Oak Ridge Cemetery. She had, after all, been present (probably sitting with the orator's wife) when Conkling said:

> Here will be deposited, side by side, the father and the son, the mother and the daughter, the brother and the sister, the husband and the wife. . . . Here many a Martha, many a Mary, will come to weep at the grave of a beloved brother.

Or, as the board had put it in its public invitation to the cemetery:

> It is a secluded and beautiful retreat, and may become the last resting places of us all. Therefore let us attend and take part in the services of the 24th with a solemnity and interest befitting the Consecration of the hours appointed for us.

So Lincoln, who delivered the most famous address at a rural cemetery, was laid to rest in the same kind of institution—and, appropriately, William Saunders, the rural architect of Gettysburg, came to Springfield to landscape the area of Lincoln's tomb.

Mount Auburn had established the rituals of dedication for these cemeteries—the procession of dignitaries, the opening prayer, an ode for the occasion, the formal address, the formula of dedication, a closing prayer, and the recessional. It was the form preserved at Gettysburg; and Lincoln was already familiar with it from the Springfield opening. The board had decreed: "The services will consist of music, prayer, an oration, a formal declaration setting apart the grounds to burial uses, and the Apostolic Benediction."

Like Conkling's oration, kept in the files of the Oak Ridge office, the published speeches of Story and Emerson move through the expected range of references used on such occasions. It is not surprising, then, that Everett drew on this repertory of nature-invocation to begin his speech at Gettysburg:

> Standing beneath this serene sky, overlooking these broad fields now reposing from the labors of the waning year, the mighty Alleghenies dimly towering before us, the graves of our brethren beneath our feet, it is with hesitation that I raise my poor voice to break the eloquent silence of God and Nature.

William Saunders, on the platform, was probably as pleased by this invocation as by Lincoln's egalitarian references. The Scottish horticulturalist had planned this cemetery to provoke contemplation. Like other promoters of the rural-cemetery movement, he used terms borrowed from Burke's treatise on the sublime:

The prevailing expression of the Cemetery should be that of *simple grandeur.* Simplicity is that element of beauty in a scene that leads gradually from one object to another, in easy harmony, avoiding abrupt contrasts and unexpected features. Grandeur, in this application, is closely allied to solemnity. Solemnity is an attribute of the sublime. The sublime in scenery may be defined as continuity of extent, the repetition of objects in themselves simple and commonplace. We do not apply this epithet to the scanty tricklings of the brook, but to the collected waters of the ocean. To produce an expression of grandeur, we must avoid intricacy and great variety of parts; more particularly must we refrain from introducing any intermixture of meretricious display or ornament. The disposition of trees and shrubs is such as will ultimately produce a considerable degree of landscape effect. Ample spaces of lawn are provided; these will form vistas, as seen from the drive, showing the monument and other prominent points. Any abridgement of these lawns by planting, further than is shown in the design, will tend to destroy the massive effect of the groupings, and in time would render the whole confused and intricate. As the trees spread and extend, the quiet beauty produced by these open spaces of lawn will yearly become more striking; designs of this character require time for their development, and their ultimate harmony should not be impaired or sacrificed to immediate and temporary interest.[12]

The function of the cemetery as a training of the sensibilities, as *paideia,* was much on Everett's mind. He even suggested that children should be kept in instructive communion with the place by volunteer work on its upkeep.

Would it not be well for the young people of Gettysburg of both kinds to form a cemetery association whose duty it should be to keep the grounds in order. There should be a suitable enclosure, trees, and walks.[13]

He is drawing on his experience as a member of the board for Mount Auburn in advising Wills on the cultural uses of the Gettysburg institution.

The dedication of Gettysburg must, therefore, be seen in its cultural context, as part of the nineteenth century's fascination with death in general and with cemeteries in particular. We tend to view it only in its connection with the Civil War and military ceremonies, which were indeed the most immediate and compelling associations. But these did not entirely obliterate the larger and longer-standing pattern of response to the recurrent rites of dedicating new parts of nature to the care of the dead.

It may strike a modern audience as odd that Everett would want young people to be drawn to the places of burial. But pensive children near a tomb were a treasured part of the century's cultural iconography, as we see in the popular mourning pictures displayed in Victorian parlors. Mark Twain made fun of this tendency in Emmeline Grangerford, the girl who specialized in death:

> Every time a man died, or a woman died, or a child died, she would be on hand with her "tribute" before he was cold. She called them tributes. The neighbors said it was the doctor first, then Emmeline, then the undertaker—the undertaker never got in ahead of Emmeline but once, and then she hung fire on a rhyme for the dead person's name, which was Whistler.[14]

Emmeline dies young and is painted by another girlish specialist in death, who also dies young. This whole sequence can be read as a satire on the taste that made thousands of people weep over Dickens's dying Little Nell or Paul Dombey, or made hundreds weep with America's women poets over the death of children.[15]

Twain made fun of the way Emmeline Grangerford's parents maintained her room as a shrine for mourning; but he did something like that when his own daughter died.[16] In the same way, Dickens had treated satirically (in *Oliver Twist*) the desire to have children mourners in the undertaking business, despite his own fiction's funereal use of children. The wonder was not the intensity of grief but the determination to prolong and caress that grief. Emerson dug up his son's body, after its decay, to contemplate it.[17] Justice Story, when he gave the dedication speech at Mount Auburn, was known to be still mourning his ten-year-old daughter's death, a fact that made his speech more deeply affecting to himself and his audience.[18]

The strong link between childhood and death in the nineteenth century is normally treated as a matter of the high rate of infant mortality. But other periods have had as high or higher death rates and not dwelt on the rituals of mourning. Frequency can indurate as well as sensitize. There is something deeper in the connection between children, death, and the healing countryside that J. Hillis Miller has traced in Dickens's novels.[19] The key to the fascination seems to be that childhood was seen as one of those *liminal* experiences that fascinated the romantics in general and the Transcendentalists in particular. The interest in dreams, revery, mesmerism, spiritualism, birth, and death shared this liminality.

Childhood was seen as a border-time on both sides of it. The child crossed the threshold of life trailing Wordsworthian memories of glory, and faced the symbolic death of innocence in adolescence (with its disillusionments). Innocence was a precarious state, wisely ignorant, of which a fetish was made by Victorian authors. Even the supposedly cynical Mark Twain became sentimental about Joan of Arc and the child "angels" in his own life.[20] Victorian authors—John Ruskin, Lewis Carroll, Henry Adams— liked to lecture young girls, playing the oracle to people who were themselves oracular with vestal secrets.[21] Childhood was poised on a frontier between youth and age, innocence and experience, vulnerability and protection.

The contemplation of nature that rural cemeteries were meant to foster was a threshold experience for the Transcendentalists. The horizon, where heaven touches earth, suggested the interplay of the ideal with the real—as did ponds mirroring heaven in the darkest groves. Afloat on such a pond, Emerson felt he was traversing a heaven of the mind: "We penetrate this incredible beauty [of water], we dip our hands in this painted element; our eyes are bathed in these lights and forms."[22] The borderlines *(limina)* in nature appealed to people who saw, figured there, the great limits to knowledge and time and history that they were meant to transcend: "In every landscape the point of astonishment is the meeting of the sky and earth."[23] Liminal experiences—twilight, dreams, daydreaming, melancholy, premonitions—were not fuzzings but intensifications of knowledge. "Margin" was a charged word, whether used of a field, lake, petal, or cloud. The *edge* of the wilderness gave meaning both to civilization and to "virgin nature." As with most romantic developments, Rousseau had pioneered this communion with nature as an opening onto other worlds. In his *Musings of a Lonely Rambler (Les Rêveries du promeneur solitaire)*, he told how he lost the sense of a division between himself and the things he impinged on. He flowed out to the world, and it flowed in. He compared this to the bliss he felt when recovering consciousness after being knocked out in an accident.[24] To recover such "transcendings" of himself, he practiced techniques of autohypnosis—rhythmic walking, "a regular and gentle motion without jolt or interruption," or the contemplation of waves whose "flux and reflux, and continued sound neither swelling nor ceasing," created interior movements as gentle and suggestive as the water's.[25] Lady Motley's description of the continual sound of birds in

Mount Auburn's "solemn but lovely shades" reveals how closely the rural cemetery aspired to the hypnotic powers to be found in nature by Rousseau's followers. Saunders, it will be remembered, said that continuity and repetition would instill a sense of the sublime.

The encouragement of dreamy half-states as revelatory led to the romantics' drastic upgrading of melancholy. Once considered a physical disorder and a theologically dangerous attitude, it now became a mark of genius.[26] That explains the nineteenth century's obsession with Hamlet as an avatar of melancholy. Ruskin had taught the American "luminists," those painters of the Transcendentalist movement, that shadows are not blank areas, pure black, but spaces of a richer color. Like melancholy, they deepen (instead of negating) life.[27] The encouragement of melancholy attitudes was supposed to be educative; so children were brought to funerals and cemeteries.

The cemetery was the supreme locus of liminality in the nineteenth century. It was the borderland between life and death, time and eternity, past and future. Justice Story even found a symbolic meaning in Mount Auburn's placement between two views, one of Harvard, the other of Boston. People came out of their ordinary places of life to view them across liberating barriers of distance. "We stand as it were, upon the borders of two worlds."[28] The distance from the bustle of ordinary life lets one consider the great frontier: "What is the grave, to us, but a thin barrier dividing time from eternity and earth from heaven?"[29] What Emerson saw in every horizon line, people less attuned to mystery were bound to experience in the awesome presence of death and nature conjoined. If the recurrences of nature can act like natural mesmerism, the sense of proximity to the dead is a form of spiritualism. As Story put it: "We return to the world, and we feel ourselves purer and better and wiser from this communion with the dead."[30] Emerson, too, in his dedication of

Sleepy Hollow, spoke of the cemetery as a place, almost, of séance: "We shall bring hither the body of the dead, but how shall we catch the escaped soul?"[31] Completing the act of contemplation the cemetery is supposed to initiate, Emerson developed his talk at Sleepy Hollow into an essay on immortality.[32]

These, then, were some of the predispositions people brought to the dedication of a cemetery in the 1860s. (Emerson's talk at Sleepy Hollow had been delivered in 1855.) Did Lincoln share in these attitudes?

He shared them in spades. He was, himself, funereal, almost to the point of caricature. Herndon wrote that "melancholy dripped from him as he walked."[33] Some fail to notice that he goes on to say this was an *attractive* quality for Lincoln's contemporaries: "His apparent gloom impressed his friends, and created sympathy for him—one means of his great success." The pose of Hamlet was suggestive of profundity. This is not to deny that Lincoln's depressions were genuine—even dangerously so, at least in earlier years, when he said that his fits of "hypo" (hypochondria) took him to the verge of suicide. Nonetheless, this was also a culturally encouraged mood, as Lincoln's fashionably mournful early poems demonstrate. These thanatopsic verses are closer to Emmeline Grangerford's than to Poe's; but they show how clearly Lincoln recognized gloom as a *liminal* state, where memory mediates between different internal states and external worlds:

> *O Memory! thou mid-way world*
> *'Twixt Earth and Paradise,*
> *Where things decayed, and loved ones lost*
> *In dreamy shadows rise.* [SW 1.120][34]

Lincoln meditates on death and madness like a young Hamlet, even echoing *Hamlet*'s words. Remembering the song of a mad young acquaintance (like Ophelia's crazed melody), Lincoln wrote:

> *To drink its strains I've stole away,*
> *All silently and still,*
> *Ere yet the rising god of day*
> *Had streak'd the Eastern hill.* [SW 1.122]

Compare the way dawn walks like a god over "yon high eastern hill" at *Hamlet* 1.1.172.

As was to be expected at this time, Lincoln's grief was acute at the death of his son in 1862. When Lincoln chose an appropriate passage from Shakespeare to read aloud to others—"I shall see my boy again" at *King John* 3.3.78—he fell into agonized sobbing before his audience.[35] Though others were mourning for their military dead at Gettysburg, Lincoln's black hatband was recognized by some as a sign of grief for the dead boy—as Justice Story's sorrow over his daughter was connected with his eloquence at Mount Auburn. When Lincoln's wife, like Mark Twain's, tried to communicate with her child through a medium, Lincoln did nothing to prevent these séances in the White House.[36] He was himself markedly alert to dreams, omens, and premonitions, writing his suggestible wife a note (the month before the battle at Gettysburg) to take care of a remaining son: "Think you better put 'Tad's' pistol away. I had an ugly dream about him" (SW 2.453). Herndon says Lincoln was superstitious about evil portents.[37] Death was a thing "o'er which his melancholy sits on brood." He was part of his age, at home in its culture of death. He went to Gettysburg as alert to all these resonances of the rural cemetery as any of those who would listen to him. The impulses behind his moping early poetry had been chastened by art, not dispelled from his psyche, when he spoke with checked emotion over the fallen young men.

In chapter 1, above, the contrasts of the speech at Gettysburg were considered as rhetorical antitheses. In the context of rural-cemetery rituals, the contrasts are those mediated by nature—life springing again from death, from the soil, in the circle of seasons. Emerson, in his address at Sleepy Hollow, had found the human race's (as opposed to the individual's) immortality pledged in the natural setting of human burial. Lincoln will not mourn the single soldier, like Everett; he looks, rather, to the birth of a *nation*'s life on this continent, its testing ordeal-by-death, and its new birth of freedom. He does not enter into the grief of the soldiers' fathers and mothers. "Our fathers" of the address are the country's founders, the explicators of doctrine who set the proposition to be tested. Mothers are not mentioned at all—only *the* mother, the continent that brought forth a nation.

We have seen how Lincoln's speech resembles Athenian Epitaphioi on this point. The Greek speeches refer to the tradition of the fathers *(progonoi)* but emphasize the motherhood of the earth itself, making Attic citizens "earth-born" *(autochthones)*. This is a common theme of patriotic attachment to a locale, and even of nationalistic religions.[38] It had created the cliché of America's founding on a "virgin continent"—a false metaphor (original Americans have to be ignored, or removed, to make the continent "virgin") but a persistent one, because it was so deep a part of American myth. Even a liberal antinationalist like Theodore Parker believed in this "clean start" for America, to stress its *intellectual* novelty:

> It is interesting to study the growth of the American people; to observe the progress of the ideas on which the government rests, and the attempts to make the idea an institution. This is one of the few great nations which can trace their history back to certain beginnings; there is no fabulous period in our annals, no mythical centuries.[39]

For Parker, too, America was "brought forth" as a proposition, with no grosser antecedents. George Bancroft voiced the same myth in his epic history: "Nothing came from Europe but a free people."[40] Male ideas came to the cloistered American continent and impregnated her.[41] As Theodore Parker put it: "Virgin America, hidden away behind the Atlantic and Pacific, is now to be married to mankind."[42] The democratic idea is thus given a kind of heavenly conception: "The new idea must come across the water to make its fortune."[43] The Spirit moves across the water to bring forth the land in Genesis 1. More important to Lincoln's terminology is the way the Spirit "overshadows" a Virgin at Luke 1.35, and she "brought forth her firstborn son" (2.7).

Lincoln's fertility-language of conception and rebirth is made especially resonant for his audience by its scriptural echoes. Don Fehrenbacher plausibly traces the form of Lincoln's opening words back to an 1861 speech in the House of Representatives, in which Galusha Grow said "Fourscore [and five] years ago . . ."[44] But all such uses echo the "four score and ten" years allotted to mankind in Psalm 90.

The Transcendentalist cult of Nature stressed its healing purity, and the idea of returning to "Mother Earth" was used in rites connected with the rural cemeteries. The ode at Mount Auburn's dedication contained the lines

> *Here to thy bosom, Mother Earth,*
> *Take back, in peace, what thou hast given;*
> *And all that is of heavenly birth,*
> *O God, in peace, recall to Heaven!*[45]

This resembles Lincoln's early poem on the earth that nurtured him:

> *The very spot where grew the bread*
> *That formed my bones, I see.*
> *How strange, old field, on thee to tread*
> *And feel I'm part of thee.* [SW 1.122]

This sense of earth as a loving mother to whom the dead are returned does not necessarily express, as Nicole Loraux claimed of the Greeks' myth of autochthony, a misogynist exclusion of the actual (human) mothers of the heroes.[46] It has been forcibly claimed that Lincoln was a misogynist; but, even if that were true, the mourning conventions of the rural cemetery brought "Mother Earth" to the fore, in ways that idealized a maternal Nature.[47]

"The fathers" are even more emphatically honored in Lincoln's speech; but modern scholars have found something false or insincere in Lincoln's constant invocation of the nation's founding fathers. True, he referred to them insistently, repeatedly, in his debates with Stephen Douglas.[48] Yet a vast literature now claims that Lincoln was hostile to "the fathers." This has colored some recent treatments of the Address.[49]

Edmund Wilson launched these speculations with his analysis of Lincoln's 1838 speech at the Young Men's Lyceum in Springfield.[50] Lincoln, attacking "mobocracy" in that talk, proposed a "political religion" of respect for law and order. "The fathers" should be revered as the fountains of law, though their heirs cannot hope to equal what they accomplished:

Their [the fathers'] ambition aspired to display before an admiring world a practical demonstration of the truth of a proposition, which had hitherto been considered, at best, no better than problematical; namely, *the capability of a people to govern themselves.* If they succeeded, they were to be immortalized; their names were to be transferred to counties and cities, and rivers and mountains; and to be revered and sung, and toasted through all time. If they failed, they were to be called knaves and fools and fanatics for a fleeting hour; then to sink and be forgotten. They succeeded. The experiment is successful; and thousands have won their deathless names in making it so. But the game is caught; and I believe it is true that, with the catching, end the pleasures of the chase. This field of glory is harvested, and the crop is already appropriated. But new reapers will arise, and *they*, too, will seek a field. It is to deny, what the history of the world tells us is true, to suppose that men of ambition and talents will not continue to spring up amongst us. And, when they do, they will as naturally seek the gratification of their ruling passion, as others have so done before them. The question, then, is: can that gratification be found in supporting and maintaining an edifice that has been erected by others? Most certainly it cannot. Many great and good men, sufficiently qualified for any task they should undertake, may ever be found, whose ambition would aspire to nothing beyond a seat in Congress, a gubernatorial or a presidential chair; *but such belong not to the family of the lion, or the tribe of the eagle.* What! think you these places would satisfy an Alexander, a Caesar, or a Napoleon? Never! Towering genius disdains a beaten path. It seeks regions hitherto unexplored. It sees *no distinction* in adding story to story, upon the monuments of fame, erected to the memory of others. It *denies* that it is glory enough to serve under any chief. It *scorns* to tread in the footsteps of *any* predecessor, however illustrious. It thirsts and burns for distinction; and, if possible, it will have it, whether at the expense of emancipating slaves, or enslaving freedom. Is it unreasonable then to expect, that some man possessed of the loftiest genius, coupled with ambition sufficient to push it to its utmost stretch, will at some time, spring up among us? And when such a one does, it will require the people to be united with each other, attached to the government and laws, and generally intelligent, to successfully frustrate his designs. [SW 1.34–35]

"It is evident," Wilson claims, "that Lincoln has projected himself into the role against which he is warning them," that of the soaring eagle, the aspiring Caesar. Harry Jaffa, the first to write a major response to Wilson, said Lincoln was not imagining himself as the Caesarian usurper but taking on himself the heroism of *resistance* to such a figure.[51] But a school of psychobiographers, agreeing with Jaffa, held that he had just found another way of stating Lincoln's oedipal resentment of "the fathers." The resentment is displaced onto an imagined "evil brother," slaying whom will assuage the conflict with the father. George Forgie claimed that when Stephen Douglas stepped into Lincoln's path, *he* became that figure in Lincoln's imagination, and Lincoln "killed" Douglas by ascribing to him a conspiracy with Pierce and Buchanan and Taney.[52] Dwight Anderson suggested that calling up this threat was Lincoln's way of beating George Washington at his own game, "killing the father."[53] Charles Strozier returned to Wilson's straightforward identification of Lincoln with the "aspiring son" resisting castration by the fathers.[54] Psychobiography had, by now, made the Lyceum speech a key not only to Lincoln's personal life but to his political ideals and significance:

> For George Washington, it can be shown, provided Lincoln with an imaginary father whom he both emulated and defied, and finally, by ceremonial apotheosis, elevated to divine rank. If the guilt that Lincoln experienced in achieving this symbolic victory over Washington haunted him like Banquo's ghost, it also provided the psychological basis for Lincoln's refoundation of political authority in the United States.[55]

Thomas Schwartz has taken a less feverish look at the Lyceum speech. The Young Men's Lyceum of Springfield was a cultural club meant to train future leaders in speaking skills. The topics and themes of its addresses tended to be set by convention—for instance, a denunciation of "mobocracy" had been voiced by a speaker in 1835.[56] And the topic of Lincoln's address was not entirely of his own choosing—it had been part of an ongoing discussion in November and December, before Lincoln delivered his oration in January.[57] In such an elocution society, Ciceronian denunciation of an aspiring Catiline was a rhetorical topos, of the sort that permeated Lincoln's culture—not least from Shakespearean denunciation of tyrants.

The importance of the Lyceum speech in Lincoln's life has more to do with his literary development than with his psyche. As calmer scholars have pointed out, the *political* point of the speech was conventional—a Whig denunciation of Jacksonian usurpations, of "King Andrew" and his high-handed ways.[58] Oratorical heroism was not something Lincoln was driven to by his internal needs. It was the currency of public address in what was considered a golden age of oratory, the age of Calhoun, Webster, and Clay—men hardly thought of as feckless descendants *(epigoni)* of the fathers.

The psychobiographers hedge their bets by making Lincoln's putative resentment of the fathers express not only his personal plight but the frustration of a "postheroic" age in general, one that felt the dying of the revolutionary generation to be a closing of some psychic frontier: there would be no more heroes.[59] There *are* many expressions of that idea. But a louder chorus of self-congratulation at America's "Manifest Destiny" is what impressed visitors like Dickens and Tocqueville. Even a native observer like Twain thought too many Americans had "the Sir Walter disease," imagining themselves the chivalrous heroes of old. Walter Scott pomposity in the South matched Jacksonian posturing in the North. John Jay Chapman called this "the era of American brag."[60] The heroes of the Mexican War, and their supporters, had no very evident feelings of inadequacy.

Lincoln is a better cultural observer in a mature speech on inventions—reworked and seriously considered at the peak of his political life—than in the one-time exercise of the Lyceum speech; and in that later speech it is the arrogant complacency of Young America, not any feeling of inferiority, that is most criticized (SW 2.3–4). It was only in one of their many moods that Americans of Lincoln's time considered themselves puny descendants of giant fathers. Very palpable heroes were felt to be in their midst. Emerson idolized Edward Everett—and though that admiration cooled, Everett's idolization of Daniel Webster never did. The Transcendentalists had many living heroes, beginning with that ideologue of hero worship, Thomas Carlyle.

It will not do, then, to say that Lincoln *must* have resented the fathers for quashing any hope of heroism in his own time. The "spirit of the age" is many-sided. What Lincoln made of it must be tested against his own words, and not just the words of one speech. When forced to go beyond the Lyceum speech for evidence of their thesis, the psychobiographers have little to adduce. On the way to his inauguration, Lincoln described to the New Jersey legislature how, as a young man, he had read Mason Weems's life of Washington and come to know the New Jersey battlefields from that account (SW 2.209). Marcus Cunliffe, a lifelong student of Weems's biography, pointed out how conventional was that single reference to Weems—yet the psychobiographers have used the reference to construct a grand spiritual drama of resistance to George Washington.[61]

It is true that this is one of very few specific references to Lincoln's childhood reading; but he seems to have singled out the book because of the occasion rather than from some deep psychic urge. Praise of Washington at a public rally has little of confessional value considered in itself. The point he draws does not concern the personality of "the father" but the heroism of his soldiers, who crossed the Delaware animated by an ideal of liberty. The actual life of Washington seems not to have interested Lincoln—in fact, biographies in general bored him.[62] His references to Washington are as few as one can reasonably expect from a politician of that time—by contrast with, for instance, Everett's marathon performances of his eulogy to the Father of His Country. Lincoln's most striking reference to Washington is in his attack on the integrity of President Polk: "Let him remember he sits where Washington sat, and, so remembering, let him answer as Washington would answer" (SW 1.168).

Another reference to Washington occurred when Lincoln himself was on his way to "sit where Washington sat." The psychobiographers make a great deal out of this sentence, spoken in farewell to the citizens of Springfield: "I now leave, not knowing when, or whether ever, I may return, with a task before me greater than that which rested upon Washington" (SW 2.199). The rivalry presupposed in comparing his task to the founding father's allows Lincoln to express, at last, his "triumph over Washington."[63] Yet the prospect of Americans fighting Americans *did* pose a greater challenge than their united war against the colonizing power. Why look for obscure psychological reasons when Lincoln is stating sober fact—where, indeed, a little hyperbole would be allowable, to brace people for a difficult time ahead? Lincoln was not obsessed with Washington. The psychobiographers are.

Indeed, so distracted are they by their own fantasies about Washington that they have not noticed the most important indicator of Lincoln's attitude to "the fathers." When he refers to the fathers, it is usually to call them the authors of the Declaration of Independence. And of course the pre-eminent father in this context is Jefferson, a man the psychobiographers neglect entirely, since Lincoln showed no resentment toward *this* "father of his country," the man who enunciated the proposition to which the country is dedicated. The act of bringing forth a new nation conceived in liberty is always an *intellectual* act for Lincoln.

Lincoln, according to Herndon, was rather stingy with his praise. But he was unstinting in his admiration for Jefferson, "who was, is, and perhaps will continue to be, the most distinguished politician in our history" (SW 1.309). And it was Jefferson's framing of the *ideal* of the nation that made him its begetter:

> The principles of Jefferson are the definitions and axioms of free society. . . . All honor to Jefferson—to the man who, in the concrete pressure of a struggle for national independence by a single people, had the coolness, forecast, and capacity to introduce into a merely revolutionary document, an abstract truth, applicable to all men and all times, and so to embalm it there, that today, and in all coming days, it shall be a rebuke and a stumbling-block to the very harbingers of reappearing tyranny and oppression. [SW 2.19]

Even Washington's soldiers crossing the Delaware were animated by Jefferson's ideal. The New Jersey remarks that began with Parson Weems quickly moved to the real point of the fathers' greatness:

> I recollect thinking then, boy even though I was, that there must have been something more than common that those men struggled for. I am exceedingly anxious that that thing which they struggled for, that something even more than National Independence, that something that held out a great promise to all the people of the world to all time to come—I am exceedingly anxious that this Union, this Constitution, and the liberty of the people shall be perpetuated in accordance with the original *idea* for which that struggle was made. [Italics added.] [SW 2.209]

One cannot intelligently discuss Lincoln's attitude toward "the fathers" unless one grasps this most basic fact about his use of the term: for him, the fathers are always the begetters of the national idea. The founders of the nation founded it on that. The fighters for the nation fought for that. The drafters of the Constitution tried to embody as much as they could of that idea. The sons of the fathers are sons only so far as they accept and perpetuate that idea. The fathers are always relevant because the idea is never old. It is life-giving every time new Americans are begotten out of it. Americans are intellectually autochthonous, having no pedigree except that of the idea. Speaking on the Fourth of July in 1858, Lincoln said there are some in America who are blood descendants of the first signers and drafters; but they have no exclusive title to the fathers' bequest:

> We have besides these men—descended by blood from our ancestors—among us perhaps half our people who are not descendants at all of these men, they are men who come from Europe— German, Irish, French and Scandinavian—men that have come from Europe themselves, or whose ancestors have come hither and settled here, finding themselves our equals in all things. If they look back through this history to trace their connection with those days by blood, they find they have none, they cannot carry themselves back into that glorious epoch and make themselves feel that they are part of us, but when they look through that old Declaration of Independence they find that those old men say that "We hold these truths to be self-evident, that all men are created equal," and then they feel that that moral sentiment taught in that day evidences their relation to those men, that it is the father of all moral principle in them, and that they have a right to claim it as though they were blood of the blood, and flesh of the flesh, of the men who wrote that Declaration, and so they are. That is the electric cord in that Declaration that links the hearts of patriotic and liberty-loving men together, that will link those patriotic

hearts as long as the love of freedom exists in the minds of men throughout the world. [SW 1.456]

Since the Revolution was not completed when national independence was won, its idea still faces people as a promise unfulfilled: "It is, now, no child's play to save the principles of Jefferson from total overthrow in this nation" (SW 2.18). As champions of that idea in a "new nation," the fathers spoke for youth and for future developments. They were what Bryant, in *Thanatopsis*, calls "patriarchs of the infant world"—like the giant trees in Parkman's "young" continent. The vision of the founders resembled the gleam of heaven that plays around the child of Wordsworth's ode. The ideal is vivid because fresh—but it must be striven for in the *adult* world. There is no longer, in the Gettysburg Address, the assumption of Lincoln's 1838 speech, that the only job is to preserve and hand on what the fathers accomplished. They did *not* accomplish the political equality they professed. They did not end slavery. They did not make self-government stable and enduring. They could not do that. The ideal is not captured at once in the real: "I had thought the Declaration contemplated the *progressive* improvement in the condition of all men everywhere" (SW 1.400, italics added).

> They [the fathers] did not mean to assert the obvious untruth, that all men were then actually enjoying that equality, nor yet that they were about to confer it, immediately, upon them. In fact, they had no power to confer such a boon. They meant simply to declare the *right*, so that the *enforcement* might follow as fast as circumstances should permit. [SW 1.398]

Since Lincoln thinks of America's claim as intellectual, the Gettysburg Address is highly abstract in its thought and language. But if the *argument* of Lincoln is abstract, generalizing, and intellectual, his *imagery* is organic and familial. This is taken from the rural cemetery's normal store of images, having to do with the fertility of nature, the life-giving earth to which the dead have returned. Reverend Stockton said in his prayer at Gettysburg: "As the trees are not dead, though their foliage is gone, so our heroes are not dead, though their forms have fallen." Even *ideas* are fertile in this setting, as Emerson noticed in his cemetery dedication: man's ability to receive notions of the ideal from nature proves that he is ideal in his own makeup. "All great men find eternity affirmed in the promise of their faculties."[64]

A nation born of an idea finds that idea life-giving. And all attempts to re-enter that idea bring it and its adherents back to life. This is the "new birth" always available to people begotten of a proposition in the first place. The "new birth of freedom" in the last sentence of the Address takes us back to the miraculous birth of the opening sentence; and behind this image, too, there is the biblical concept of people "born again" (John 3.3–7). Elsewhere Lincoln made the theological imagery of spiritual regeneration more explicit:

> Our republican robe is soiled, and trailed in the dust. Let us repurify it. Let us turn and wash it white, in the spirit, if not the blood, of the Revolution. [SW 1.339–40]

The Declaration of Independence has replaced the Gospel as an instrument of spiritual rebirth. The spirit, not the blood, is the *idea* of the Revolution, not its mere temporal battles and chronological outcome. The "great task remaining" at the end of the Address is not something inferior to the great deeds of the fathers. It is the *same* work, always being done, and making all its champions the heroes of the nation's permanent ideal. In the last sentence of the Address, he is saying, in more concentrated form, what he said in his 1854 speech on the Kansas-Nebraska Act.

Let us re-adopt the Declaration of Independence, and, with it, the practices and policy which harmonize with it. Let north and south—let all Americans—let all lovers of liberty everywhere—join in the great and good work ["the unfinished work" of the Address]. If we do this, we shall not only have saved the Union, but we shall have so saved it as to make and to keep it forever worthy of the saving. We shall have so saved it that the succeeding millions of free happy people, the world over, shall rise up and call us blessed to the latest generations. [SW 1.340]

The last sentence draws more openly on Luke's tale of Jesus' miraculous birth than does the opening of the Address ("henceforth all generations shall call me blessed" [1.48]). And therein lies the greater power of the Address. It is made compact and compelling by its ability to draw on so many sources of verbal energy—on a classical rhetoric befitting the democratic burial of soldiers, on a romantic nature-imagery of birth and rebirth expected at the dedication of rural cemeteries, on biblical vocabulary for a chosen nation's consecration and suffering and resurrection, on a "culture of death" that made mourning serve life. In the crucible of the occasion, Lincoln distilled the meaning of the war, of the nation's purpose, of the remaining task, in a statement that is straightforward yet magical. No wonder the Chicago *Times* chafed impatiently at the Gettysburg Address. Lincoln argues, but he also casts a spell; and what can a rebuttal do to incantation?

The Transcendental
Declaration

S ome of the omissions of Lin-
coln's speech have already been mentioned. It is brief, one might
argue, because it is silent on so much that one would expect to
hear about. The Gettysburg Address does not mention Gettysburg. Nor slavery. Nor—more surprising—the Union. (Certainly
not the South.) The other major message of 1863, the Emancipation Proclamation, is not mentioned, much less defended or
vindicated. The "great task" mentioned in the Address is not
emancipation but the preservation of self-government. We assume, today, that self-government includes self-rule by blacks as
well as whites; but at the time of his appearance at Gettysburg
Lincoln was not advocating, even eventually, the suffrage for
African Americans. The Gettysburg Address, for all its artistry
and eloquence, does not directly address the prickliest issues of
its historic moment.

Lincoln was accused during his lifetime of clever evasions and key silences. He was especially indirect and hard to interpret on the subject of slavery. That puzzled his contemporaries, and has infuriated some later students of his attitude. Theodore Parker, the Boston preacher who was the idol of Lincoln's partner, William Herndon, found Lincoln more clever than principled in his 1858 Senate race, when he debated Stephen Douglas:

> In the Ottawa [Illinois] meeting, to judge from the *Tribune* report, I thought Douglas had the best of it. He questioned Mr. Lincoln on the great matters of slavery, and put the most radical questions, which go to the heart of the question, before the people. Mr. Lincoln did not meet the issue. He made a technical evasion: "he had nothing to do with the resolutions in question" [against slavery]. Suppose he had not, admit they were forged. Still, they were the vital questions pertinent to the issue, and Lincoln dodged them. That is not the way to fight the battle of freedom.[1]

Parker supported William Seward for president in 1860, since he found Seward more forthright than Lincoln in his opposition to slavery.[2] But Seward probably lost the Republican nomination *because* of that forthrightness. Lincoln was more cautious and circuitous. The reasons for his reserve before his nomination are clear enough—though that still leaves the omissions of the Gettysburg Address to be explained.

Lincoln's political base, the state of Illinois, runs down to a point (Cairo) farther south than all of what became West Virginia, and farther south than most of the states of Kentucky and Virginia. The "Negrophobia" of Illinois led it to vote overwhelmingly, in 1848, just ten years before the Lincoln-Douglas debates, to amend the state constitution so as to deny freed blacks all right of entry to the state.[3] The average vote of the state was 70 percent for exclusion, though southern and some central counties voted over 90 percent for it. Lincoln knew the racial geography of his own state well, and calibrated what he had to say about slavery according to his audience.

> His speeches were noticeably more receptive to antislavery senti-ment in northern Illinois. As he moved to central and southern portions of the state, his manner of expression appeared to corre-spond more favorably to the conservative attitude of these peo-ples.[4]

This shiftiness troubled Richard Hofstadter as recently as the 1940s:

> It is not easy to decide whether the true Lincoln is the one who spoke in Chicago or the one who spoke in Charleston. Possibly the man devoutly believed each of the utterances at the time he delivered it; possibly his mind too was a house divided against itself.[5]

But there is no sign of confusion in Lincoln's least defensible speech, delivered in Charleston, Illinois, as he ran unsuccessfully against Douglas. He sorts out his priorities in prose as clear, balanced, and precise as anything he ever wrote.

> *I will say then*
> *that I am not*
> *nor ever have been*
> *in favor of bringing about*
> *in any way*
> *the social and political equality*
> *of the white and black races—*
> *that I am not*
> *nor ever have been*

> *in favor of making voters or jurors of negroes*
> *nor of qualifying them to hold office,*
> *nor of intermarrying with white people;*
> *and I will say, in addition to this,*
> *that there is a physical difference*
> *between the white and black races*
> *which I believe will for ever forbid the two races*
> *living together on terms of political and social equality.*
> *And inasmuch as they cannot so live,*
> *while they do remain together*
> *there must be the position of superior and inferior,*
> *and I*
> *as much as any other man*
> *am in favor of having the superior position*
> *assigned to the white race.*
> *I say upon this occasion*
> *I do not perceive*
> *that because the white man is to have the superior*
> *position*
> *the negro should be denied everything.*
> *I do not understand*
> *that because I do not want a negro woman*
> *for a slave*
> *I must necessarily want her*
> *for a wife.* [SW 1.636][6]

This language is carefully studied to *avoid* conflict with anything Lincoln was saying elsewhere. Hofstadter is pursuing a false issue when he talks about contradiction between "the two Lincolns" in this period. The degree of *explicitness* in Lincoln's opposition to slavery, on the one hand, or his resignation to it, on the other, is greater or less from place to place. The fault in Charleston was less in the position he took than in his willingness to tickle the racism of his audience in a passage like the following:

My understanding is that I can just let her [a black woman] alone. I am now in my fiftieth year [actually his forty-ninth], and I certainly never had a black woman for either a slave or a wife. So it seems to me quite possible for us to get along without making either slaves or wives of negroes. I will add to this that I have never seen to my knowledge a man, woman or child who was in favor of producing a perfect equality, social and political, between negroes and white men. I recollect of but one distinguished instance that I ever heard of, so frequently as to be entirely satisfied of its correctness—and that is the case of Judge Douglas's old friend Col. Richard M. Johnson [who had acknowledged that his children were born of a mulatto].

[laughter]

I will also add to the remarks I have made (for I am not going to enter at large upon this subject), that I have never had the least apprehension that I or my friends would marry negroes if there was no law to keep them from it,

[laughter]

but as Judge Douglas and his friends seem to be in great apprehension that they might, if there were no law to keep them from it,

[roars of laughter]

I give him the most solemn pledge that I will to the very last stand by the law of this State, which forbids the marrying of white people with negroes.

[continued laughter and applause]

I will add one further word, which is this, that I do not understand there is any place where an alteration of the social and political relations of the negro and the white man can be made except in the State Legislature—not in the Congress of the United States— and as I do not really apprehend the approach of any such thing myself, and as Judge Douglas seems to be in constant horror that some such danger is rapidly approaching, I propose as the best means to prevent it that he be kept at home and placed in the

State Legislature to fight the measure. [uproarious laughter and applause]. [SW 1.637]

By drawing out the consequences of Douglas's alleged obsession, Lincoln indulges a kind of logical fantasy. He feigns concern for the friend *too* interested in black equality, for Douglas's susceptibility to black women, for his need to maintain a legislative protection against his own promptings. The easy flow of the last long sentence—going where the listeners foresee, but carrying them along with nudges and expansive savorings—is a masterpiece of casual lampooning. Alas, it is also demagogic. David Davis, Lincoln's adviser on Illinois politics, who was urging him to maintain his distance from the abolitionists, was delighted by the Charleston speech.[7]

Lincoln knew it was useless to promote the abolitionist position in Illinois—even the far "softer" stand of Seward proved too politically risky. He wanted to establish some common ground to hold together the elements of his fledgling Republican party. Even as a lawyer, Herndon says, he concentrated so fiercely on the main point to be established ("the nub") that he would concede almost any ancillary matter. Leonard Swett, a lawyer who had faced Lincoln in court, described his method:

As he entered the trial, where most lawyers would object he would say he "reckoned" it would be fair to let this in, or that; and sometimes, when his adversary could not quite prove what Lincoln knew to be the truth, he "reckoned" it would be fair to admit the truth to be so-and-so. When he did object to the Court, and when he heard his objections answered, he would often say, "Well, I reckon I must be wrong." Now, about the time he had practiced this three-fourths through the case, if his adversary didn't understand him, he would wake up in a few minutes learning that he had feared the Greeks too late and find himself beaten. He was wise as a serpent in the trial of a cause, but I have had too many scars from his blows to certify that he was harmless as a dove. When the whole thing was unraveled, the adversary would begin to see that what he [Lincoln] was so blandly giving away was simply what he couldn't get and keep. By giving away six points and arguing the seventh, he traded away everything which would give him the least aid in carrying that. Any man who took Lincoln for a simple-minded man would very soon wake up with his back in a ditch.[8]

Lincoln's accommodation to the prejudice of his time did not imply any agreement with the points he found it useless to dispute. One sees his attitude in the disarming concessions he makes to Horace Greeley, in order to get to the "nub" of their disagreement:

> I have just read yours of the 19th addressed to myself through the New York Tribune. If there be in it any statements, or assumptions of fact, which I may know to be erroneous, I do not, now and here, controvert them. If there be in it any inference which I may believe to be falsely drawn, I do not, now and here, argue against them. If there be perceptable [sic] in it an impatient and dictatorial tone, I waive it in deference to an old friend, whose heart I have always supposed to be right. [SW 2.357–58]

Obviously, Lincoln did not agree with the aspersions on his character; but those were not matters he could usefully pursue "now and here." In the same way, Lincoln preferred agnosticism about the blacks' intellectual inferiority to whites, and went along with the desire to keep them socially inferior. As George Fredrickson points out, agnosticism rather than *certainty* about blacks' intellectual disability was the "liberal" position of that time, and there was nothing Lincoln or anyone could do about social mixing.[9] Lincoln refused to let the matter of *political* equality get tangled up with such emotional and (for the time) irresolvable issues. What, for him, was the nub, the realizable minimum—which would be hard enough to establish in the first place?

At the very least, it was wrong to treat human beings as property. Lincoln reduced that position to absurdity by spelling out its consequences:

> If it is a sacred right for the people of Nebraska to take and hold slaves there, it is equally their sacred right to buy them where they can buy them cheapest; and that undoubtedly will be on the coast of Africa . . . [where a slave trader] buys them at the rate of about a red cotton handkerchief per head. This is very cheap.

Why do people not take advantage of this bargain? Because they will be hanged like pirates if they try. Yet if slaves are just one form of property like any other,

> it is a great abridgement of the sacred right of self-government to hang men for engaging in this profitable trade! . . . You never thought of hanging men for catching and selling wild horses, wild buffaloes or wild bears.

Not only had the federal government, following international sentiment, outlawed slave trade, but the domestic slave barterer was held in low esteem, even in the South:

> You do not recognize him as a friend, or even as an honest man. Your children may not play with his. . . . Now why is this? You do not so treat the man who deals in corn, cattle, or tobacco.

And what kind of *property* is "set free"? People do not "free" their houses, horses, or manufactures to fend for themselves. But there were almost half a million freed blacks in Lincoln's America:

> How comes this vast amount of *property* to be running about without owners? We do not see free horses or free cattle running at large. [SW 1.326–30]

Lincoln said that in 1854, three years before Chief Justice Taney declared, in the Dred Scott case, that slaves were movable property like any other chattel goods. The absurd had become law. No wonder Lincoln felt he had to fight for even minimum recognition of human rights.

If the black man owns himself and is not another person's property, then he has rights in the product of his labor:

> I agree with Judge Douglas he [the Negro] is not my equal in many respects—certainly not in color, perhaps not in moral or intellectual endowment. But in the right to eat the bread, without leave of anybody else, which his own hand earns, he is my equal and the equal of Judge Douglas and the equal of every living man. [SW 1.512]

Lincoln, as often, is using a Bible text, and one with a sting in it. The *curse* of mankind in general, that "in the sweat of thy face shalt thou eat bread" (Genesis 3.19), is, at the least, a sardonic *right* for blacks.

Lincoln tried to use one prejudice against another. There was, in Americans, a prejudgment in favor of anything biblical. There was, also, antimonarchical bias. Lincoln put the text about eating the bread of one's own sweat in an American context of antimonarchism:

> That is the issue that will continue in this country when these poor tongues of Judge Douglas and myself shall be silent. It is the

98

eternal struggle between these two principles—right or wrong—
throughout the world. They are the two principles that have stood
face to face from the beginning of time; and will ever continue to
struggle. The one is the common right of humanity and the other
the divine right of kings. It is the same principle in whatever
shape it develops itself. It is the same spirit that says, "You work
and toil, and earn bread, and I'll eat it." [Loud applause]. No
matter in what shape it comes, whether from the mouth of a king
who seeks to bestride the people of his own nation and live by the
fruit of their labor, or from one race of men as an apology for
enslaving another race, it is the same tyrannical principle. [SW
1.810–11]

In these two minimum ways, then, slavery is wrong. One cannot
own human beings, and one should not be in the position of a
king over human beings. Mark Twain, too, relied on this latter
prejudice when he introduced fake royalty onto Huck's raft, to
deepen the relationship between Huck and Jim. The King and
the Dauphin demand servile labor from their "subjects," who
must kneel to their "betters" when bringing them food. Paradoxically, the man already a slave is the first to rebel: "Dese [two] is
all I kin stan.' "[10] Huck and Jim are made allies yearning for a
joint freedom from "royalty," and it is in this situation that
Huck, hearing the story of Jim's deaf daughter, first makes the
startling admission: "I do believe he cared just as much for his
people as white folks does for their'n."[11] Then, when Huck sees
others truckling to the poseurs, he says, with an irony he does not
yet sense, though the reader does: "Well, if I ever struck anything like it, I'm a nigger."[12]

Lincoln and Twain both knew how to sneak around the
frontal defenses of prejudice and find a back way into agreement
with bigots. This explains, at the level of tactics, the usefulness
of the Declaration of Independence for Lincoln. That revered

document was antimonarchical in the common perception, and, so far as that took the reader, unchallengeable. But because it indicted King George III in terms of the equality of men, the Declaration committed Americans to claims even more at odds with slavery than with kingship—since kings do not, necessarily, claim to *own* their subjects. Put the claims of the Declaration as mildly as possible, and it still cannot be reconciled with slavery:

> I, as well as Judge Douglas, am in favor of the race to which I belong having the [socially] superior position. I have never said anything to the contrary, but I hold that, notwithstanding all this, there is no reason in the world why the negro is not entitled to all the natural rights enunciated in the Declaration of Independence, the right to life, liberty, and the pursuit of happiness. [Loud cheers]. I hold that he is as much entitled to these as the white man. [SW 1.512]

> I think the authors of that notable instrument [the Declaration] intended to include *all* men, but they did not intend to declare all men equal *in all respects*. They did not mean to say all were equal in color, size, intellect, moral development, or social capacity. They defined, with tolerable distinctness, in what respects they did consider all men created equal—equal in "certain unalienable rights, among which are life, liberty, and the pursuit of happiness." This they said, and this they meant. [SW 1.398]

Americans at that time were reverent toward (prejudiced in favor of) the Declaration of Independence; yet many of them were also prejudiced in favor of slavery. Lincoln kept arguing, in ingenious ways, that they must, in consistency, give up one or the other prejudice. The two cannot coexist in the same mind once their mutual enmity is recognized.

Stephen Douglas insisted that he did not have to make that

choice. Thomas Jefferson had not. The very author of the Declaration continued to own slaves. Moreover, the Constitution countenanced slavery, and the Constitution, not the Declaration, is the working law of the land.

It was at this point in the argument that Lincoln distinguished between the Declaration as the statement of a permanent ideal and the Constitution as an early and provisional embodiment of that ideal, to be tested against it, kept in motion toward it. The provisionality of the Constitution Lincoln found in the language devoted to slavery, a language so shamefaced as to call, by its very obliquity, for an end to the matter it treats as an anomaly:

At the framing and adoption of the constitution, they forbore to so much as mention the word "slave" or "slavery" in the whole instrument. In the provision for the recovery of fugitives, the slave is spoken of as a "PERSON HELD TO SERVICE OR LABOR." In that [provision] prohibiting the abolition of the African slave trade for twenty years, that trade is spoken of as "The migration or importation of such persons as any of the States NOW EXISTING, shall think, proper to admit," &c. These are the only provisions alluding to slavery. Thus, the thing is hid away, in the constitution, just as an afflicted man hides away a wen or a cancer, which he dares not cut out at once, lest he bleed to death; with the promise, nevertheless, that the cutting may begin at the end of a given time. Less than this our fathers COULD not do; and MORE they WOULD not do. But this is not all. The earliest Congress, under the constitution, took the same view of slavery. They hedged and hemmed it in to the narrowest limits of necessity.

In 1794, they prohibited an out-going slave-trade—that is, the taking of slaves FROM the United States to sell.

In 1798, they prohibited the bringing of slaves from Africa, INTO the Mississippi Territory—this territory then comprising what are now the States of Mississippi and Alabama. This was TEN YEARS before they had the authority to do the same thing as to the States existing at the adoption of the constitution.

In 1800 they prohibited AMERICAN CITIZENS from trading in slaves between foreign countries—as, for instance, from Africa to Brazil.

In 1803 they passed a law in aid of one or two State laws, in restraint of the internal slave trade.

In 1807, in apparent hot haste, they passed the law, nearly a year in advance, to take effect the first day of 1808—the very first day the constitution would permit—prohibiting the African slave trade by heavy pecuniary and corporal penalties.

In 1820, finding these provisions ineffectual, they declared the trade piracy, and annexed to it the extreme penalty of death. While all this was passing in the general government, five or six of the original slave States had adopted systems of gradual emancipation; and by which the institution was rapidly becoming extinct within these limits.

Thus we see, the plain unmistakable spirit of that age, towards slavery, was hostility in the PRINCIPLE, and toleration ONLY BY NECESSITY. [SW 1.337–38]

By invoking the "spirit of the age" (the *Zeitgeist*), Lincoln is using terminology familiar to *his* age. But he thinks the Declaration somehow escaped the constraints that bound the Constitution. It was free to state an ideal that transcended its age, one that serves as a touchstone for later strivings:

They [the fathers who issued the Declaration] meant to set up a standard maxim for free society, which should be familiar to all, and revered by all; constantly looked to, constantly labored for, and even though never perfectly attained, constantly approximated, and thereby constantly spreading and deepening its influence, and augmenting the happiness and value of life to all people of all colors everywhere. [SW 1.398]

The ideal is so general and time-free that it does not merely affect Americans—rather, its influence radiates out to *all* people *everywhere*. By setting up this dialectic of the ideal with the real, Lincoln has reached, already, the very heart of his Gettysburg Address, where a nation conceived in liberty by its dedication to the Declaration's critical proposition (human equality) must test that proposition's survivability in the real world of struggle.

Lincoln is no longer able to think of the Declaration as Jefferson did. Jefferson, a philosophical materialist, did not believe in metaphysical abstractions. For him, the right to equality and happiness was an empirically tested and measurable law of nature, inherent in the workings of society. His friend the Marquis de Chastellux wrote a two-volume work on *Public Happiness* studying the increase of political efficiency by the reduction of social friction.[13] That is the kind of Enlightenment project Jefferson had in mind in his own "political science," as one can see from the *Notes on the State of Virginia*.

Lincoln, like Jefferson, was a man of his own age; but his age was the romantic era, which breathes through the melancholy and brooding poetry he wrote in the 1840s. More to the point, his dialectic of ideals struggling for their realization in history owes a great deal to the primary intellectual fashion of his period, Transcendentalism. The Transcendentalists were theological Unitarians who, largely through the influence of Carlyle, adapted German Idealism to the study of American society. They saw the permanent ideal shining through the particulars of nature. "Nature," as Emerson put it, "is the incarnation of a thought. . . . The world is mind precipitated."[14] Lincoln was bound to be affected by the rhetoric, assumptions, and conscious ideals of the men who shaped his culture. This shows in his language, and can partially be traced in direct and indirect influences on his thinking. He knew, in different degrees, the work of the Transcendentalists—by minimal contact with Emerson himself, limited but deep contact with the thought of George Bancroft, and extensive exposure to Theodore Parker's views.

Lincoln had attended one of the public lectures in which Emerson—imitating his teacher Edward Everett—spread the Transcendentalist message. Emerson, after visiting President Lincoln in the White House, wrote in his diary for January 31, 1862: "When I was introduced to him, he [Lincoln] said, 'O Mr. Emerson, I once heard you say in a lecture, that a Kentuckian seems to say by his manners, "Here I am, if you don't like me, the worse for you." ' "[15] Emerson, like Parker, thought Lincoln had temporized on the slavery issue before the war, but he praised the Emancipation Proclamation in Transcendentalist terms very like Lincoln's own description of the way the Declaration's "maxim" must be progressively approximated according to the spirit of the age:

> The extreme moderation with which the President advanced to his design—his long-avowed expectant policy, as if he chose to be strictly the executive of the best public sentiment of the country, waiting only till it should be unmistakably pronounced—so fair a mind that none ever listened so patiently to such extreme varieties of opinion—so reticent that his decision has taken all parties by surprise, whilst yet it is just the sequel of his priorities—the firm tone in which he announces it, without inflation or surplusage—all these have bespoken such favor to the act that, great as the popularity of the President has been, we are beginning to think that we have underestimated the capacity and virtue which the Divine Providence has made an instrument of benefit so vast.[16]

George Bancroft's Transcendentalism suffused the ten-volume *History of the United States* for which he is best remembered now.[17] But Lincoln, who met Bancroft in 1854, knew the text Perry Miller chooses as the essential statement of Bancroft's Transcendentalism—the 1854 lecture on "The Necessity, the Reality, and the Promise of the Progress of the Human Race." This served as the model for Lincoln's own most ambitious philological-philosophical exercise of the 1850s, his lecture on inventions.[18] Bancroft, who had imbibed the elements of Transcendentalism from Friedrich Schleiermacher in Berlin, expressed his political creed in the 1854 lecture: "In public life, by the side of the actual state of the world, there exists this ideal state toward which it should tend." The historian's task, he felt, is to follow "the clashing between the fact and the higher law."[19] In the case of the United States, this meant tracing the fulfillment of the great American idea enunciated in the Declaration of Independence. In the climactic last pages of his eighth volume, published in the year of Lincoln's election, Bancroft uses typically Transcendentalist language concerning the Declaration:

> The bill of rights which it promulgates is of rights that are older than human institutions, and spring from the eternal justice. . . . The heart of Jefferson in writing the Declaration, and of Congress in adopting it, beat for all humanity; the assertion of right was made for the entire world of mankind and all coming generations, without any exceptions whatever.

This is the belief of Lincoln—that the Declaration is a pledge "to all people of all colors everywhere" (SW 1.398).

But Transcendentalism was not, for Lincoln, just a matter of famous texts by famous men. It was something he encountered, living and breathing, every time he went into his Springfield office and talked with his partner, "Billy" Herndon, a homespun idealist, the disciple of that most militant Transcendentalist, Theodore Parker, whom Emerson called "our Savonarola."[20] Herndon had metaphysical ardors that Lincoln rarely shared—one reason, perhaps, for Herndon's judgment that the older man was "cold." Few would now read Herndon's letters for their Transcendentalist flights:

> Come let us leap up into the uncolumned air and rest upon the spongy foundation, and there let us see satellite, planet, and sun; sea, air, and land. What do you see? Coexistences and successions, powers and forces, and consciously God—no Laws; but all, all governed by constant modes of operation, God the immediate cause.[21]

But the writings of Parker himself, which Herndon pushed upon Lincoln, were far more down-to-earth, and chimed with many of Lincoln's own preoccupations. Parker, a polymath who mastered twenty languages, was nonetheless a devout American patriot. He responded to the plight of slaves in the spirit of his grandfather, who had fought on the green at Lexington (where Parker was born):

> My grandfather drew the first sword in the Revolution; my father fired the first shot; the blood which flowed there was kindred to this which courses in my veins today. Besides that, when I write in my library at home, on the one side of me is the Bible which my fathers prayed over, their morning and evening prayer, for nearly a hundred years. On the other side there hangs the firelock my grandfather fought with in the old French war, which he carried at the taking of Quebec, which he zealously used at the battle of Lexington, and beside it is another, a trophy of that war, the first gun taken in the Revolution, taken also by my grandfather. With these things before me, these symbols; with these memories in me, when a parishioner, a fugitive from slavery, a woman, pursued by the kidnappers, came to my house, what could I do less than take her in and defend her to the last?[22]

Parker's great love of "the fathers" was concentrated on what he considered their finest legacy, the Declaration of Independence. That was "the American idea" by which all later history had to be judged.

The great political idea of America, the idea of the Declaration of Independence, is a composite idea made up of three simple ones 1. Each man is endowed with certain unalienable rights. 2. In respect of these rights all men are equal. 3. A government is to protect each man in the entire and actual enjoyment of all the unalienable rights. Now the first two ideas represent ontological facts, facts of human consciousness; they are facts of necessity. The third idea is an idea derived from the two others, is a synthetic judgment *a priori;* it was not learned from sensational experience; there never was a government which did this, nor is there now. Each of the other ideas transcended history; every unalienable right has been alienated, still is; no two men have been actually equal in actual rights. Yet the idea is true, capable of proof by human nature, not of verification by experience; as true as the proposition that three angles of a triangle are equal to two right angles; but no more capable of a sensational proof [based on the physical senses] than that. The American Revolution, with American history since, is an attempt to prove by experience this transcendental proposition, to organize the transcendental idea of politics. The idea demands for its organization a democracy—a government of all, for all, and by all. . . .[23]

Those last words bring to mind the point on which most historians grant Parker's influence on Lincoln. The great preacher constantly used a triple refrain describing government of, by, and for the people. Herndon was certain that Lincoln read one such formulation, and there were many of them scattered through Parker's writings.[24] But the real importance of Parker cannot be reduced to a tag, to one phrase in one or another text. There was a much larger consonance of the two men's thinking, certainly in politics and probably in wider areas as well. Herndon quotes the judgment of Jesse Fell, who elicited Lincoln's 1859 autobiographical sketch: "If, from my recollections on this subject, I was called upon to designate an author whose views most nearly represented Mr. Lincoln's on this subject [religion], I would say that author was Theodore Parker."[25] Whether that is true or not, it has much to do with Herndon's famous contention that Lincoln had rejected dogmatic Christianity. Edmund Wilson, Gore Vidal, and others take that to mean Lincoln was irreligious. For Herndon, it means that Lincoln was "a thoroughly religious man, not a Christian"—the kind of man a Transcendentalist could admire.[26]

Most Transcendentalists went beyond even the broad theology of their Unitarian upbringing. Some ceased to be Christians in any sense, but Parker kept to his pulpit because he contrasted the *ideal* Jesus with all the provisional expressions of that ideal in biblical texts or church doctrines.[27] Thus Parker drew his all-important theological-political analogy: as Jesus is to the Bible (the ideal to the limited reality), so is the Declaration to the Constitution:

> By Christianity, I mean that form of religion which consists of piety—the love of God, and morality—the keeping of His laws. That is not the Christianity of the Christian church, nor of any sect. It is the ideal religion which the human race has been groping for. . . . By Democracy, I mean government over all the people, by all the people, and for the sake of all. . . . This is not the democracy of the parties, but it is that ideal government, the reign of righteousness, the kingdom of justice, which all noble hearts long for, and labor to produce, the ideal whereunto mankind slowly draws near.

Here is the American programme of political principles: All men are endowed by their Creator with certain natural rights; these rights can be alienated only by the possessor thereof; in respect thereto all men are equal. . . . But the means to that end, the Constitution itself, is by no means unitary; it is a provisional compromise between the ideal political principle of the Declaration, and the actual selfishness of the people North and South.[28]

Parker says, in the harsher terms of the preacher, what the politic Lincoln put more gently: "The [Constitutional] Convention was ashamed of the whole thing, and added hypocrisy to its crime: it did not dare mention the word slave."[29]

Herndon said that Lincoln believed in "evolution," a pre-Darwinian use of the word to mean human *progress*.[30] Parker, too, saw the world progressing toward the realization of the supreme value, human freedom. For him there were four great leaps forward toward the realization of that ideal—the birth of Jesus, the Protestant Reformation, the puritan societies of New England, and the Declaration of Independence.[31] In each case, mere fact is made to express, at last, transcendent aspirations and ideals:

First comes the Sentiment—the feeling of liberty; next the idea— the thought become a thing. Buds in March, blossoms in May, apples in September—that is the law of historical succession.

Even when the Declaration was adopted, it just set the stage for further progress:

It would not be historical to expect a nation to realize its own Idea at once, and allow all men to be "equal" in the enjoyment of their "natural and unalienable rights." Still, there has been a great progress towards that.[32]

This is exactly Lincoln's notion of the continual approximation to the Declaration. It stands as a test for all other things (even the Constitution), since it is outside American history while being inside it.

> Our national ideal out-travels our experience, and all experience. We began our national career by setting all history at defiance— for that said, "A republic on a large scale cannot exist." Our progress since has shown that we were right in refusing to be limited by the past. *The political ideas of the nation are transcendent, not empirical.* Human history could not justify the Declaration of Independence and its large statements of the new idea: the nation went behind human history and appealed to human nature. [Italics added].[33]

Lincoln has been described as making a cult of the Declaration. Parker demonstrates how natural that attitude could be in the Transcendentalist period. He also shows that one can be even more enthusiastic in one's devotion to the document than Lincoln himself.

And, like Lincoln, Parker progressed in his own life toward the views he finally expressed on equality. He, too, was culturally constrained. Despite his firebrand quality as an abolitionist (the quality that made Lincoln resist overt identification with Parker, despite all Herndon's efforts), he had as constricted a view of black *social* rights as Lincoln himself had. His best biographer notes: "Parker's estimate of the negro, intellectually and morally, was low. He exaggerated the sensuality of the negro as he did that of the Jew [and, one might add, the Catholic]. . . . Moreover the negro had for him a certain physical repulsion."[34] And, like Lincoln, Parker did not show an early concern for the slave issue. But the Fugitive Slave Act of 1850, which Parker called the Government Kidnapping Act, made the patriot preacher feel the nation was surrendering even the hitherto-compromised devotion to its own animating idea. Without that idea, expressed in the Declaration, America had no moral identity at all.

So even Parker's grasp on the ideal he espoused was imperfect, like Lincoln's. But both men recognized attacks on the ideal, and were driven to deeper realization of its implications as they responded to those attacks. In 1854, when Stephen Douglas canceled the Missouri Compromise of 1821 (which had excluded slavery in new territories above the latitude of 36° 30′), throwing open the whole Nebraska territory, Parker felt that an idea *opposite* to the American idea was now on the march, the Despotic Idea advanced by the Slave Power, and that the two ideas were engaged in a battle that one or the other must shortly win. Equality, once the ground of agreement, was now openly challenged and going backward:

> At first, Slavery was an exceptional measure, and men tried to apologize for it, and excuse it. Now it is a normal [normative] principle, and the institution must be defended and eulogized.[35]

Parker, who had always been interested in the historiography of his country, forged in the 1850s a powerful analysis of recent events, from which he made the prediction that the Slave Power, if not stopped, would extend its reign over all the nation.[36] He saw its past steps—the silencing of the presidency, the swaying of the Supreme Court, the Fugitive Slave Act, the Kansas-Nebraska Act—as leading to future victories: the addition of Cuba and Haiti to slave territories, the revival of the slave trade on the world market, the protection of slave "property" in free states.[37] In 1857, the Dred Scott decision went far toward making this last prediction come true—if a slave was movable property in the territories, why not in free states as well? Property is property, and the right to it is innate.

Parker's description of the Slave Power's plot to defeat the Declaration is especially important to the student of Lincoln, whose own charge that there was a "conspiracy" of the slave interests has been dismissed, even by many of Lincoln's admirers, as exaggerated if not deceptive. J. G. Randall called the alleged conspiracy "quite fanciful and non-existent."[38] Allan Nevins called it "an absurd bogey," since "no Court would have dared such folly" as restoring slavery in the free states.[39] David Zarefsky, while granting that charges of conspiracy were common in the 1860s, says that Lincoln went beyond what anyone else was charging:

> Lincoln made two major contributions to the conspiracy argument. He presented elaborate explanations of the legal means by which the conspiracy could work its will, and he linked Douglas to the plot. . . . The "news" in Lincoln's use of the argument was his assertion that Douglas was in on the plot.[40]

But, in fact, Parker often vilified Douglas as an agent of the Slave Power, and his description of the legal machinery and strategy of that Power precedes Lincoln's and corresponds with it in every part. The Slave Power, according to Parker, controlled the Supreme Court under Justice Taney, the presidency under Pierce and Buchanan, and the legislature through Douglas. These are the four men Lincoln attacked in his famous House Divided Speech of 1858. In a virtuoso single sentence, which itself shifts and fits parts together constructively, enacting the process it describes, Lincoln saw design in the separate acts of Stephen [Douglas] and Franklin [Pierce] and Roger [Taney] and James [Buchanan]:

> But when we see a lot of framed timbers, different portions of which we know have been gotten out at different times and places

and by different workmen—Stephen, Franklin, Roger, and James, for instance—and when we see these timbers joined together, and see they exactly make the frame of a house or a mill, all the tenons and mortises exactly fitting, and all the lengths and proportions of the different pieces exactly adapted to their respective places, and not a piece too many or too few—not omitting even scaffolding—or, if a single piece be lacking, we can see the place in the frame exactly fitted and prepared to yet bring such piece in—in *such* a case, we find it impossible to not *believe* that Stephen and Franklin and Roger and James all understood one another from the beginning, and all worked upon a common *plan* or *draft* drawn up before the first lick was struck. [SW 1.431]

Even before Buchanan was elected, Parker saw the conspiracy taking shape (in 1854):

The Slave Power controls the President, and fills all the offices. Out of twelve elected Presidents, four have been from the North, and the last of them might just as well have been taken by lot at the South anywhere. Mr. Pierce, I just now said, was Texan in his latitude. His conscience is Texan; only his cradle was New Hampshire. Of the nine judges of the Supreme Court, five are from the slave states—the Chief Justice [Taney] from the slave States.[41]

And Douglas was a prominent part of this cabal in Parker's eyes. Speaking of his role in the Kansas-Nebraska Act, he said, "no man has done us such harm."[42] In his role as clergyman, with a professional's knowledge of his own trade, he said of Douglas: "Amongst men not clerical, I have heard but one speaker lie with such exquisite adroitness, and make the worse appear the better reason."[43]

As for the legal means the cabal would use, Lincoln lists the same moves Parker had—revive the slave trade, introduce slavery in the North, and extend the institution to Cuba and other parts of the Caribbean (SW 1.433, 2.196). The tactic would be to use slave property in the territories to establish similar property rights in the free states. Both men saw that Judge Taney's formulae in the Dred Scott decision (defended by Douglas) lent themselves to this future use.[44] Lincoln traced the logic of the decisions that could follow on the words of Justice Taney:

> Nothing in the Constitution or laws of any State can destroy a right distinctly and expressly affirmed in the Constitution of the United States.
>
> "The right of property in a slave [quoting Taney] is distinctly and expressly affirmed in the Constitution of the United States."
>
> Therefore, nothing in the Constitution or laws of *any* State can destroy the right of property in a slave. [SW 1.714]

Parker was equally certain that this was the direction of the Court:

> The first [step] is to establish Slavery in all the Northern States— the Dred Scott decision has already put it in all the territories. . . . I have no doubt The Supreme Court will make the [subsequent] decisions.[45]

Justice Taney said a man does not forfeit his property right over a slave just by traveling to a territory. Why, in logic, should he forfeit that basic right when traveling in a Northern state?

Recent historians have been less ready to charge Lincoln with exaggeration or special pleading when he talked of conspiracy. For one thing, it is now known that President Buchanan was secretly communicating with the Supreme Court and timing his own acts and words in expectation of the decision that was handed down on Dred Scott—a key contention in Lincoln's

House Divided Speech.[46] The modern historian Kenneth Stampp sounds quite conspiratorial himself: "Thus, three southern [Supreme Court] justices, one compliant northern justice, and the President-elect [Buchanan] secretly made a pawn of Dred Scott in a game of judicial politics."[47]

Besides, there was real pressure to expand slavery into the Caribbean and to revive the slave trade.[48] Lincoln argued that confining slavery to its Southern bastion would put it "in course of extinction"—would "ring it with fire," as Parker said.[49] Southerners themselves proved they shared this view by their desperation to expand south and west. James Oakes argues that there is an economic imperative for slavery to expand, one reflected in the priorities of the Southern states:

> The needs of the slave economy and the rights of slaveholders were invoked to justify the war with Mexico, imperial escapades in the Caribbean, and "border ruffianism" in Kansas and Nebraska. . . . By the 1850s slavery was far more than a negative frame of reference among free-labor ideologues. It was an imminent threat. . . . Centuries of western history had also demonstrated slavery's insatiable urge to expand.[50]

Oakes's extended analysis gives in argument what Parker presented as an image:

> There is an old story told by the Hebrew rabbis, that before the flood there was an enormous giant, called Gog. After the flood had got into the full tide of successful experiment, and every man was drowned except those taken into the ark, Gog came striding along after Noah, feeling his way with a cane as long as the mast of the "Great Republic." The water had only come up to his girdle. It was then over the hill-tops and was still rising—raining night and day. The giant hailed the Patriarch. Noah put his head out of the

115

window, and said, "Who is there?" "It is I," said Gog. "Take us
in; it is wet outside!" "No," said Noah, "you're too big; no room.
Besides, you're a bad character. You would be a very dangerous
passenger, and would make trouble in the ark; I shall not take you
in. You may get on top if you like"; and he clapped to the
window. "Go to thunder," said Gog; "I will ride, after all." And
he strode after him, wading through the waters; and mounting on
the top of the ark, with one leg over the larboard and other over
the starboard side, steered it just as he pleased, and made it rough
weather inside. Now, in making the Constitution, we did not care
to take in slavery in express terms. It looked ugly. We allowed it
to get on the top astride, and now it steers us just where it
pleases.[51]

Lincoln, too, felt that temporizing with slavery was the great
historical weakness of America:

> Has anything ever threatened the existence of this Union save and
> except this very institution of slavery? What is it that we hold
> most dear amongst us? Our own liberty and prosperity. What has
> ever threatened our liberty and property save and except this
> institution of slavery? If this is true, how do you propose to
> improve the condition of things by enlarging slavery—by spread-
> ing it out and making it bigger? You may have a wen or a cancer
> upon your person and not be able to cut it out lest it bleed to
> death; but surely it is no way to cure it, to engraft it and spread
> it over your whole body. [SW 1.808]

Lincoln has been criticized for continuing to treat Douglas
as part of the proslavery conspiracy even after the Illinois senator
broke with his own Democratic party leader, President Buchanan, over the Lecompton Constitution—a proslavery constitution for Kansas drawn up by a rump convention. Psychobiographers, as we have seen, claim that this demonstrates Lincoln's

oedipal compulsion to "kill" Douglas as a sibling rival. But Parker demonstrates that distrust of Douglas, even when he disagreed with his own party on a measure so extreme as to be farcical, was not a private obsession confined to Lincoln.[52]

> If he were President, he would do as Buchanan does, only more so. . . . He knows he cannot be re-elected [to the Senate] unless he changes course. So he alters his measures and provisionally favors freedom, but not its principles. . . . I know it is said, "Any stone is good enough to throw at a dog"; but this is a stone that will scale in its flight, veer off, and finally hit what you mean not to hurt but to defend.[53]

Douglas, to soften his break with Buchanan, said he attacked the Lecompton Constitution only on procedural grounds (because it was not a valid expression of real preference), not on substantive grounds. He said he did not care how the people voted on slavery, up or down, so long as they voted freely. Lincoln seized on the "I do not care" language in a way that Douglas's defenders consider unfair.[54] But Lincoln lamented the fact that even when people opposed, on tactical grounds, an extreme measure of the Slave Power, they felt a need to stress that they were not speaking ill of slavery itself. The South, which had imposed a ban on antislavery speech in its own confines, and had tried to extend it in "gag rules" even to the North, had extorted a kind of complicity by silence, one that made open disapproval of slavery a form of civic provocation.[55]

> And if there be among you anybody who supposes that he as a Democrat, can consider himself "as much opposed to slavery as anybody," I would like to reason with him. You never treat it as a wrong. What other thing that you consider as a wrong, do you deal with as you deal with that? Perhaps you *say* it is wrong, *but*

117

your leader never does, and you quarrel with anybody who says it is wrong. Although you pretend to say so yourself you can find no fit place to deal with it as a wrong. You must not say anything about it in the free States, *because it is not here.* You must not say anything about it in the slave States, *because it is there.* You must not say anything about it in the pulpit, because that is religion and has nothing to do with it. [SW 1.809]

Parker had denounced the same intimidation of people on a matter considered too "inflammatory" to be discussed:

The Slave Power, thus controlling the slaves and slaveholders at the South, and the Democratic party at the North, easily manages the Government at Washington. The Federal officers are marked with different stripes—Whig, Democrat, and so on. They are all owned by the same master, and lick the same hand. So it controls this nation. It silences the great sects, Trinitarian, Unitarian, Nullitarian: the chief ministers of this American Church—threefold in denominations, one in nature—have naught to say against Slavery; the Tract Society dare not rebuke "the sum of all villainies," the Bible Society has no "Word of God" for the slave, the "revealed religion" is not revealed to him. Writers of schoolbooks "remember the hand that feeds them," and venture no word against the national crime that threatens to become also the national ruin. In no nation on earth is there such social tyranny of opinion. . . . The Democratic hands of America have sewed up her own mouth with an iron thread.[56]

For a Transcendentalist like Parker, this checking of the *expression* of the American idea of equality is the deepest kind of defeat. How can events be made to approximate an ideal that people are afraid to express? If Douglas feels he can only be elected by professing indifference to human equality, the battle is almost over. Lincoln said the conspiracy was being advanced by some who were not conscious agents of it. It can succeed if enough people become tacitly complicitous, never voicing the one ideal opposed to it:

> In this I think I argue fairly (without questioning motives at all) that Judge Douglas is most ingeniously and powerfully preparing the public mind to take that [next Dred Scott style] decision when it comes; and not only so, but he is doing it in various other ways. In these general maxims about liberty—in his assertions that he "don't care whether Slavery is voted up or voted down," that "whoever wants Slavery has a right to have it," that "upon principles of equality it should be allowed to go everywhere," that "there is no inconsistency between free and slave institutions." In this he is also preparing (whether purposely or not) the way for making the institution of slavery national. I repeat again, for I wish no misunderstanding, that I do not charge that he means it so; but I call upon your minds to inquire, if you were going to get the best instrument you could, and then set it to work in the most ingenious way, to prepare the public mind for this movement, operating in the free States, where there is now an abhorrence of the institution of Slavery, could you find an instrument so capable of doing it as Judge Douglas, or one employed in so apt a way to do it? [SW 1.717]

Government by the people cannot exist where those who believe in equality are asked to sacrifice that belief (and its expression) in the name of social concord. Douglas had quoted against Lincoln Henry Clay, who feared the muzzling of cannon and the blowing out of moral lights; but Lincoln asked who could more effectively do both things than the person who abandons the expression of the American creed?

> And I do think—I repeat, though I said it on a former occasion—that Judge Douglas, and whoever like him teaches that the negro has no share, humble though it may be, in the Declaration of

Independence, is going back to the era of our liberty and independence, and, so far as in him lies, muzzling the cannon that thunders its annual joyous return; that he is *blowing out the moral lights around us,* when he contends that whoever wants slaves has a right to hold them; that he is penetrating, so far as lies in his power, the human soul, and eradicating the light of reason and the love of liberty, when he is in every possible way *preparing the public mind,* by his vast influence, for making the institution of slavery perpetual and national. [SW 1.717–18]

"Preparing the public mind" is a thing of great importance in an age of Transcendentalism. To fall silent, or to silence others, on the very notion of equality is the ultimate self-betrayal of a land that was dedicated to a *proposition.* Lincoln does not exaggerate the crisis of the house divided if one accepts his premise—and Parker's—that the only ground of legitimate union for the American nation is the American idea enunciated in the Declaration of Independence.

Lincoln was able to achieve the loftiness, ideality, and brevity of the Gettysburg Address because he had spent a good part of the 1850s repeatedly relating all the most sensitive issues of the day to the Declaration's supreme principle. If all men are created equal, they cannot be property. They cannot be ruled by owner-monarchs. They must be self-governing in the minimal sense of self-possession. Their equality cannot be denied if the nation is to live by its creed, and voice it, and test it, and die for it. All these matters are now contained in the pregnant formulae of the Address. Nothing more specific needs to be mentioned, because a nation free to proclaim its ideal is freed, again, to approximate that ideal over the years, in ways that run far beyond any specific or limited reforms, even one so important as emancipation. A return to the ideal is an *escape* from distracting particulars, a recovery of the long-term tasks of equality and self-government.

Revolution
in Thought

Close as was Lincoln's thinking to that of Theodore Parker, one insuperable barrier lay between them. Parker had no qualms about separation of the Union. Better secession of the South, he felt, than further spreading of its poisons to the North. The Union was not worth preserving if that just gave infection a larger body to pervade. Parker, who raised funds to support the crusade of John Brown, was ready to let the division come, violently if necessary, rather than submit to further aggressions from the Slave Power.

Parker's increasingly frenetic crusade against slavery reached its height in the late 1850s, when speaking, publishing, organizing, and fund-raising broke his health. Traveling abroad to repair it, he died in 1860, aged fifty, just before he could witness the breakup of the Union. Though he had been disappointed that Lincoln tried to finesse Douglas instead of denouncing him in the 1858 debates, he would probably have come around, like Emerson, to Lincoln's view of things by the time of the Emancipation Proclamation.[1] Parker's own candidate for the presidency, William Seward, had gone into the Lincoln Cabinet, by then, as a close adviser and supporter.

Parker realized that practicing politicians could not be as fierce as could free-lance reformers of his sort. He pardoned Seward's tactical maneuvers with these words:

> I think that the anti-Slavery men have not always done quite justice to the political men. See why. It is easy for Mr. Garrison and Mr. Phillips or me to say all of their thought. I am responsible to nobody, and nobody to me. But it is not easy for Mr. Sumner, Mr. Seward, and Mr. Chase to say all of their thought; because they have a position to maintain, and they must keep that position.[2]

But there was one politician Parker would never forgive, the one he considered the great betrayer of New England—and that politician was the one whose style and arguments Lincoln used as models all through his political life: Daniel Webster. When the Compromise of 1850 was put together by Henry Clay, Webster supported it, Seward opposed. Part of that complex package of five bills was the Fugitive Slave Act. Nothing, in Parker's eyes, could counterbalance that concession to the Slave Power. For the last two years of Webster's life, Parker hounded him in his home city of Boston, making Faneuil Hall ring with attacks on the man whose fame had been nurtured there. When Webster died in 1852, people flocked to Parker's church, where a eulogy was announced, curious to see if Parker would soften at the memory of Webster's earlier achievements. For three hours Parker held them in a spell of horror as he painted the man darker and darker with sardonic tributes.

Did men honor Daniel Webster? So did I. I was a boy ten years old when he stood at Plymouth Rock, and never shall I forget how his clarion words rang in my boyish breast. I was but a little boy when he spoke those brave words in behalf of Greece. I was helped to hate slavery by the lips of that great intellect; and now that he takes back his words, and comes himself to be slavery's slave, I hate it tenfold harder, because it made a bondman out of that proud, powerful nature.[3]

Lincoln, as an admirer of both Clay and Webster, did not oppose the Compromise of 1850. Parker dated the climactic campaign of the Slave Power from that year. Lincoln thought the final onslaught began in 1854, with Douglas's passage of the Kansas-Nebraska Act. Parker was disappointed by Lincoln's performance against Douglas since Lincoln refused to be pinned down on repeal of the 1850 Fugitive Slave Act. Partly, of course, this was a matter of Lincoln's constituency. Henry Clay, the author of the Compromise, was still a figure to reckon with in Illinois politics, and Douglas fought with Lincoln for the possession of Clay's mantle in 1858. Lincoln had delivered a long and ambitious eulogy to Clay at his death in 1852 (SW 1.259–72).

But there was also, for Lincoln, a point of principle in his devotion to the memories of Clay and Webster. All their tacking and maneuver in the period of sectional compromise was dictated by their effort to preserve the Union. Lincoln felt they proved that one can remain opposed to slavery while making temporary concessions to the South in order to keep the nation together. The one thing Lincoln would not surrender, as Douglas had, was the continued identification of slavery as an evil, no matter how necessary. Lincoln praised Clay as a way of clearing similar space for his own career. Clay, in Lincoln's view of the man, opposed *both* the abolitionists for their cavalier readiness to divide the nation *and* those who would deny the plain meaning of the Declaration to mollify slaveholders:

> Those who would shiver into fragments the Union of these States, tear to tatters its now venerated Constitution; and even burn the last copy of the Bible, rather than slavery should continue a single hour, together with all their more halting sympathizers, have received, and are receiving their just execration; and the name, and opinions, and influence of Mr. Clay, are fully, and, as I trust, effectively and enduringly, arrayed against them. But I would also, if I could, array his name, opinions, and influence against the opposite extreme—against a few but an increasing number of men who, for the sake of perpetuating slavery, are beginning to assail and to ridicule the white man's charter of freedom—the declaration that "all men are created free and equal." [SW 1.269]

Clay and Webster were important symbols to Whigs of Lincoln's background. Coming from different regions, divided in temperament, made rivals by their similar ambition, they offered the hope that a slaveholding Southerner like Clay could agree with a New England celebrant of the Pilgrims like Webster on the importance of finding ways to keep the nation together. Clay picked his way through the political swamp like a flamboyant heron, where Webster dashed in like a moody bull, splashing mud on himself and others—but each, by his own route, reached common ground, and Lincoln was loath to jeopardize that last space of united endeavor.

As a fellow Kentuckian, as one whose political career lay in a state bordering Missouri, Lincoln found Clay the more useful man to cite and celebrate before his constituents.[4] (Parker, for his part, excoriating Webster as a renegade New Englander, entirely neglected Clay because he never expected statesmanship from a slaveholder.) But Webster provided Lincoln with the arguments and reasoning he needed for placing such importance on the concept of union.

Some think, to this day, that Lincoln did not really have *arguments* for union, just a kind of mystical attachment to it. That was the charge of Southerners, who felt they had a better constitutional case for secession than he had for compelling states to remain. Alexander Stephens, who had served as vice-president of the Confederacy, was an influential formulator of the view that Lincoln's attitude was not reachable by mundane arguments: "The Union with him, in sentiment, rose to the sublimity of a religious mysticism."[5] But even Northerners like Whitman felt that "the only thing like passion or infatuation in the man [Lincoln] was the passion for the Union of these states."[6] Edmund Wilson was following a long tradition when he called his Lincoln essay (later included in his book on the Civil War) "The Union as Religious Mysticism."

Yet Lincoln drew much of his defense of the Union from the speeches of Webster, and few if any have considered Webster a mystic. He was thought of as the leading constitutional lawyer of his day. He argued 180 cases before the Supreme Court, including some of the most famous constitutional cases in our history. In fact, he pleaded almost as many landmark cases as John Marshall decided—*Dartmouth College* v. *Woodward* (1818), *McCullough* v. *Maryland* (1818), *Gibbons* v. *Ogden* (1824), *Ogden* v. *Saunders* (1827), *Swift* v. *Tyson* (1842), *Luther* v. *Borden* (1849).[7] Theodore Parker, trying to belittle Webster's legal acumen, said he borrowed much of it from his friend on the Court, Justice Joseph Story (whom we have already met as the dedicator of the Mount Auburn Cemetery).

I know that much of his present reputation depends on his achievements as a lawyer; as an "expounder of the Constitution." Unfortunately, it is not possible for me [in Webster's eulogy!] to say how much credit belongs to Mr. Webster for his constitutional arguments, and how much to the late Judge Story. . . . From 1816 to 1842 Mr. Webster was in the habit of drawing from that deep and copious well of legal knowledge, whenever his own bucket was dry. Mr. Justice Story was the Jupiter Pluvius [Raingod] from whom Mr. Webster often sought to elicit peculiar thunder for his speeches and private rain for his own public tanks of law.[8]

It is quite true that Story and Webster collaborated in ways inconceivable now for a Supreme Court justice and a senator pleading before the Court; but this does not weaken Webster's claims as an expert on the Constitution. Story was the leading academic expositor of that document in his day. He held the Dane Professorship of Law at Harvard even while he continued sitting on the Court, and his three-volume commentary on the Constitution, the product of that lectureship, appeared to great acclaim in the 1830s. Lincoln knew and used Justice Story's commentary.[9] It did not hurt Webster's reputation for authority on the Constitution that it was (correctly) rumored that Justice Story read and helped strengthen Webster's major speeches before they were given.[10]

Webster's doctrine of constitutional union was forged to answer the subtlest case formulated in defense of the Southern view—John C. Calhoun's. In the late 1820s and early 1830s, Calhoun and Webster fenced with each other in an intellectual duel that set the terms of argument for the next thirty years. The struggle precipitated each man's masterpiece—Calhoun's *Disquisition on Government* (not published till 1853) and Webster's Reply to Hayne (1830).

We know what Lincoln thought of these two men's arguments. Though he usually refrained from attack on individual Southerners, out of regard for sectional unity, the following passage was aimed at Calhoun, the "metaphysician" of the South, a muser whose theory of "concurrent majorities" was in fact a system of multiple vetoes:

> They have him [the Negro] in this prison house; they have searched his person, and left no prying instrument with him. One after another they have closed the heavy iron doors upon him, and now they have him, as it were, bolted in with a lock of a hundred keys, which can never be unlocked without the *concurrence* of every key; the keys in the hands of a hundred different men, and they scattered to a hundred different and distant places; and they stand musing as to what invention, in all the dominions of mind and matter, can be produced to make the impossibility of his escape more complete than it is. [Italics added.] [SW 1.396–97][11]

About Webster, Lincoln's views could not be more different. He thought his Reply to Hayne the greatest American speech, and he consulted it in composing his House Divided Speech and the First Inaugural.[12] Echoes of it can be found in other Lincoln speeches, including the Gettysburg Address. It would be hard to find any other text, except the Declaration of Independence, which Lincoln used with such familiarity and respect. This is not surprising in a man whose intellectual formation took place during the 1830s, when the Webster speech was everywhere printed, quoted, and praised. The published version was distributed in at least a hundred thousand copies, with subsidized emphasis on the West, where its themes were especially relevant.[13]

Webster's great performance arose from a matter trivial in itself—congressional requisitions for Western surveying in 1830. But the West was the arena being contended for by slave and free factions, and Calhoun had threatened in 1828 that the South might nullify laws it considered injurious. Calhoun could not engage Webster directly in Senate debate, in 1830, since the former was serving as Andrew Jackson's vice-president, which

meant that he presided in the Senate as the animosity mounted—
Thomas Hart Benton speaking for the pro-Southern West; Senator Robert Hayne, Calhoun's South Carolina cat's-paw, speaking
for the South; and everyone awaiting Webster's reply, presumably to be spoken for the East.

The reply was delivered on January 27, before a packed
gallery; and Calhoun cannot have watched from his presiding
chair with any comfort as Webster, hour after hour, took apart
the case that had been made by Hayne. Webster refused to speak
for the East. He spoke for the nation. It was a single people, he
argued, that rallied to Washington in the Revolution, heroes
from Bunker Hill dying in the South, Southern leaders following
Washington north. Men of Massachusetts and South Carolina
fought together: "Shoulder to shoulder they went through the
Revolution, hand in hand they stood round the administration of
Washington, and felt his own great arm lean on them for support."[14] Webster will not confine his pride as an American to
Concord, Lexington, or Bunker Hill:

I shall not acknowledge that the honorable member [Hayne] goes
before me in regard for whatever of distinguished talent, or distinguished character, South Carolina has produced. I claim part of
the honor, I partake in the pride of her great names. I claim them
for countrymen, one and all, the Laurenses, the Rutledges, the
Pinckneys, the Sumpters, the Marions, *Americans* all, whose
fame is no more to be hemmed in by State lines, than their talents
and patriotism were capable of being circumscribed within the
same narrow limits. . . . Him whose honored name the gentleman
himself bears [Isaac Hayne, Robert's uncle, whose hanging by the
British caused patriotic fulminations during the Revolution],
does he esteem me less capable of gratitude for his patriotism, or
sympathy for his sufferings, than if his eyes had first opened upon
the light of Massachusetts, instead of South Carolina? Sir [to

Calhoun presiding, himself from South Carolina], does he suppose it in his power to exhibit a Carolina name so bright as to produce envy in my bosom?[15]

Webster is deftly making Southerners traitors to their own Revolutionary heroes if they tear apart a nation those ancestors built. If all his speech had been based on such appeals to sentiment, then he, too, might have been charged, like Lincoln, with a merely sentimental or "mystical" attachment to Union—one that reached a climax in the famous conclusion to this speech, "Liberty *and* Union, now and forever, one and inseparable."[16]

But Webster had legal and constitutional arguments to make for the singleness of the nation. Hayne, like Calhoun, treated the nation as a league of "sovereign states" bound only by a pact (the Constitution). Webster argued that Americans had constituted themselves a single people long before the Constitution was drafted or ratified. The single people forged in the Revolution, which declared its independence in 1776, which formed a "perpetual union" in the Articles of Confederation, adopted a new form of government for itself (*not* a pact between different peoples) in the Constitution:

> Is it [the government] the creature of the State legislature, or the creature of the people? . . . It is, Sir [Calhoun again], the people's Constitution, the people's government, made for the people, made by the people, and answerable to the people. . . . I hold it to be a popular government, erected by the people; those who administer it responsible to the people; and itself capable of being amended and modified, just as the people may choose it should be. . . . We are here to administer a Constitution emanating immediately from the people, and trusted by them to our administration. It is not the creature of the State governments.[17]

This is Lincoln's doctrine in the First Inaugural, where he admits that some states have spoken for disunion, but not "my rightful masters, the American people" (SW 2.218). The people's existence precedes and makes possible the Constitution. Otherwise, "The United States [would] be not a government proper, but an association of States in the nature of a contract [or pact] merely" (SW 2.217).

According to Lincoln and Webster—and, as we shall see, to Story—the Declaration of Independence was closer to being *the* founding document of the United States than was the Constitution. Webster made the point in many of his writings, as in "The Constitution Not a Compact" (1833):

> At least as far back as the first Congress, in 1774, they [the United States] had been in some measure, and for some national purposes, united together. Before the Confederation of 1781, they had declared independence jointly, and had carried on the war jointly, both by sea [a trans-state arena] and land; and this not as separate States, but as one people. When, therefore, they formed the Confederation, and adopted its articles as articles of perpetual union, they did not come together for the first time; and therefore they do not speak of the States as acceding to the Confederation, as though it was a league, and nothing but a league, and rested on nothing but plighted facts for its performance. Yes, even then, the States were not strangers to each other; there was a bond of union already subsisting between them; they were associated, united States; and the object of the Confederation was to make a stronger and better bond of union.[18]

And here is Lincoln speaking at his inauguration.

> Descending from these general principles, we find the propositions that, in legal contemplation, the Union is perpetual, confirmed by the history of the Union itself. The Union is much older

than the Constitution. It was formed, in fact, by the Articles of Association of 1774. It was matured and continued by the Declaration of Independence in 1776. It was further matured, and the faith of all the then thirteen States expressly plighted and engaged that it should be perpetual, by the Articles of Confederation in 1778. And finally, in 1787, one of the declared objects for ordaining and establishing the Constitution, was "to form a more perfect union." [SW 2.217–18]

Of course, the "states' rights" school of constitutional interpretation did not—and does not—accept this view of the founding process. To this day we hear that, as President Reagan liked to put it, "the federal government hadn't created the states; the states had created the federal government."[19] But another body of theory, the Federalist party's, had existed since 1790, when James Wilson delivered the first set of academic lectures on constitutional law. Justice Story continued and developed Wilson's body of legal thinking. This school of constitutional law, and not a vague sentiment, is what Lincoln relied on in his defense of the Union. Among other things, it emphasized his beloved Declaration of Independence, which Webster called "the title deed of their [Americans'] liberties."[20] Story emphasizes the importance of the Declaration precisely as a *founding* document:

It was "a declaration by the representatives of the United States of America in Congress assembled"—"by the delegates of the good people of the colonies," as in a prior declaration of rights they were called. It was not an act done by the State governments then organized, nor by persons chosen by them. It was emphatically the act of the whole *people* of the united colonies, by the instrumentality of their representatives, chosen for that among other purposes. It was not an act competent to the State governments, or any of them, as organized under their charters, to adopt. These charters neither contemplated the case nor provided

for it. It was an act of original, inherent sovereignty by themselves, resulting from their right to change the form of government, and to institute a new one, whenever necessary for their
safety and happiness. . . . From the moment of the Declaration of
Independence, if not for most purposes at an antecedent period,
the united colonies must be considered as being a nation *de facto*,
having a general government over it, created and acting by the
general consent of the people of all the colonies.[21]

Lincoln did not cease to regard the Declaration as the expression of a transcendent ideal to be approximated. But the
further conception, of the Declaration as a *founding document*,
gave him considerations to keep in mind that were of no importance to Theodore Parker. In Parker's view, if the South was
untrue to the American vision, then those resolved upon following the vision could just leave the South behind, extruding it
from a Union in which it had become a contaminant. But if the
Declaration is the sovereign act of a single people, that people
could not rend itself when brought to face a problem that affected
the whole. It will be noticed that Webster, like Parker, used
triple formulations about government of, for, by the people; but
for Webster the people had a grittier historical reality than for
Parker. The term meant, for Webster, the *one* people that
brought itself into being while issuing the Declaration. Regard
for that sovereign enunciator of the doctrine, and not just for the
nobility of the high ideals expressed, is part of the constitutional
reality he honored. Both these aspects of the Declaration are
affirmed in the conclusion of the Gettysburg Address, since both
of them animated Lincoln's words and acts from his moment of
taking office, when he spoke of "my rightful masters, the American people."

Lincoln's constitutional view had concrete legal consequences that are hard, almost impossible, to understand if one

treats his devotion to the Union as a mystical notion or sentiment. Only in this context can one assess as he did the legal
aspect of belligerency and his emancipation measures. Both of
these matters must be seen in the light of the Union created by
the Declaration.

1. THE STATUS OF BELLIGERENTS.

On this, Lincoln never wavered. The problem, for him, was
insurrection, not war. The South could not be a body of foreign
belligerents. He was as insistent, at the end of the war, that
"seceded states" was a misnomer (SW 2.699) as he was, in his
inaugural address, that "the Union is unbroken" (ibid., p. 218).
The states *had* not seceded since they *could* not. It is wrong,
therefore, to say, as James McPherson does, that Lincoln came to
accept the view that the Civil War was a foreign war and not a
civil insurrection.[22] It is true that the North had to adopt belligerent procedures (e.g., for exchange of prisoners), in large part
because of dealings with foreign powers under international law
(e.g., in administering a blockade that affected foreign flags). But
these were legal fictions to Lincoln, who thought of Jefferson
Davis's army as an outlaw band preying on the South. As he told
John Hay after Gettysburg:

> Davis is right. His army is his only hope, not only against us, but
> against his own people. If that were crushed, the people would be
> ready to swing back to their old bearings.[23]

It may be said that this was wishful thinking on Lincoln's part;
but if so, he persisted in it. He refused to speak of the states as
rejoining the Union; he spoke, rather, of restoring "their proper
practical relation" (SW 2.699)—the "old bearings" of his com-
ment to Hay.

All Lincoln's military measures were taken, in his own

mind, to "insure domestic tranquility," as opposed to "providing for the common defense." The proper constitutional parallel is George Washington's response to the Whiskey Rebellion—or even Lyndon Johnson's response to the urban riots of the late 1960s—rather than any foreign war. As commander-in-chief of the armed forces, Washington had sent federalized militia to Pennsylvania—just as Johnson sent federal troops to Detroit—without a declaration of war. "Martial law" was declared. Citizens were put under curfew, under restriction of their movements, and under arrest for impeding the military. Martial law is more expected in the case of domestic insurrection than of mobilization against a foreign enemy.

Lincoln's suspension of habeas corpus when Baltimore blocked the transit of troops is often compared to the war measures of later presidents like Franklin Roosevelt.[24] Lincoln is not necessarily exonerated from blame if one thinks, rather, in terms of restoring domestic tranquillity; but one comes closer to his own conception of the matter. People normally consider only his legal action against Northerners in this respect—on the assumption, apparently, that anything done to Southerners must be counted action against an *enemy*. For Lincoln, however, Northerners and Southerners were equally citizens, and support for the insurrection was the same crime no matter where it occurred. He could suspend habeas corpus in the North by the *same* authority he used in repressing armed insurrection to the South. (In foreign wars, domestic discipline is subordinate to and different from belligerency abroad.)

In wartime, internal supporters of the enemy are called traitors. Lincoln not only refused to use that term about Northern supporters of insurrection; he usually avoided it when referring to Southerners, though it was the favorite term of ardent Unionists. As we have seen, he would not even use the term "seceders" without a disclaiming phrase like "so called." He was equally quick to pardon Southerners and Northerners, since their basic category was the same in either case: they were citizens.[25]

It is true that Lincoln was severe, even ruthless, in putting down the insurrection. He hoped to do this swiftly, to prevent it from spreading, and he used carrot-tactics with border states while making the stick a menace not only to dissident states but to some hesitating ones. His frustration with dilatory generals, his agony after Gettysburg when Lee escaped the trap, came from his desire to put down the domestic disorder with rapid finality. But it is misleading to call this a policy of "unconditional surrender," as McPherson does. "Unconditional surrender" is a term in international law for the cessation of hostilities with foreign belligerents. Since Lincoln never thought of the Southerners as foreign belligerents, his attitude was that of a policeman dealing with criminal bands. In arresting them, all necessary force is permissible, and the law they are breaking is not negotiable (as are points of dispute between countries). On the other hand, criminals who "give themselves up" are not thought to be surrendering their basic rights, as an enemy gives up not only war aims but certain rights to an exigent conqueror.

In nothing has Lincoln's constitutional role, as conceived by himself, been so misunderstood, with such unhealthy consequences, as in his use of his *military* authority. He so often invoked this power that he is seen as extending presidential prerogative by this means. Arthur Schlesinger is just one of many historians who make this judgment: "The war power flowed into the Presidency most particularly, as Lincoln saw it, in the presidential role as Commander in Chief. This marked the beginning of a fateful evolution."[26] One of the most typical aspects of that sentence is the shortening of the title—an error Lincoln did not make. When he issued the Emancipation Proclamation, for instance, he did it "by virtue of the power in me vested as *Com-*

*mander-in-Chief of the Army and Navy of the United States in
time of actual armed rebellion against authority and government of the United States,* and as a fit and necessary war measure
for suppressing said rebellion." He has hedged his authority
about very carefully in terms of extent (over armed services),
temporal duration (of *actual* and *armed* rebellion), and criteria
(only the *necessary* acts for suppressing the rebellion).

In doing this, he was saying nothing more than what the
Constitution does. It has become customary to refer to the President as "Commander in Chief" *tout court*—and even citizens
now refer to him as "our Commander in Chief."[27] But the Constitution makes it very clear whom he commands in that role:

> The president shall be commander in chief of the army and navy
> of the United States, and of the militia of the several States, when
> called into the actual service of the United States. . . . [Article II,
> Section 2]

By referring to the *time when* actual rebellion was in process,
Lincoln specified his power to use regular and militia troops
against rebellion (as Washington had). He was, legally, no less the
commander-in-chief of military men in the South (including Lee)
than of Northern troops. When he emancipated slaves as a *military* measure, it was as federal troops seized houses in Detroit
during the 1967 riot there. By emancipating slaves *as commander-in-chief of the army and navy*, Lincoln was making it
clear that he did not act with any other of his (civilian) presidential powers—only Congress and the states could do that, by
amending the Constitution. In fact, his critics among the diehard
abolitionists attacked him *because* he used such limited authority. And even soberer judges have been harsh on him in this
matter. Richard Hofstadter wrote in 1948:

The Emancipation Proclamation of January 1, 1863 had all the moral grandeur of a bill of lading. It contained no indictment of slavery, but simply based emancipation on "military necessity." It expressly omitted the loyal slave states from its forms. Finally, it did not in fact free any slaves. For it excluded by detailed enumeration from the sphere covered in the Proclamation all the counties in Virginia and parishes in Louisiana that were occupied by Union troops and into which the government actually had the power to bring freedom. It simply declared free all slaves in "the States and parts of States" where the people were in rebellion—that is to say, precisely where its effect could not reach. Beyond its propaganda value the Proclamation added nothing to what Congress had already done in the Confiscation [of *captured* slaves] Act.[28]

This brings us to the second area where Lincoln's mind can be understood only if we appreciate what Union meant to him. Paradoxically, the Declaration as a *founding* document tied Lincoln's hands with regard to slavery.

2. EMANCIPATION.

Lincoln had often said that he would do nothing individually to disturb slavery in its protected area—because it was protected there by the Constitution, the document adopted by the whole people that came into existence at the time of the Declaration of Independence. It is true that he considered the Constitution imperfect in its treatment of slavery. Its own language he thought shamefaced and provisional, meant to exist only as slavery was "in course of extinction." But it *was* the enactment of the *whole* (single) people, and could be changed only by the whole people—through the amendment process. As the South could not unilaterally secede, the North could not unilaterally emancipate. The opponents of slavery could criticize it, work for amendment, refuse to accept its morality, point to its inconsistency with the Declaration. But *while* the Constitution's provisions were in effect, they could not ignore them.

Lincoln had many ways of framing this constitutional barrier to forcible emancipation. Arguing for the exclusion of slavery from new territories, he put in vivid terms the different status of slavery as considered in itself and in each of the three relevant jurisdictions of America:

> If I saw a venomous snake crawling in the road, any man would say I may seize the nearest stick and kill it. [Slavery in itself.]
>
> But if I found that snake in bed with my children that would be another question. I might hurt the children more than the snake, and it might bite them. [Slavery in the South.]
>
> Much more, if I found it in bed with my neighbor's children, and I had bound myself by a solemn oath not to meddle with his children under any circumstances, it would become me to let that particular mode of getting rid of the gentleman alone. [Slavery in the South as seen from the North.]
>
> But if there was a bed newly made up, to which the children were to be taken, and it was proposed to take a batch of young snakes and put them there with them, I take it no man would say there was any question how I ought to decide. [Slavery in the territories.] [SW 2.137]

Lincoln was very careful in framing these parallels (delivered to a Connecticut audience early in 1860). He does not speak of Southerners as belonging to different states, but as "neighbors" with whom one has a solemn agreement. Nor does he palliate the evil of slavery—it is a snake no matter where one finds it, and it endangers the Southerners' children. But in denouncing the evil, in trying to contain it, in hoping for new agreements, Lincoln will not divide the "one people" that declared itself united in the Declaration—long before it made the temporary arrangements of the Articles of Confederation or the Constitution. So basic was his commitment not to interfere with slavery, so long as it could be contained, that he gave this extraordinary assurance to the South in his First Inaugural:

> I understand a proposed amendment to the Constitution [the Crittenden Amendment]—which amendment, however, I have not seen—has passed Congress, to the effect that the federal government shall never interfere with the domestic institutions of the States, including that of persons held to service. To avoid misconstruction of what I have said, I depart from my purpose not to speak of particular amendments, so far as to say that, holding such a provision to now be implied constitutional law, I have no objection to its being made express and irrevocable. [SW 2.222]

Though Lincoln had privately told his aides and supporters not to work for the Crittenden Amendment, he made his own pledge not to work against it as a last way of showing the South he was committed to preserving the Union, not to emancipating slaves by unilateral Northern action, outside the agreed processes of the Constitution.

Once the South rejected even this last plea, many took the attitude that "all bets are off." The South had broken the Constitution; it no longer applied to them. Southerners could not plead the slavery provisions in a document whose other terms they had rejected. Lincoln never took this view. For him, the Constitution was still in force throughout the nation. When his generals talked of protecting "our soil" in the North, Lincoln was furious: "The whole country is our soil."[29]

Since the Constitution was still in effect, the Southerners

were still in the Union (as any rioters or criminals are still in the polity whose laws they break), and Lincoln, too, was still bound by the Constitution, even by its slave provisions. General John C. Frémont, in the border state of Missouri, responded to raids by Southern guerrillas like William Quantrill by freeing the slaves of anyone who supported the marauders. Lincoln had to instruct Frémont that he was doing the work of Quantrill, helping to scare border states away from the Union. But abolitionists did not understand how Lincoln could *re-enslave* people freed by Frémont. It was even more difficult for Lincoln when General David Hunter, a year later, freed slaves in the Southern states he was responsible for—freed those in the dissident states themselves. At this time Lincoln was working for voluntary emancipation in Missouri, and he again revoked a military emancipation. But he did it in terms that show how he conceived his own authority to emancipate (a step he was already preparing to take):

> I further make known that whether it be competent for me, as Commander-in-Chief of the Army and Navy [the longer title, notice] to declare the Slaves of any state or states free, and whether at any time, in any case, it shall have become a necessity indispensable to the maintenance of the government to exercise such supposed power, are questions which, under my responsibility, I reserve to myself, and which I can not feel justified in leaving to the decision of commanders in the field. These are totally different questions from those of police regulations in armies and camps. [SW 2.318–19]

He distinguishes two military situations here—and both are distinguished from civilian action. As civilian leader Lincoln cannot choose a course he thinks desirable or morally commendable, apart from what the Constitution he is upholding dictates. Nor, as commander-in-chief of the army and navy, can he delegate or countenance the freeing of slaves for military *convenience* (to the better conduct of armies in field and camp). Only looking at the highest military *necessity*—to that which is *indispensable to the maintenance of the government*—could he take such a step. By maintenance of government, of course, he does not mean the saving of Washington as opposed to Richmond; he is pledged to maintain the government of the United States, North *and* South, against armed rebellion. He must, he is asserting ahead of time, be able to show that such maintenance will be an absolute *military* impossibility, without freeing the slaves being used in support of rebellion.

That, and that only, was what Lincoln threatened to do in September of 1862 (only four months after revoking General Hunter's emancipation, which had *not* claimed absolute military necessity to the whole endeavor). The South was given until the new year to prevent this *military* move by desisting from insurrection. Even within its limited military form, emancipation could have been prevented by a return to compliance with the law. Then, on January 1, 1863, Lincoln issued the military proclamation which Hofstadter denounces for having all the eloquence of a bill of lading. The master of political rhetoric, who relied on the word for his influence over others, deliberately made this document so unlikely to stir moral sentiment that J. G. Randall says it is "more often admired than read."[30] Lincoln did not present this as a moral document, or even a political one. It did not free slaves in the nation at large, but only in the theater of active insurrection and only as a "necessary war measure for suppressing said rebellion" (SW 2.424).

Lincoln does everything possible to treat the South's slaves as *commodities of war*:

It [emancipation] is not a question of sentiment or taste, but one of physical force, which may be preserved and estimated as horsepower, and steam power, are measured and estimated. And by measurement, it [black support] is more than we can lose, and live. [SW 2.621]

Over and over, and always, Lincoln talks of the emancipation as a *purely* military act he *had* to resort to in order to *restore order* in the Southern part of the United States (his task as the President of the entire nation) against armed insurrection. Ironically, he was restricting himself, as a military leader, to the view of slaves as *property* that the Southerners themselves professed:

> Is there—has there ever been—any question that, by the law of war, property, both of friends and enemies, may be taken as needed? [SW 2.497]

But why would the Southerners' slaves, seized and used while war was on, remain free *after* the military crisis passed? Because *this* kind of property can only be *used* if it cooperates, and it will not cooperate as a mule does, but as a man or woman.

> Nor is it possible for any Administration to retain the service of these people with the express or implied understanding that, upon the first convenient occasion, they are to be re-enslaved. It *can* not be; and it ought not to be. [SW 2.631]

Lincoln could not be more insistent that his act was taken only out of military necessity, a necessity that was absolute.

> The original proclamation has no constitutional or legal justification except as a military measure. [SW 2.501]

> According to our political system, as a matter of civil administration, the general government had no lawful power to effect eman-

cipation in any State, and for a long time it had been hoped that
the rebellion could be suppressed without resorting to it as a
military measure. [SW 2.550]

I believed the indispensable necessity for military emancipation
and arming the blacks would come, unless averted. [SW 2.586]

Some, who feel that Lincoln was exaggerating the military need
for his own purposes, follow Lincoln's early generals in suppos-
ing he led only the North. The blacks were clearly not needed to
protect Washington. But since Lincoln thought of himself as the
President of the South as well, restoring rightful order everywhere was a task that *did* call for military resources of every sort,
and on a large scale. This was true, as Lincoln said, even considering slave power as a physical commodity like horse and steam
power. It was true for equally important military reasons of
morale—and that in a double sense. The threat of emancipation,
and then its fulfillment, damaged Southern morale and strengthened Northern hopes. Union troops would have more to fight
with (as well as for), and the Southerners would have less:

There is a witness in every white man's bosom that he would
rather go to the war having the negro to help him, than to help
the enemy against him. . . . It [failing to offer military emancipa-
tion] is simply giving a large force to the enemy, for *nothing* in
return. [SW 2.621]

He could answer a critic: "You say you will not fight to free
negroes. Some of them seem willing to fight for you" (SW 2.498).
Hofstadter and others deplore this "low" motive for emancipation. But a new generation of black historians finds in it a realism,
a recognition of the black contribution, that avoids the conde-
scension of doing things *for* the slaves.[31] If the slaves were

needed, they *earned* their freedom. Lincoln recognized a *superiority* of black "freedom fighters" to white shirkers from all mankind's struggle:

> And then [when peace comes], there will be some black men who can remember that, with silent tongue, and clenched teeth, and steady eye, and well-poised bayonet, they have helped mankind on to this consummation; while, I fear, there will be some white ones, unable to forget that, with indignant heart and deceitful speech, they have strove [sic] to hinder it. [SW 2.499]

This was one of many ancillary benefits to the constitutional scruple Lincoln observed in *limiting* emancipation to his reach as commander-in-chief of the army and navy. By keeping his pledge to the South, not to interfere with their institutions through the civil power, he made the claim against them as bearable as possible, not indulging moralistic tirades against them. He meant to *govern* these people when order was restored. Meanwhile, the strictly military measure did not contaminate (though it increased indirect pressure for) voluntary emancipation in the border states and the fostering of the civil procedure that would lead to passage of the Thirteenth Amendment, freeing all slaves, in 1865.[32]

Above all, by avoiding a unilateral (civil) emancipation, while insisting there could be no unilateral secession, Lincoln kept the Constitution intact (slave clauses and all) for the whole people. Lincoln was expressing in every way possible his determination that the nation remain united.[33] By grounding that Union in the Declaration as the founding document of a single nation, he took from his favored document *both* values that Webster had expressed at the end of his Reply to Hayne: "Liberty *and* Union, now and forever, one and inseparable!"

If we did not know the actual Address Lincoln gave, most

of us would consider it natural, almost inevitable, to mention the Emancipation that had occurred in the same year as the battle at Gettysburg. (Everett *did* mention it.) But now, I hope, it is clear why Lincoln not only did not but *would* not mention it. He meant to rise above the particular, the local, the divisive. The Emancipation had been only a military measure, an exigency of the war. Lincoln was looking beyond the war to "the great task remaining before us" as a nation trying to live up to the vision in which it was conceived.

James McPherson describes Lincoln as a revolutionary in terms of the economic and other physical changes he effected, whether on purpose or not—a valid point sensibly discussed.[34] But Lincoln was a revolutionary in another sense, as well, the one Willmoore Kendall denounced him for—he not only put the Declaration in a new light as a matter of founding *law*, but put its central proposition, equality, in a newly favored position as a principle of the Constitution (which, as the Chicago *Times* noticed, never uses the word). What had been a mere theory of lawyers like James Wilson, Joseph Story, and Daniel Webster— that the nation preceded the states, in time and importance— now became a lived reality of the American tradition. The results of this were seen almost at once. Up to the Civil War, "the United States" was invariably a plural noun: "The United States are a free government." After Gettysburg, it became a singular: "The United States is a free government." This was the result of the whole mode of thinking Lincoln expressed in his acts as well as his words, making *union* not a mystical hope but a constitutional reality. When he spoke at the end of the Address, about government "of *the* people, by *the* people, for *the* people," he was not just praising "popular government" as a Transcendentalist's ideal, like Theodore Parker. Rather, like Webster, he was saying that America is *a* people addressing its great assignment as that was accepted in the Declaration. This people was "conceived" in

1776, "brought forth" as an entity whose birth was datable ("four score and seven" years back) and placeable ("on this continent"), something that could receive a "new birth of freedom."

By giving this language a place in our sacred documents, Lincoln changed the way people thought about the Constitution. For a states'-rights advocate like Willmoore Kendall, for an "original intent" advocate like Edwin Meese, our politics has all been misdirected since that time. The Fourteenth Amendment was, for them, later "bootlegged" into the Bill of Rights. But, even before that, the Amendment was doing its harm in the eyes of strict constructionists. As Robert Bork put it:

> Unlike the [Amendment's] other two clauses, it [the due-process clause] quickly displayed the same capacity to accommodate judicial constitution-making which Taney had found in the fifth amendment's version.[35]

Bork, too, thinks equality as a *national* commitment has been sneaked into the Constitution. There can be little doubt about the principal culprit. As Kendall put it, Lincoln's use of the Declaration's phrase about all men being equal is an attempt "to wrench from it a single proposition and make that our supreme commitment."[36]

> We should not allow him [Lincoln]—not at least without some probing inquiry—to "steal" the game, that is, to accept his interpretation of the Declaration, its place in our history, and its reasoning as "true," "correct," and "binding."[37]

But, as Kendall himself admits, the professors, the textbooks, the politicians, the press *have* overwhelmingly accepted Lincoln's vision.[38] The Gettysburg Address has become an authoritative expression of the American spirit—as authoritative as the Declaration itself, and perhaps even more influential, since it determines how we read the Declaration. For most people now, the Declaration means what Lincoln told us it means, as a way of correcting the Constitution itself without overthrowing it. It is this correction of the spirit, this intellectual revolution, that makes attempts to go back beyond Lincoln to some earlier version so feckless. The proponents of states' rights may have arguments, but they have lost their force, in courts as well as in the popular mind. By accepting the Gettysburg Address, its concept of a single people dedicated to a proposition, we have been changed. Because of it, we live in a different America.

Revolution
in Style

Lincoln's speech at Gettysburg worked several revolutions, beginning with one in literary style. Everett's talk was given at the last point in history when such a performance could be appreciated without reservation. It was made obsolete within a half-hour of the time when it was spoken. Lincoln's remarks anticipated the shift to vernacular rhythms that Mark Twain would complete twenty years later. Hemingway claimed that all modern American novels are the offspring of *Huckleberry Finn.*[1] It is no greater exaggeration to say that all modern political prose descends from the Gettysburg Address.

The Address looks less mysterious than it should to those who believe there is such a thing as "natural speech." All speech is unnatural. It is artificial. Believers in "artless" or "plain" speech think that rhetoric is added to some prior natural thing, like cosmetics added to the unadorned face. But human faces are *born*, like kitten faces. Words are not born in that way. Human babies, unlike kittens, produce a later artifact called language, and they largely speak in jingles, symbols, tales, and myths during the early stages of their talk. Plain speech is a later development, in whole cultures as in individuals. Simple prose depends on a complex epistemology—it depends on concepts like "objective fact."[2] Language reverses the logic of horticulture: here the blossoms come first, and *they* produce the branches.

Lincoln, like most writers of great prose, began by writing bad poetry. Early experiments with words are almost always stilted, formal, tentative. Economy of words, grip, precision come later (if at all). A Gettysburg Address does not precede rhetoric, but burns its way through the lesser toward the higher eloquence, by a long discipline. Lincoln not only exemplifies this process, but studied it, in himself and others. He was a student of the word.

One of the more teasing entries in John Hay's diary of his service with Lincoln was made on July 25, 1863. Hay had ridden out with the Tycoon (as he called the President in the privacy of his journal) to the Retired Soldiers Home—a federal property on a wooded height outside Washington, which Lincoln used as an early version of Camp David, a retreat from Washington's swamp-fever summers. The twenty-five-year-old secretary who lived in the Executive Mansion was often favored by the President with late-night visits and long talks. These talks could become more relaxed and discursive when the two were away from their respective offices. On this night, three weeks after the disappointment of Meade's actions after Gettysburg, the subject was a recurring one: "I rode out to Soldier's Home with the Tycoon tonight. . . . Had a talk on philology for which the T. has a little-indulged inclination" (p. 72).

Philology, the study of words, was a bond between the

President and this man half his age. Hay would later tell Mark Twain, after they had become friends, that he was born like Twain on the Mississippi (at Spunky Point, Illinois), and Hay would help along the vernacular revolution when, in the early 1870s, he published dialect poems of the Bret Harte sort.[3] But Hay had also gone to Brown University (where he was Class Poet), and he would become a newspaper editor, a member of Henry Adams's exclusive circle (The Five of Hearts), and Secretary of State to Presidents William McKinley and Theodore Roosevelt. He was sure enough of his own taste to argue with "the Tycoon," and even to catch Lincoln out when the President reverted to earlier bad habits.

Hay, who admired Lincoln without succumbing to a debilitating awe, wrote about one of his boss's famous effusions:

> His last letter is a great thing. Some hideously bad rhetoric—some indecorums that are infamous—yet the whole letter takes its solid place in history, as a great utterance of a great man. [P. 91.]

Hay is just in his praise and just in his reproach. Lincoln's letter to James C. Conkling has shrewd criticisms of Conkling's desire to hasten emancipation, but its description of military successes goes from grandiosity to mushy cuteness:

> The Father of Waters again goes unvexed to the sea. Thanks to the great North-West for it. Nor yet wholly to them. Three hundred miles up, they meet New-England, Empire, Key-Stone, and Jersey, hewing their way right and left. The Sunny South too, in more colors than one, lent a hand. On the spot, their part of the history was jotted down in black and white. The job was a great national one; and let none be banned who bore an honorable part in it. And while those who have cleared the great river may well be proud, even that is not all. It is hard to say that anything has

been more bravely and well done than at Antietam, Murfreesboro, Gettysburg, and on many fields of lesser note. Nor must Uncle Sam's Web-feet [marines] be forgotten. At all the watery margins they have been present. Not only on the deep sea, the broad bay, and the rapid river, but also up the narrow muddy bayou, and wherever the ground was a little damp, they have been, and made their tracks. Thanks to all. For this great republic—for the principle it lives by, and keeps alive—for man's vast future,—thanks to all. [SW 1.498]

Though this was written only three months before the Gettysburg Address, it has the poeticisms of Everett ("watery margins"), the nature lore of Waugh's John Boot in *Scoop* ("featherfooted through the plashy fan"), and the comic formality of Claudius and Gertrude:

—Thanks, Rosencrantz and gentle Guildenstern.
—Thanks, Guildenstern and gentle Rosencrantz.

Hay, whose narrow-set eyes gave him a perpetual air of intense scrutiny, was merciless in spotting such weaknesses. It is a measure of Lincoln's desire for honest literary discussion that he became ever more intimate with Hay.

Hay appreciated the ironies in this arrangement. Despite his own frontier birth, the small, trim Hay was a bit of a dandy. In the photograph of Lincoln with Hay and his young friend John Nicolay, the two presidential secretaries look like oversized (and overdressed) Lilliputians guarding a morose Gulliver. In Hay's and Nicolay's corner room on the second floor of what we now call the White House, the contrast was even more striking: Lincoln would wander in late at night to read something he had just come across. Hay records one scene, after midnight, as he was writing that day's entry in his diary: Lincoln was utterly unconscious that he with his short shirt hanging above his long legs and setting out behind like the tail feathers of an ostrich was infinitely funnier than anything in the book he was laughing at [p. 179].

Of another such bare-legged apparition, Hay wrote that he

complimented him [Lincoln] on the amount of underpinning he still has [fifty-five looks old to one still in his twenties] & he said he weighed 180 pds. Important if true [p. 181].

The critic is apparent in those two last words.

Lincoln liked to attend the theater with the foppish Hay—opera *(Martha)*, plays (several with John Wilkes Booth), and, especially, Shakespeare. Hay, like Lincoln, admired the Shakespearean actor James Hackett, who was invited to the White House and favored with a presidential correspondence.[4] Hay defended the way Hackett emphasized a word while playing Falstaff:

The President criticized H.'s reading of a passage where Hackett said "Mainly *thrust* at me," the President thinking it should read "Mainly thrust at *me*." I told the Pres^t I tho't he was wrong: that "mainly" merely meant "strongly," "fiercely." [P. 139.]

Hay is right on the narrower matter—"mainly" here is "with might and main." But Falstaff's account of his imaginary fight at Gad's Hill is funnier if he gives a plaintive emphasis to "[poor] *me*"—as in his earlier line from the same scene: "two or three and fifty upon poor old Jack" (*1 Henry IV*, 2.4.184). Orson Welles, playing Falstaff in *Chimes at Midnight*, reads the disputed line Lincoln's way, not Hay's. There was very little Hay, or any other man, could teach Lincoln about how to milk a comic remark for maximum effect.

Arguments like this, over the exact meaning of (and stress on) a single word, make us wish that Hay had described the discussions on philology held with Lincoln at the Soldiers Home. The closest we can come to that is a lecture on the subject that Lincoln wrote, and delivered several times, and wished to see in print. This began as a speech in the 1850s praising modern inventions. It was patterned after a similar performance by the historian George Bancroft.[5] The effort shows that Lincoln, like Mark Twain, like many aspiring authors of the mid-century, hoped to become a paid lecturer. But the changes he made in the text show, even more clearly, what Lincoln considered the supreme inventions of mankind—language and its modes of dissemination (writing and printing). In that age of a dawning technology, he thought the principal mark of human ingenuity was still the ancient "trick" of verbal communication. No wonder his *words* made sense of the merely destructive work of advanced weaponry in the Civil War. It is impossible, reading this early lecture, to doubt that Lincoln knew language is a human glory *because* it is "artificial," an invention:

When we remember that words are *sounds* merely, we shall conclude that the idea of representing those sounds by marks, so that whoever should, at any time after, see the marks would understand what sounds they meant, was a bold and ingenious conception, not likely to occur to one man of a million in the run of a thousand years. And, when it did occur, a distinct mark for each word, giving twenty thousand different marks first to be learned and afterwards remembered, would follow as the second thought, and would present such a difficulty as would lead to the conclusion that the whole thing was impracticable. But the *necessity* still would exist; and we may readily suppose that the idea was conceived, and lost, and reproduced, and dropped, and taken up, again and again, until at last the thought of dividing sounds into parts, and making a mark not to represent a whole sound but only a part of one, and then of combining these marks, not very many in number, upon the principles of permutation, so as to represent any and all of the whole twenty thousand words, and even any additional number, was somehow conceived and pushed into practice. This was the invention of phonetic writing, as distinguished from the clumsy picture writing of some of the nations. That it was difficult of conception and execution is apparent, as well by the foregoing reflections as by the fact that so many tribes of men have come down from Adam's time to ours without ever having possessed it. Its utility may be conceived by the reflection that to *it* we owe everything which distinguishes us from savages. Take it from us, and the Bible, all history, all science, all government, all commerce, and nearly all social intercourse, go with it. [SW 2.7–8]

Lincoln's early experiments with language have an exuberance that is almost comic in its playing with contrivances. His showy 1838 speech to the Young Men's Lyceum is now usually studied to support or refute Edmund Wilson's claim that it contains "oedipal" feelings. But its most obvious feature is the desire to express a complex situation in neatly balanced structures.

> *Theirs was the task*
> *(and nobly they performed it)*
> *to possess themselves,*
> *and through themselves, us,*
> *of this goodly land;*
> *and to uprear upon its hills*
> *and its valleys*
> *a political edifice of liberty*
> *and of equal rights;*
> *'tis ours only*

> to transmit these,
> > the former, unprofaned by the foot of an
> > invader,
> > the latter, undecayed by the lapse of time,
> > untorn by usurpation—
> > > to the latest generation that fate shall permit
> > > the world to know. [SW 1.28]

This is too labored to be clear. One has to look a second time to be sure that "the former" refers to "this goodly land" and "the latter" to "a political edifice." But the exercise is limbering Lincoln up for subtler uses of such balance and antithesis. The parenthetic enriching of a first phrase is something he would use to give depth to his later prose:

> Theirs was the task
> > (and nobly they performed it)
> to possess themselves
> > (and through themselves us)
> > of this goodly land.

It is the pattern of

> The world will little note
> (nor long remember)
> > what we do here. [SW 2.536]

Or of:

> Fondly do we hope
> > (fervently do we pray)
> > that this mighty scourge of war
> > may speedily pass away. [SW 2.687]

Or:

> with firmness in the right
>   (as God gives us to see the right)
>   let us strive on to finish
>   the work we are in. [SW 2.687]

To end, after complex melodic pairings, with a strong row of monosyllables, was an effect he especially liked. Not only "what we do here" and "the work we are in" and "the world to know" of the above examples, but:

> Trusting in Him,
>   who can go with me,
>   and remain with you
>   and be everywhere for good,
> let us confidently hope
>   that all will yet be well. [SW 2.199]

Or this, from the Second Inaugural:

> Both parties deprecated war;
>   but one of them would make war
>   rather than let the nation survive;
>   and the other would accept war
>   rather than let it perish.
>   And the war came. [SW 2.686]

Or, from the 1862 message to Congress:

> In giving freedom to the slave,
>   we assure freedom to the free—
> honorable alike in what we give,
>   and what we preserve.
> We shall nobly save,
>   or meanly lose
>   the last best hope of earth. [SW 2.415]

The closing of Lincoln's early Lyceum sentence ("to the latest generation") also gives a premonition of famous statements to come.

> *The fiery trial through which we pass*
> *will light us down*
>   *(in honor or dishonor)*
>   *to the latest generation.* [SW 2.415]

Those words to Congress in 1862 were themselves forecast in Lincoln's Peoria address of 1854:

If we do this,
   we shall not only have saved the Union,
   but we shall have so saved it
      as to make and to keep it
      forever worthy of the saving.
We shall have so saved it
   that the succeeding millions
   of free happy people
      (the world over)
   shall rise up
   and call us blessed to the latest generations. [SW 1.340]

It would be wrong to think that Lincoln moved toward the plain style of the Gettysburg just by writing shorter, simpler sentences. Actually, that Address ends with a very long sentence—eighty-two words, almost a third of the whole talk's length. So does the Second Inaugural Address, Lincoln's other most famous piece of eloquence: its final sentence runs to seventy-five words. Because of his early experiments, Lincoln's words acquired a flexibility of structure, a rhythmic pacing, a variation in length of words and phrases and clauses and sentences, that make his sentences move "naturally," for all their density and scope.[6] We get inside his verbal workshop when we see how he recast the suggested conclusion to his First Inaugural given him by William Seward.[7] Every sentence is improved, in rhythm, emphasis, or clarity:

Seward	Lincoln
I close.	I am loth to close.
We are not, we must not be, aliens or enemies, but fellow-countrymen and brethren.	We are not enemies, but friends. We must not be enemies.
Although passion has strained our bonds of affection too hardly, they must not, I am sure they will not, be broken.	Though passion may have strained, it must not break our bonds of affection.
The mystic chords which, proceeding from so many battle-fields and so many patriot graves, pass through all the hearts and all the hearths in this broad continent of ours, will yet harmonize in their ancient music when breathed upon by the guardian angels of the nation.	The mystic chords of memory, stretching from every battlefield and patriot grave, to every living heart and hearthstone, all over this broad land, will yet swell the chorus of the Union, when again touched, as surely they will be, by the better angels of our nature. [SW 2.224]

Lincoln's lingering monosyllables in the first sentence seem to cling to the occasion, not wanting to break off the communication on which the last hopes of union depend. He simplifies the next sentence using two terms (enemies/friends) where Seward had used two *pairs* (aliens - enemies/fellow countrymen - brethren), but Lincoln repeats "enemies" in the urgent words "We *must* not be enemies." The next sentence is also simplified, to play off against the long, complex image of the concluding sentence, and to repeat the urgent "must." The *bonds* of affection become the *cords* of memory in Lincoln. The bonds and the strings are equally *physical* images. The "chords" are not musical *sounds*. Lincoln spelled "chord" and "cord" indiscriminately—they are the same etymologically. He uses the geometric term "chord" for the line across a circle's arc—as the cord on a tortoise shell gave Apollo his lute.[8] On the other hand, he spelled the word "cord" when calling the Declaration of Independence an electrical *wire* sending messages to American hearts: "the electric cord in that Declaration that links the hearts of patriotic and liberty-loving men together" (SW 1.456).

Seward knew the cord to be breathed on was a *string* (of harp or lute), though his "chords *proceeding from* graves" is grotesque. Lincoln stretches the cords *between* graves and living hearts, as in his image of the Declaration. Seward also gets ethereal when he talks of harmonies that come from breathing on the cords. Lincoln is more believable (and understandable) when he has the better angels of our nature *touch* the cords to swell the chorus of union. Finally, Seward made an odd picture to get his jingle of chords passing *through* "hearts and hearths." Lincoln stretches the lines from graves *to* hearts *and* hearthstones. He gets rid of the crude rhyme by making a chiastic (a-b-b-a) cluster of "*living*-hearts, hearth-*stone*"; the vital heart is contrasted with the inert hearth-stuff. Seward's clumsy image of stringing these two different items on a single cord has disappeared. Lincoln gives to Seward's fustian a pointedness of imagery, a euphony and interplay of short and long sentences and phrases, that lift the conclusion almost to the level of his own best prose.

Lincoln was not abandoning rhetoric in a passage like that, but taking the formal ideals of the past into the modern era, where the pace of life does not allow for the leisurely style of Lincoln's rhetorical forebears. He perfected a new classicism in this effort, since economy had always been the ancient ideal. Hugh Blair, who was still the respected expositor of ancient rhetoric in Lincoln's time, had written:

> The first rule which I shall give for promoting the strength of a sentence is to prune it of all redundant words. . . . The exact import of precision may be drawn from the etymology of the word. It comes from *precidere*, to cut off. It imports retrenching all superfluities and turning the expression so as to exhibit neither more nor less than an exact copy of his ideas who uses it.[9]

Lincoln may have known Blair directly; he certainly knew his principles from derivative texts when he undertook what Joshua Speed called "his study for composition . . . to make short sentences and a compact style."[10] His work seems the very embodiment of Blair's ideal. Take, for instance, the opening to the House Divided Speech of 1858. Don Fehrenbacher has identified the debt this speech owes to Daniel Webster's Reply to Hayne.[11] This makes the contrast in their opening paragraphs more startling. Webster began this way:

> When the mariner has been tossed for many days in thick weather and on an unknown sea, he naturally avails himself of the first pause in the storm, the earliest glance of the sun, to take his latitude, and ascertain how far the elements have driven him from his true course. Let us imitate this prudence, and, before we float farther on the waves of this debate, refer to the point from which we departed, that we may at least be able to conjecture where we now are.[12]

Here is Lincoln's simple exordium:

> If we could first know *where* we are, and *whither* we are tending,
> we could then better judge *what* to do, and *how* to do it. [SW
> 1.426]

One might read this as an implicit criticism of Webster,
though Lincoln had praised Webster as one who "talked excel-
lent sense and used good language," and he quarried thoughts as
well as phrases for several of his own speeches out of the Reply
to Hayne.[13] In fact, Lincoln admired all three of the giants in his
own "golden age of oratory"—Clay and Calhoun as well as Webster.

The spare quality of Lincoln's prose did not come naturally
but was worked at. Blair taught that it was not enough to be plain.
The proper words must be thrown into prominence, even if that
meant inverting the normal order of a sentence.[14] Twain said that
even in swearing you must study to put the "crash-words" in
emphatic places.[15] The young Lincoln attacked this problem with
a kind of verbal athleticism: "Broken by it, I, too, may be; bow
to it I never will" (SW 1.64). He remained fond of grammatical
inversion throughout his life, but learned to make it look less
studied. In the Second Inaugural, he does not say "We fondly
hope and fervently pray," but "Fondly do we hope, fervently do
we pray."

Blair recommended defining by balanced antitheses. He
gave Pope's famous example:

> Homer was the greatest genius; Virgil the better artist: in the one,
> we most admire the man; in the other, the work. Homer hurries
> us with a commanding impetuosity; Virgil leads us with an attrac-
> tive majesty. . . .[16]

Lincoln describes the hostile sections the nation had fallen into by 1854:

> The South, flushed with triumph and tempted to excesses; the North, betrayed, as they believe, brooding on wrong and burning for revenge. One side will provoke; the other resent. The one will taunt, the other defy; one aggresses, the other retaliates. [SW 1.335]

Lincoln even "shortens his members," as the rhetoricians put it, to suggest the quickening pace toward disaster.

But Blair taught that all such devices will be self-defeating if not used with honest intent to make meaning clearer and truth more compelling:

> For we may rest assured that, whenever we express ourselves ill, there is, besides the mismanagement of language, for the most part some mistake in our manner of conceiving the subject. Embarrassed, obscure and feeble sentences are generally, if not always, the result of embarrassed, obscure and feeble thought. Thought and language act and react upon each other mutually. Logic and rhetoric have here, as in many other cases, a strict connection; and he that is learning to arrange his sentences with accuracy and order is learning, at the same time, to think with accuracy and order. . . .[17]

This, surely, is the secret of Lincoln's eloquence. He not only read aloud, to think his way into sounds, but wrote as a way of ordering his thought. He had a keenness for analytical exercises. He was proud of the mastery he achieved over Euclid's Elements, which awed Herndon and others.[18] He loved the study of grammar, which some think the most arid of subjects.[19] Some claimed to remember his gift for spelling, a view that our manuscripts disprove.[20] Spelling as he had to learn it (apart from etymology) is more arbitrary than logical. It was the logical side of language—the principles of order as these reflect patterns of thought or the external world—that appealed to him.

He was also, Herndon tells us, laboriously precise in his choice of words. He would have agreed with Mark Twain that the difference between the right word and the nearly right one is that between the lightning and a lightning bug.[21] He said, debating Douglas, that his foe confused a similarity of words with a similarity of things—as one might equate a horse chestnut with a chestnut horse (SW 1.511).

Herndon's description of Lincoln's attitude toward words suggests Hugh Blair's standards. Here is Blair:

> The words which a man uses to express his ideas may be faulty in three respects. They may either not express that idea which the author intends, but some other which only resembles it or is akin to it; or they may express that idea, but not quite fully or completely; or they may express it together with something more than he intends. . . . Hardly in any language are there two words that convey precisely the same idea; a person thoroughly conversant in the propriety of the language will always be able to observe something that distinguishes them. . . . The bulk of writers are very apt to confuse them with each other, and to employ them carelessly, merely for the sake of filling up a period or of rounding and diversifying the language, as if their signification were exactly the same, while in truth it is not. Hence a certain mist, and indistinctness, is unwarily thrown over style.[22]

Twain and Herndon both used the same image, of a mist over the sentence, to suggest what the "right word" dispels. Here is Twain:

A powerful agent is the right word: it lights the reader's way and makes it plain; a close approximation to it will answer, and much traveling is done in a well-enough fashion by its help, but we do not welcome it and applaud it and rejoice in it as we do when *the* right one blazes out on us. . . . One has no time to examine the [right] word and vote upon its rank and standing, the automatic recognition of its supremacy is so immediate. There is a plenty of acceptable literature which deals largely in approximations, but it may be likened to a fine landscape seen through the rain; the right word would dismiss the rain, then you would see it better. It doesn't rain when Howells is at work.[23]

Neither, Herndon says, did it rain when Lincoln was at work:

He saw all things through a perfect mental lens. There was no diffraction or refraction there. He was not impulsive, fanciful, or imaginative; but cold, calm, and precise. He threw his whole mental light around the object, and, after a time, substance and quality stood apart, form and color took their appropriate place, and all was clear and exact in his mind. . . . In the search for words Mr. Lincoln was often at a loss . . . because there were, in the vast store of words, so few that contained the exact coloring, power, and shape of his ideas.[24]

Lincoln was merciless in pointing out his opponents' loose use of words. When Stephen Douglas said that Winfield Scott's nomination posed a peril to the Union, Lincoln replied:

Well, we ought all to be startled at the view of "peril to the Union," but it may be a little difficult for some shortsighted mortals to perceive such peril in the *nomination* of Scott. Mark you, it is the *nomination* and not the *election* which produces the peril. The Judge does not say the election, and he cannot mean the election, because he constantly assures us there is no prospect of Scott's election. He could not be so alarmed at what he is so sure will never happen. In plain truth I suppose he did mean the election, so far as he meant anything; but, feeling that his whole proposition was mere nonsense, he did not think of it distinctly enough to enable him to speak with any precision. [SW 1.277]

Like other logicians, like Lewis Carroll and Edgar Poe, Lincoln saw fantasy in the illogical use of words. Douglas accused Winfield Scott of entertaining reservations about the Whigs' platform because he had said, "I accept the nomination, with the resolution annexed."

In the North it will be said he accepts the nomination notwithstanding the platform; that he accepts it although he defies the platform; that he accepts it although he spits upon the platform.

"Verily," Lincoln rejoined, "these are wonderful substitutes for the word 'with' "—and he suggested they be substituted for "with" in a Bible verse like "Enoch walked with [although he spat upon?] God." In a dizzy exercise, he turns Douglas's exegetical tool on his own words.

As another example, take from Judge Douglas's ratification speech a sentence in relation to the democratic platform and the democratic ticket, Pierce and King, which is as follows:
"With such a platform, and with such a ticket, a glorious victory awaits us."
Now, according to the Judge's rule of criticizing General Scott's language, the above sentence of his will, without perversion of meaning, admit of being read in each of the following ways:
"*Notwithstanding* such a platform, and notwithstanding such a ticket, a glorious victory awaits us."
"*Although we defy* such a platform, and although we defy such a ticket, a glorious victory awaits us."

"*Although we spit upon* such a platform and although we spit upon such a ticket, a glorious victory awaits us." [SW 1.277–80][25]

Lincoln's responsive Whig audience could anticipate where he was going, yet there was a natural climax in the way he ordered Douglas's "synonyms," giving this passage an inexorable air of letting nonsense work itself out to its own demise.

When the Dred Scott decision said that the Constitution applied only to free subjects in the eighteenth century, Lincoln took Douglas's defense of that position and did another of his word substitutions, to reduce his opponent to absurdity:

Suppose after you read it [the Declaration of Independence] in the old-fashioned way, you read it once more with Judge Douglas' version. It will run thus: "We hold these truths to be self-evident, that all British subjects who were on this continent eighty-one years ago, were created equal to all British subjects born and *then* residing in Great Britain." [SW 1.400]

Parker had made a similar substitution in 1848: "To make our theory accord with our practice, we ought to recommit the Declaration to the hands which drafted that great state paper and declare that 'All men are created equal, and endowed by their Creator with certain unalienable rights if born of white mothers; but if not, not.' "[26]

In his quest to use the right words himself, Lincoln often achieved a clarity that is its own source of aesthetic satisfaction. There is no better description of this effect than Blair's:

Perspicuity in writing is not to be considered as only a sort of negative virtue, a freedom from defect. It has a higher merit. It is a degree of positive beauty. We are pleased with an author, we consider him as deserving praise, who frees us from all fatigue of searching for his meaning, who carries us through his subject without any embarrassment or confusion, whose style flows always like a limpid stream where we see to the very bottom.[27]

In a text like Lincoln's famous letter to Horace Greeley, even the sentence structure seems to present its own case. The grammar argues. By ordering a series of simple and disjunctive sentences, Lincoln patiently exhausts all alternatives. Beginning his sentences with repeated "If"'s (anaphora), Lincoln rings all changes on the concessive clause (granting irrelevant assertions or assumptions for now) and the hypothetical clause (posing case after case for its own treatment). The analysis of every permutation of the subject seals off misunderstandings as if Lincoln were quietly closing door after door. The points are advanced like a series of theorems in Euclid, as clear, as sequential, as compelling:

I have just read yours of the 19th instant, addressed to myself through the *New York Tribune*.

If there be in it any statements or assumptions of fact which I may know to be erroneous, I do not now and here controvert them.

If there be in it any inferences which I believe to be falsely drawn, I do not now and here argue against them.

If there be perceptible in it an impatient and dictatorial tone, I waive it, in deference to an old friend whose heart I have always supposed to be right.

As to the policy I "seem to be pursuing," as you say, I have not meant to leave anyone in doubt. I would save the Union. I would save it the shortest way under the Constitution.

The sooner the national authority can be restored, the nearer the Union will be—the Union as it was.

167

If there be those who would not save the Union unless they could at the same time save slavery, I do not agree with them.

My paramount object in this struggle is to save the Union, and not either to save or destroy slavery.

If I could save the Union without freeing any slave, I would do it; if I could save it by freeing all the slaves, I would do it; and if I could save it by freeing some and leaving others alone, I would also do that.

What I do about slavery and the coloured race, I do because I believe it helps to save the Union; and what I forbear, I forbear because I do not believe it would help to save the Union.

I shall do less whenever I shall believe that what I am doing hurts the cause; and I shall do more whenever I shall believe doing more will help the cause.

I shall try to correct errors where shown to be errors, and I shall adopt new views as fast as they shall appear to be true views.

I have here stated my purpose according to my views of official duty, and I intend no modification of my oft-expressed personal wish that all men everywhere be free.[28]

This is the highest art, which conceals itself. The opening sentences perform the classical role of an exordium, limiting one's task, disarming hostility, finding common ground with one's audience. The traditional *captatio benevolentiae* (claim on good will) could not be better exemplified than in Lincoln's address to his old friend's heart.

While making his own position clear, Lincoln professes a readiness to alter course if he is proved wrong. But he promises to do that only within the framework he has constructed. (He will change *only* if the change saves the Union.) He sounds deferential rather than dogmatic, yet he is in fact precluding all norms but his own. It is the same kind of rhetorical trap he used in his most famous statement of alternative possibilities:

"A House divided against itself cannot stand."

I believe this government cannot endure, permanently half *slave* and half *free*.

I do not expect the Union to be *dissolved*—I do not expect the house to *fall*—but I *do* expect it will cease to be divided.

It will become *all* one thing or *all* the other.

Either the *opponents* of slavery will arrest the further spread of it, and place it where the public mind shall rest in the belief that it is in course of ultimate extinction; or its *advocates* will push it forward, till it shall become alike lawful in *all* the states, *old* as well as *new*—*North* as well as *South*.

Have we no *tendency* to the latter condition? [SW 1.426]

Lincoln's own underlinings reinforce sentence structure in suggesting that these two and only these two outcomes are possible.

The language seems stripped of all figurative elements—though Lincoln has begun with a biblical figure that seems to pre-empt criticism of its premise. Lincoln's logic can be, and has been, challenged; but the ordering of the words *seems* logical, perspicuous. It is also, in its clipped quality, urgent. The rapid deployment of all options seems to press on the reader a need to decide. Lincoln's language is honed to a purpose.

Looking back to the nineteenth century's long speeches and debates, we might deplore the more disjunct "blips" of communication in our time. Television and other modern developments are blamed for a shortening of the modern attention span. But a similar process was at work in Lincoln's time, and he welcomed it. The railroad, the telegraph, the steamship had quickened the pace of events. Thoughts and words took on new and nervous rhythms. Lincoln, who considered language the world's great invention, welcomed a cognate invention, telegraphy. He used the telegraph to keep up with his generals—he even experimented with telegraph wires strung to reconnaissance balloons.[29]

As president, Lincoln worked intimately with the developer of telegraphy in America, Joseph Henry, the president of the Smithsonian Institution.[30] He had praised the lightning "harnessed to take his [man's] tidings in a trifle less than no time" (SW 2.3). Lincoln spent long hours in the telegraph center at the War Department, and was impatient with the fumbling and imprecise language still being used on this instrument, which demands clarity as well as concision.[31] Hay reflects Lincoln's relief when he found an efficient user of modern language in one of his military engineers:

> This is Herman Haupt, the railroad man at Alexandria. He has, as Chase says, a Major General's head on his shoulders. The President is particularly struck with the business-like character of his dispatch, telling in the fewest words the information most sought for, which contrasted strongly with the weak, whiney, vague, and incorrect dispatches of the whilom General-in-Chief [McClellan]. [P. 46.][32]

Lincoln's respect for General Grant came, in part, from the contrast between McClellan's waffling and Grant's firm grasp of the right words to use in explaining or arguing for a military operation. Lincoln sensed what Grant's later publisher, Mark Twain, did, that the West Pointer who once taught mathematics was a master of expository prose. Sitting his horse during a pause in battle, Grant could write model instructions for his subordinates—a skill John Keegan compares to the Duke of Wellington's. Keegan even says: "If there is a single contemporary document which explains 'why the North won the Civil War,' that abiding conundrum of American historical inquiry, it is *The Personal Memoirs of U. S. Grant*."[33] In an answering hyperbole, James McPherson has claimed that Lincoln won the war by his language.[34] The two half-truths contain at least one whole truth—

that well-focused words were the medium through which Grant and Lincoln achieved their amazing degree of mutual sympathy and military accord.[35]

There was no possibility of misunderstanding a dispatch like Lincoln's of August 17, 1864, "Hold on with a bull-dog gripe, and chew & choke, as much as possible"—a message that made Grant burst into laughter and say, "The President has more nerve than any of his advisers."[36] Lincoln's telegraphic eloquence has a monosyllabic and staccato beat:

Have none of it. Stand firm. [SW 2.190]

On that point hold firm, as with a chain of steel. [CW 4.151]

Watch it every day, and hour, and force it. [SW 2.615]

Events were moving too fast for the more languid phrases of the past. As a speaker, Lincoln grasped ahead of time Twain's insight of the postwar years: "Few sinners are saved after the first twenty minutes of a sermon."[37] The trick, of course, was not simply to be brief but to say a great deal in the fewest words. Lincoln justly boasted, of his Second Inaugural's six hundred words, "Lots of wisdom in that document, I suspect."[38] The same is even truer of the Gettysburg Address, which uses roughly half that number of words.

The unwillingness to waste words shows up in the Address's telegraphic quality—the omission of most coupling words—that rhetoricians call asyndeton.[39] Triple phrases sound as to a drum-beat, with no "and" or "but" to slow their insistency:

we are engaged . . .
We are met . . .
We have come . . .

171

we can not dedicate . . .
we can not consecrate . . .
we can not hallow . . .

that from these honored dead . . .
that we here highly resolve . . .
that this nation, under God . . .

government of the people,
by the people,
for the people . . .

Despite the suggestive images of birth, testing, and rebirth, the speech is surprisingly bare of ornament. The language is itself made strenuous, its musculature easily traced, so even the grammar becomes a form of rhetoric. By repeating the antecedent as often as possible, instead of referring to it indirectly by pronouns like "it" or "they," or by backward referential words like "former" and "latter," Lincoln interlocks his sentences, making of them a constantly self-referential system. This linking up by explicit repetition amounts to a kind of hook-and-eye method for joining the parts of his address. The rhetorical devices are almost invisible, since they use no figurative language or formal tropes.

Four score and seven years ago our fathers brought forth on this continent, *a new nation, conceived* in Liberty *and dedicated* to the proposition that all men are created equal.

Now we are engaged in A GREAT CIVIL WAR, testing whether *that nation,* or any nation *so conceived and so dedicated,* can long endure.

We are met on a great <u>*battle-field*</u> of THAT WAR.

We have come to <u>dedicate</u> a portion of <u>*that field,*</u> as a final resting place for those who here gave their lives that *that nation* might live. It is altogether fitting and proper that we should do this.

But, in a larger sense, we can not <u>dedicate</u>—we can not <u>consecrate</u>—we cannot hallow—this ground.

The brave men, living and dead, **who struggled here,** have <u>consecrated</u> it, far above our poor power to add or detract. The world will little note, nor long remember, what we say here, but it can never forget what they did here.

It is for us, the living, rather, to be <u>dedicated</u> here to the unfinished work which they **who fought here** have thus far so nobly advanced. It is, rather, for us to be here <u>dedicated</u> to the great task remaining before us—that from **THESE HONORED DEAD** we take increased devotion to that cause for which they gave the last full measure of devotion—

that we here highly resolve that **THESE DEAD** shall not have died in vain—that this nation, under God, shall have a new birth of freedom—and that government of the people, by the people, for the people, shall not perish from the earth.

Each of the paragraphs printed separately here is bound to the preceding and the following by some resumptive element. Only the first and last paragraph do not (because they cannot) have this two-way connection to their setting. Not all of these "pointer" phrases replace grammatical antecedents in the technical sense. But Lincoln makes them perform analogous work. The nation is declared, again, to be "consecrated" and "dedicated" before each of these terms is given a further two (separate) uses for individuals present at the ceremony, who repeat (as it were) the national consecration. By this reliance on a few words in different contexts, the compactness of the themes is emphasized. A similar linking process is performed, almost subliminally, by the repeated pinning of statements to *that* field, *these* dead, who died *here,* for *that* (kind of) nation. The reverential touching, over and over, of the charged moment and place leads Lincoln to use "here" six times in the short text, the adjectival "that" five times, "this" four times.[40] The spare vocabulary is not impoverishing because of the subtly interfused constructions, in which Charles Smiley identifies "six antitheses, six instances of balanced sentence structure, two cases of anaphora, and four alliterations." "Plain speech" was never *less* artless. Lincoln forged a new lean language to humanize and redeem the first modern war.

Some have claimed, simplistically, that Lincoln achieved a "down-to-earth" style by using short Anglo-Saxon words rather than long Latin ones in the Address. Such people cannot have read the Address with care. Lincoln talks of a nation "conceived in Liberty," not born in freedom; of one "dedicated to [a] proposition," not vowed to a truth; of a "consecrated" nation whose soldiers show their "devotion"—Latinate terms all. Lincoln was even criticized, in the past, for using so "unliterary" a word as "proposition."[41] These criticisms are based on a misunderstanding. Though Lincoln used fertility *imagery* from the cemetery movement, his *message* was telegraphic (itself a Latin term, from the Greek). He liked to talk of the theorems and axioms of democracy, comparing them to Euclid's "propositions" (SW 2.19). He was a Transcendentalist without the fuzziness. He spoke a modern language because he was dealing with a scientific age, for which abstract words are appropriate. His urgency was more a matter of the speech's internal "wiring" and *workability* than of anything so crude as "calling a spade a spade." He was not addressing an agrarian future but a mechanical one. His speech is economical, taut, interconnected, like the machinery he tested and developed for battle. Words were weapons, for him, even though he meant them to be weapons of peace in the midst of war.

This was the perfect medium for changing the way most Americans thought about the nation's founding acts. Lincoln does not argue law or history, as Daniel Webster did. He *makes* history. He does not come to present a theory, but to impose a symbol, one tested in experience and appealing to national values, with an emotional urgency entirely expressed in calm abstractions (fire in ice). He came to change the world, to effect an intellectual revolution. No other words could have done it. The miracle is that these words did. In his brief time before the crowd at Gettysburg he wove a spell that has not, yet, been broken—he called up a new nation out of the blood and trauma.

Epilogue

THE OTHER ADDRESS

It is tempting to think that Lincoln went too far when he cleansed the morally infected air of Gettysburg. By turning all the blood and waste into a hygienic testing of an abstract proposition, he may have ennobled war, the last thing he wanted to do in other contexts. Slavery was not mentioned, because he wanted to lift his ideal of America as the Declaration's nation above divisive particulars. But the war was not just an intellectual affair, and the burden of slavery could not be ignored. That is why the Gettysburg Address, weighty as it is with Lincoln's political philosophy, fails to express the whole of Lincoln's mind. It must be supplemented with his other most significant address, the Second Inaugural, where *sin* is added to the picture.

Lincoln was the least romantic man where war was concerned. He served as a militia officer in that Indian hunt called the Black Hawk War (1832)—a skirmish which did not change his low opinion of the President (Andrew Jackson) conducting it. He was even harsher on President Polk for the greed and mendacity that drew Mexico into war in 1846. As a congressman, he earned some enduring animosity for the bitterness of his assault on Polk.

I more than suspect already that he is deeply conscious of being in the wrong—that he feels the blood of this war, like the blood of Abel, is crying to Heaven against him. That originally having some strong motive—what, I will not stop now to give my opinion concerning—to involve the two countries in a war, and trusting to escape scrutiny, by fixing the public gaze upon the exceeding brightness of military glory—that attractive rainbow that rises in showers of blood—that serpent's eye that charms to destroy—he plunged into it and has swept *on* and *on* till, disappointed in his calculation of the ease with which Mexico might be subdued, he now finds himself he knows not where. How like the half insane mumbling of a fever-dream is the whole war part of his late message! . . . His mind, tasked beyond its power, is running hither and thither, like some tortured creature on a burning surface, finding no position on which it can settle down and be at ease. [SW 1.168, 170]

Lincoln found it impolitic to name Polk's motives, because, very probably, he agreed with those who claimed that the Slave Power was seeking new territories for reintroducing slavery (which even Mexico had abolished). Modern historians doubt that was the original motive, but it soon became the ominous result; and Lincoln no doubt shared Theodore Parker's conspiratorial view that this outcome had been in the President's mind all along. As Parker noted, "This was the first time that America had ever established slavery in any land whence any government had positively driven it out."[1] General Grant, who knew the war was evil while he fought in it, considered the Civil War a logical consequence of the Mexican War:

> The occupation, separation, and annexation were, from the inception of the movement to its final consummation, a conspiracy to acquire territory out of which slave states might be formed for the American Union. . . . Nations, like individuals, are punished for their transgressions. We got our punishment in the most sanguinary and expensive war of modern times.[2]

Lincoln mocked his own part in the Black Hawk War (SW 1.214) and described the swaggering of veterans:

> Among the rules and regulations, no man is to wear more than five pounds of cod-fish or epaulets, or more than thirty yards of bologna sausage for a sash, and no two men are to dress alike, and if any two should dress alike the one that dresses most alike is to be fined. [SW 1.288]

Lincoln recognized the evils of war even in the "best wars." The Mexican War was evil throughout. But the Revolution, the war of "the fathers," was also a dark and cruel transaction:

> It breathed forth famine, swam in blood, and rode on fire; and long, long after, the orphan's cry and the widow's wail continued to break the sad silence that ensued. [SW 1.89]

Lincoln, the war leader, was nonviolent in most ways. He knew how violence works people beyond their original intent. He was deeply ashamed that he let himself be drawn into preparation for a duel, and he rebuked a hotheaded officer:

> The advice of a father, "Beware of entrance to a quarrel, but being in, bear it that the opposed may beware thee" [*Hamlet* 1.3.65–67], is good, and yet not the best. Quarrel not at all. No man resolved to make the most of himself can spare time for personal contention. Still less can he afford to take all the consequences, including the vitiating of his temper and loss of self-control. Yield larger things to which you can show no more than equal right, and yield lesser ones, though clearly your own. Better give your path to a dog than be bitten by him in contesting for the right. Even killing the dog would not cure the bite. [SW 2.530–31][3]

Lincoln told lawyers not to encourage litigiousness, and he conceded as many points as possible in his own practice (SW 1.245–46). He tried to avoid sectional insult even when attacking the spread of slavery. Unlike Theodore Parker, who subsidized John Brown, he feared resort to violence in opposition to slavery. He predicted in 1854 the results of abandoning the Compromise of 1850:

> The spirit of mutual compromise—that spirit which first gave us the constitution, and which has thrice saved the Union—we shall have strangled and cast from us forever. And what shall we have in lieu of it? The South, flushed with triumph and tempted to excesses; the North, betrayed, as they believe, brooding on wrong and burning for revenge. One side will provoke; the other resist. The one will taunt, the other defy; one aggresses, the other retaliates. [SW 1.335]

The mechanism by which hostilities ratchet each other up, higher and higher, is something Lincoln had witnessed in the barroom brawls of his young wrestling days. It is a fearsome process when whole societies indulge in it. Thucydides described what happens: "Suspicion of prior atrocities drives men to *surpass* report in their own cruel innovations, either by subtlety of assault or extravagance of reprisal."[4]

Lincoln analyzed this process in language as searing as that of Thucydides.

> Actual war coming, blood grows hot, and blood is spilled. Thought is forced from old channels into confusion. Deception breeds and thrives. Confidence dies, and universal suspicion reigns.[5] Each man feels an impulse to kill his neighbor, lest he first be killed by him.[6] Revenge and retaliation follow. And all this, as before said, may be among honest men only. But this is

not all. Every foul bird comes abroad, and every dirty reptile rises up. These add crime to confusion. Strong measures, deemed indispensable but harsh at best, such men make worse by maladministration. Murders for old grudges, and murders for self, proceed under any cloak that will best cover the occasion. [SW 2.523]

This was written, in the year of Gettysburg, about a war Lincoln was himself conducting. He has no illusions about war's "nobility." It is a cover for other crimes. And the longer it goes on, the more it outraces any rational purpose. Even noble yearnings serve savagery—as Lee's power to inspire made sure that the South would be more thoroughly drained of its best men and treasure.[7] Lincoln's descriptions show that he understood the inner dynamics of war, what Clausewitz called *Wechselwirkung*—the way each side is wrought upon by the other: "Each side, therefore, compels its opponent to follow suit; a reciprocal action [*Wechselwirkung*] is started which must lead, in theory, to extremes."[8] Superficially, at least, not only the Civil War, but Lincoln's conduct of it, serves to confirm this gloomy observation. After all, General Grant was just following the President's lead when he adopted what is known to military historians as a "strategy of annihilation."[9] And James McPherson, as we have seen, argued that Lincoln escalated his demands toward "a policy of unconditional surrender."

No one doubts that Lincoln was personally humane, that he softened the rigors of war whenever he could use his pardoning and amnesty powers:

The case of Andrews is really a very bad one, as appears by the record already before me. Yet before receiving this I had ordered his punishment commuted to imprisonment for during the war at hard labor, and had so telegraphed. I did this, not on any merit

in the case, but because I am trying to evade the butchering business lately. [SW 2.565]

Hay noted in his 1863 diary:

Today we spent 6 hours deciding on Court Martials, the President, Judge Holt, & I. I was amused at the eagerness with which the President caught at any fact which would justify him in saving the life of a condemned soldier. He was only merciless in cases where meanness or cruelty were shown. Cases of cowardice he was especially averse to punishing with death. He said it would frighten the poor devils too terribly, to shoot them. On the case of a soldier who had once deserted & reenlisted he indorsed, "Let him fight instead of shooting him." [P. 68.]

But Lincoln was ruthless in his determination to end the insurrection as swiftly as possible, never blunting at all the hard edge of *that* determination. He would give no signals of flexibility. Told in 1862 that General Phelps was harsh in his occupation of Louisiana, he responded:

If they can conceive of anything worse than General Phelps, within my power, would they not better be looking out for it? They very well know the way to avert all this is simply to take their place in the Union upon the old terms. If they will not do this, should they not receive harder blows rather than lighter ones? [SW 2.344]

It would have been natural—it seems almost inevitable—for Lincoln to grow more extreme as war wrought its mutual transformations in the warring parties. This *does* often lead to demands for unconditional surrender, which are reciprocated by a determination to fight "to the last man." Even the rational Pericles, who delivered the serene-sounding Funeral Oration, is shown by Thucydides in his next speech talking like a man trapped:

> This fight is for your empire. Its loss would subject you to all the hatreds incurred by your administration of it. There is no giving it up, anymore, though some would like to adopt a humane policy out of fear, and become neutral. You hold your empire as a usurped power—wrong perhaps to have taken, but deadly to give back.[10]

Bernard Knox has compared the speech to Hitler's address in his bunker. If we put "slavery" for "empire," it also represents the position of Lee and other Southern leaders. War becomes an all-or-nothing matter. As Clausewitz observed, hatred *(Hass)* becomes a necessary force for nerving combatants to the grisly actions of war.[11]

But Lincoln was exceptional in that his goals and rhetoric did *not* escalate. It is inaccurate to say that he moved to a position of crushing the rebellion at its source. James McPherson finds in later stages of the conflict an embrace of "total war."[12] But we have already seen that Lincoln did not treat the suppression of insurrection as war with a foreign people. If it were appropriate to talk of "surrender" in terms of international law rather than of domestic disturbances, his provisional emancipation proclamation was a *conditional*-surrender proposal: if states returned to the Union in the next several months, they would retain their slaves.

Edmund Wilson could not have erred more basically than in his claim that Lincoln became a Lenin or a Bismarck in the course of the war, an "uncompromising dictator" who felt the inevitability of his cause.[13] Lincoln's distinctive mark, one almost unique in the history of war leadership, was his refusal to indulge in triumphalism, righteousness, or vilification of the foe. He professed to be preserving the Union by suppression of rebellion, and any other effects were providential—the work of a mysterious, not a manifest, Providence:

> If I had had my way, this war would never have been commenced; if I had been allowed my way, this war would have ended before this, but we find it still continues; and we must believe that He permits it for some wise purpose of his own, mysterious and unknown to us; and though with our limited understandings we may not be able to comprehend it, yet we cannot but believe that He who made the world still governs it. [CW 5.478][14]

Nothing could be farther from the crusading righteousness of Julia Ward Howe in her "Battle Hymn of the Republic."[15] Lincoln's submission to Providence is made in a spirit of humility, reflected in the series of Fast Day and Thanksgiving Day proclamations issued throughout the war, where the people as a whole are called on to repent the sins that led to violence:

> When our own beloved Country, once, by the blessing of God, united, prosperous and happy, is now afflicted with faction and civil war, it is peculiarly fit for us to recognize the hand of God in this terrible visitation, and in sorrowful remembrance of our own faults and crimes as a nation and as individuals, to humble ourselves before Him, and to pray for His mercy—to pray that we may be spared further punishment, though most justly deserved; that our arms may be blessed and made effectual for the re-establishment of law, order and peace, throughout the wide extent of our country; and that the inestimable boon of civil and religious liberty earned, under His guidance and blessing, by the labors and sufferings of our fathers, may be restored in all its original excellence. [SW 2.264][16]

In a situation where heightening animosities *(Wechselwirkung)* tend to ratchet up the rhetoric, the demands, the righteousness

of combatants, Lincoln deliberately ratchets *down* the claims that can be made by himself and the nation. He asks people to fight a *repenting* war:

> May we not justly fear that the awful calamity of civil war, which now desolates the land, may be but a punishment, inflicted upon us, for our presumptuous sins, to the needful end of our national reformation on a whole people? [CW 6.156]

It is this counterrhetoric of joint responsibility for the historical sin of slavery that gives Lincoln's last great statement on the war its tortured radiance. It was inappropriate, at Gettysburg, to talk about the *sins* of the men to whom he was paying tribute. He talked of rebirth from blood, there, but not of washing away the crimes of the past, as he does in the Second Inaugural Address. In this last speech, war is made to pay history's dues in a prophet's ledger, where scales balance precisely the blood drawn by the lash and by the bayonet.

The verse of scripture Lincoln used at the climax of the Second Inaugural was not implicit, like the Lukan references in the Gettysburg Address, nor worn to a cliché like the parable of the House Divided. Lincoln quotes verbatim from Matthew 18.7: "Woe unto the world because of offenses." Jesus says that even when offenses are bound to come, the punishment of them will be strict. Lincoln's phrases are weary and resigned:

> *The prayer of both*
> *could not be answered;*
> *that of neither*
> *has been answered fully.*
> *The Almighty has his own purposes.*
> *"Woe unto the world*
> *because of offenses!*

185

For it must needs be
that offenses come;
but woe to that man
by whom the offense cometh!" [SW 2.687]

Four sentences follow, three of them long and periodic, suggestive of the historical law being worked out in the divagations of
the national past:

If we shall suppose
that American Slavery is one of those offenses
which, in the providence of God,
must needs come,
but which, having continued through His appointed time,
He now wills to remove
and that He gives
to both North and South
this terrible war as the woe due
to those by whom the offense came,
shall we discern therein
any departure from those divine attributes
which the believers in a Living God
always ascribe to Him?

It should be noticed that Lincoln speaks of "*American* Slavery"
as a single offense ascribed to the whole nation—a point he spells
out even further in "both North and South." There is one agent
by which the offense came, just as in the text of Matthew's
Gospel, and that agent is the undifferentiated American people.
In the Gettysburg Address, the people was consecrated as a
whole; it could overthrow its government only as a whole (in the
constitutional theory of Webster and others). Now we see that it
sins in solidarity as well. Lincoln began this passage with the
notion that neither side's prayers were answered. Now both sides

pray, and only what they *both* pray for can come true—the nation's restoration, as the consecrated child of equality and freedom.

> *Fondly do we hope—*
> *fervently do we pray—*
> *that this mighty scourge of war*
> *may speedily pass away.*

But a price must be paid for that outcome. Here is the second of the careful periods Lincoln is marshaling toward his grandest conclusion:

> *Yet, if God wills that it continue*
> *until all the wealth*
> *piled by the bond-man's two hundred and fifty years*
> *of unrequited toil*
> *shall be sunk,*
> *and until every drop of blood*
> *drawn with the lash*
> *shall be paid by another*
> *drawn with the sword,*
> *as it was said three thousand years ago,*
> *so still it must be said,*
> *"the judgments of the Lord, are true*
> *and righteous altogether."*

The inner correspondences of this passage suggest the precision of the price being exacted—as the final quote from Psalm 19 precludes any appeal from the exaction:

> *until all the wealth*
> *until every drop*
> *piled by*

> *drawn with*
> *drawn with*
> *shall be sunk*
> *shall be paid.*

Even "sunk," neatly paralleled with "paid" here, is an *accounting* term in its nineteenth-century use. In phrases like "the sinking fund," it means the extinguishing of financial debts.

Turning from this vision of blood, Lincoln brings redemption in his final period:

> *With malice toward none;*
> *with charity for all;*
> *with firmness in the right,*
>   *as God gives us to see the right,*
> *let us strive on*
>   *to finish the work we are in;*
>   *to bind up the nation's wounds;*
>   *to care for him who shall have borne the battle,*
>   *and for his widow,*
>   *and his orphan—*
>   *to do all which may achieve*
>   *and cherish*
> *a just,*
>   *and a lasting*
> *peace, among ourselves,*
>   *and with all nations.*

There is a characteristic limitation on Lincoln's own claim to knowledge—"as God gives us to see the right." This is almost a refrain of this period:

> in the light which he affords *me* . . . [CW 5.478]
>   *as we understand it* . . . [SW 2.130]

[God's will] if I can learn what it is . . . [SW 2.361]
in the best light He gives us . . . [SW 2.627]

Lincoln calls on a united people "to finish the work we are in"—not the war, but "the unfinished work" of the first dedication to a proposition, "the great task remaining before us." This statement complements and completes the Gettysburg Address. It is the only speech worthy to stand with it.

I

What Lincoln Said: The Text

Short as is the Gettysburg Address, its exact wording is hard to pin down. What should be counted the authoritative text? What Lincoln actually said on the spot? Stenographic accounts differ on that. The text he spoke from—his delivery text? It is not certain that we have that; but if we do, then he clearly departed from it. His revised later texts? There are at least four of these. Which should be preferred? The final one is usually accepted, *faute de mieux*. A text more closely linked to the actual event would, if it could be established, take precedence in modern editorial practice.

1. NEWSPAPER ACCOUNTS

There were four known newspaper copyists at work in Gettysburg, of whom the representatives of the Associated Press (Joseph L. Gilbert) and the Boston *Daily Advertiser* (Charles Hale) are the most accurate.[1] Joseph Gilbert actually consulted Lincoln's delivery text briefly after the ceremony, which makes his version more authoritative for some scholars. But William Barton argues that Hale should be preferred because he relied *only* on what was said. Gilbert may have returned to the text where Lincoln had departed from it in his actual delivery.[2]

Two other transcripts, generally inferior, seem to have caught the word "poor" (in "our poor power to add or detract"), which both Gilbert and Hale missed. But all these four accounts have "under God," confirming that it was actually said, though it is missing from what seem to be the earliest texts in Lincoln's hand. Lincoln's later copies of the speech are closer to the newspaper accounts than to those apparently earlier drafts; his secretary, John Nicolay, says he consulted the AP report of his speech when making these copies.[3] Those who want to construct an authoritative text from the newspaper account thus have strong grounds for their project. They usually base their text mainly on Gilbert, supplemented with "poor" from the other accounts and correcting "refinished" to "unfinished work."

2. THE NICOLAY TEXT ("FIRST DRAFT")
This autograph, at the Library of Congress, is called the First Draft by Roy Basler, David Mearns, and Lloyd Dunlap.[4] They mean, obviously, the first *surviving* draft, since it is too clean to have been the composition draft. We have to assume that there were one or more drafts in which Lincoln worked out his ideas on paper.[5] (Mearns and Dunlap think the "Second Draft" retains or re-creates such fumblings toward the final version.) The reasons for treating this as the delivery text are:

1. Nicolay, who owned the draft, says it was what Lincoln held in his hand.

2. The first page has the Executive Mansion's letterhead, which the New York *Tribune* reporter says he saw while Lincoln was reading.

3. The second page is in pencil, and several witnesses say they saw Lincoln completing his address in pencil on the morning of his delivery.

4. The two sheets of this draft have fold lines, and witnesses at the cemetery say Lincoln took the speech out of his pocket and unfolded it.

The arguments seem strong, and have convinced many of the best students of the matter that these are the very sheets Lincoln was holding as he made his greatest speech. But there are counterarguments.

1. This text does not have three important phrases that the joint newspaper accounts prove he actually spoke. Despite Lincoln's dislike for extemporizing, did he depart from this short and considered text three times in three minutes? That seems unlikely when we consider the phrases themselves.[6]

2. The first omission occurs at the meld between the first page, written in ink, and the second one, done in pencil. The transition is garbled and ungrammatical, besides dropping an entire clause. The last line on page one goes: "It is rather for us, the living, to stand here." In pencil, "to stand here" is crossed out and "we here be dedica-" written above it. The result is this: "It is rather for us, the living, we here be dedicated to the great task remaining before us—" This is not only garbled; it omits "dedicated here to the unfinished work that they have thus far so nobly carried on," which comes before "It is rather for us to be here dedicated to the great task remaining before us" in the newspaper (and Lincoln's own later) accounts. To suppose that this is the delivery text we have to assume (a) that Lincoln was so careless in preparing his short speech that he linked the second page to the first in an ungrammatical way and left it to the spur of the moment to straighten out the sentence; (b) that he not only dropped a clause in the process, but (c) remembered the clause in delivery, without having bothered to put it on paper, or else (d) he improvised the whole sentence by adding a new clause ad lib. This goes against what we know, from Herndon's testimony and Lincoln's practice elsewhere, about his careful preparation and desire for a perfected text. The casual way these two pages are united makes it unlikely that Lincoln relied on them to make an address he had taken great pains over, traveling early to make sure he could deliver it. The second page is the more objectionable one, causing the ungrammatical nexus and the dropped clause.

3. Yet even the first page is vulnerable. It is obviously an early

stage (not the earliest) in the evolution of the text. Its version of the *dignum et justum* clause is different from the one delivered. This text says: "This we may, in all propriety do." But the newspaper (and Lincoln's own later) accounts have: "It is altogether fitting and proper that we should do this." Again, did Lincoln just make his changes in his head, on the spot, as he turned the written words in his hand into the spoken words being taken down by reporters? It is unlikely that such stylistic revision would have been put off to the moment itself. Lincoln had time to rework his short text; he was seen writing the night before and the morning of the ceremony, and most people feel he came to Gettysburg with a text all-but-completed anyway.

4. The third disparity between the written text and the reported speech is the most famous—the insertion of "under God" after "this nation shall" (later moved back before the "shall"). This is a far easier change than the other two, which involve simultaneous deletion of some material and substitution of replacements, or the rearrangement of grammar. Dropping two words into an otherwise undisturbed text would not be difficult. But neither would it have been difficult to pencil it into the text if, as some assume, the new words occurred to him during the spoken prayer, the sung poems, or Everett's long oration. Unless we assume a divine afflatus striking him at the very moment of delivering "this nation," there was no need for improvising where so simple a last-minute alteration could have been made in the text itself. Taken in isolation, the "under God" change is not impossible; but in conjunction with the other differences from what was said, it shows uncharacteristic behavior on Lincoln's part, making his text a set of notes for him to play live variations on in front of a huge audience.

5. Another consideration, not conclusive in itself but suggestive in combination with the earlier points, is that Lincoln liked to underline the words he would emphasize in delivery. It did not matter that these words were somewhat obvious in their antitheses—e.g., the House Divided Speech's *"old* as well as *new—North* as well as *South."* The "First Draft" has none of the expected cues, even where we would most expect them ("what we *say* here, as what they *did* here," or would it have been "what *we* say . . . what *they* did"?). There is a back-and-forth

stroke of a pencil roughly positioned under *"did"*—without the customary underlining of the correlative "said." But it is made by harder and sharper lead than the soft one Lincoln uses elsewhere in this text.[7] It could have been added later, but why? There is, of course, no handwriting test for underlinings, so we cannot be sure Lincoln was the wielder of the different pencil.

Though it is hard to prove a negative, and there is no *physical impossibility* that this draft is the delivery text, it is unproved that it *is,* and unlikely that it is. It could have been folded in Lincoln's jacket when he left the Executive Mansion to catch his train, as part of a composition process whose end product was probably closer to what was actually said in the cemetery. Sergeant James A. Robert saw Lincoln shuffling several pages in pencil on the morning of the speech—the penciled page we have could have been one of those, without being part of the delivery text. Nicolay, who was in the room that morning, could have picked up this draft and confused it later on with others handled back at the White House. The possibilities are endless. The probabilities are more limited. It is improbable that we have the delivery text.

3. THE WILLS TEXT (LITTLE, BROWN?)

What happened to the delivery text? The last time we see it, that text is in the hand of the AP reporter Joseph Gilbert; but he only had it a short time. Others probably asked to look at it, in Gettysburg or on the train back to Washington. It was not, presumably, left behind in Gettysburg, since David Wills, Lincoln's host and the ceremony's impresario, wrote to Washington asking for the delivery text (which he called "the original") to be preserved among the official records of the event. Presumably Lincoln made some response, which has been lost—as was his response to the invitation to attend the ceremony in the first place.

Wills's first invitation to Lincoln was not only to say a few words at the dedication, but to stay with him overnight at the house—an invitation extended in a separate letter. It is unlikely that Lincoln failed to answer this formal offer of hospitality in writing—he responded to less substantial expressions of respect and hospitality. The few remains of Wills's papers have been scattered to various repositories, and obviously reflect a mere fraction of the heavy correspondence he carried on with seventeen governors and their agents—with contractors as well as with speakers, poets, marshals, and others—in connection with the business of the cemetery, its dedication, and its future governance. We get one glimpse of his hasty attention to detail in the late telegram he fired off to Governor Curtin urging him to bring the state flag with him to the dedication.[8] So it would not be terribly surprising if the Address Lincoln sent to Wills were lost, exactly as the response to his invitation had been. Wills would later say he had a lithograph of a copy he had seen—not, apparently, the one Lincoln sent him.[9]

One possibility has not enough been explored: he may have sent the Lincoln draft to Everett in Boston. Six days after the dedication, while Everett was still in Washington, he wrote to Wills about the proposed publication of all the speeches. Everett said that his own publisher in Boston was "one of the best, if not the very best printer in the United States," and made this offer:

> If you would furnish me with whatever you would wish to include in the pamphlet, I will with pleasure superintend the publication, causing such a number to be struck off or furnished at cost, as might be wished for distribution among the States interested.[10]

Wills asked for further information on the printing proposal, and Everett replied from Boston on November 28, saying (among other things):

> I have no particular wish to have Mr. Houghton print the pamphlet beyond the convenience of correcting the proof sheets & a desire to have it extremely well done. It would be better to have the publication made by some bookseller in Philadelphia, but that need not prevent the employment of Mr. Houghton as printer. He does work both for the Philadelphia & New York publishers.[11]

Everett, whose text was far the longest, wanted to control its proper reproduction—he was wary of printers, from long experience. For that

very reason, he asked that the other speeches be sent him—he did not trust newspaper accounts. Wills complied, sending separately the minister's invocation. The fact that Everett was handling the memorial publication—with Little, Brown, as it turned out, not Houghton—was sufficiently known in Washington for the State Department to write the publisher asking that Secretary Seward's speech, given the night before the dedication, be included. Everett asked for Wills's approval of this suggestion—which he rather liked—on January 2, 1864. He delayed the print run for Wills's reply—which is lost but was obviously in the negative, since the Seward speech was not included. It was not till January 30 that Everett was able to send Lincoln what he calls "the authorized edition" of the two men's speeches, with other material on the creation and dedication of the cemetery.[12]

Did Wills send the copy Lincoln had given him to Everett? That goes against the purpose he had given in his request, to have a place where all the speeches given could be kept—an archive of the event. But that plan seems to have been superseded by Everett's proposal to reprint the authorized account in Boston. Wills no longer asks for Everett's speech to place in the Gettysburg file. Rather, he sends things off to him. It must be remembered, here also, how pressed Wills was with the business of continuing the burials in the period—two thousand more to be completed—and setting up the machinery of state payment and government of the committee, which still had many tasks before it (beginning with the soliciting of designs for the monument). Wills seems to have been happy to turn responsibility for the texts over to Everett, payment to whom for printing costs ($1,357.00) was reported by Wills to Governor Curtin on March 22, 1864.[13]

If Wills did not send the Lincoln text to Everett, where did Everett get the text he used? The only other ones available to him were newspaper accounts, which he distrusted.[14] Besides, the text printed by Little, Brown does not exactly correspond with any of the newspaper versions.[15] Wills supplied the other material provided in the book—the prayers, the dirge, even the music for the dirge. Wills himself wrote for inclusion a new letter, at Everett's suggestion, saying that the orator's long description of the battle was desired and appreciated in Gettysburg. This is the text Everett calls "the authorized edition" of all the information relating to the dedication. The title page says:

PUBLISHED FOR THE BENEFIT OF THE
CEMETERY MONUMENT FUND

It should be remembered that all the three succeeding holographs of the Lincoln speech were supplied for charitable purposes. If Everett used the Wills copy, it would be the first text put to such use.

If, as seems possible, Everett printed the text Lincoln sent to Wills in November, then this would be the text we can date closest to the event, and the preferred version of what was *said*. It is close to the newspaper accounts, yet it is not identical with them. (For instance, it includes "under God," but in the place where the newspapers put it: "the nation shall, under God . . .")

If this is the Wills text, then the hunt for it among his papers is useless. The texts were all handled for printing in Boston, not in Gettysburg, and there is no record in Everett's carefully kept papers that he returned anything to Wills (or was expected to). When he acknowledges the late receipt of Dr. Baugher's benediction, he makes no reference to returning it.

4. THE HAY TEXT ("SECOND DRAFT")

Mearns and Dunlap suggested that Lincoln never sent a copy in response to Wills's letter of November 23. Why on earth would that have been Lincoln's reaction to a reasonable request? He sent copies to people with far less claim on him. Besides, he wanted his speech to be given the attention and recognition that would make it do its work, and one way of accomplishing this was to encourage such memorials as Wills seemed to be planning.

Mearns and Dunlap need to direct the Wills copy into John Hay's possession, since they believe that his text is the *kind* of thing Lincoln might have drafted with a view to answering Wills's request. They propose that he gave it instead to Hay, whose family preserved it. Hay's text was unknown to the public until 1906, when the news of its existence was published. Nicolay, who discussed the text of the Address using his own copy, seems not to have known about his friend Hay's.

When a facsimile of the Hay copy was published in 1909, it led to a debate over what Mearns and Dunlap call "the most inexplicable of the five copies Lincoln made." On the face of it, this text seems earlier than the clean Nicolay "First Draft," since it has a number of rewritings, as if it were a composition draft—which some took it for. The man who first revealed the text's existence, a collector named William Harrison Lambert, assumed that this composition draft was left in Washington when Lincoln went to Gettysburg carrying a fair copy of it. But others, who notice that Hay's text is closer to newspaper reports of what was actually said than is the Nicolay text, think Hay's must be a later version than Nicolay's. This view would conform with a Hay family tradition that it was copied out specially for John Hay.

Then why did Mearns and Dunlap think it was written for Wills and given, for some odd reason, to Hay instead? Their reasoning is complex. Wills had asked for "the original"—meaning, most obviously, the delivery text; but Mearns and Dunlap take this to mean the composition draft, and they suppose that Lincoln set out to *reconstruct* that draft, either from memory, or from an existing rough draft he did not want to give up. In this view, the Hay copy is a *fake* draft.

Why would Lincoln create such a thing? Mearns and Dunlap have a parallel to offer. Lincoln was asked for the composition draft of the Emancipation Proclamation, to be used at the Cincinnati Sanitary Fair of December 8, 1863. He sent a copy of that draft, including changes made in it, explaining that the original was too damaged to send. But in that case Lincoln explained what he was doing, and why; and the request was for an original of a printed text, not for the speaking copy of an address.

Yet all these mystifications are beside the point. What Mearns and Dunlap take as compositional changes are probably copyists' corrections—there is no attempt to reproduce changes made while creating the text in the first place. The clearest example of this is the omission of words that are supplied, above the line, with a caret: "the unfinished [∧ work] which" and "task remaining before [∧ us]." The phrases are meaningless without the missing word, and an author composing is not likely to put down such phrases and only then notice he had left out a key word. That is what happens when one is *copying* a text, especially if one is doing it rapidly.

Given that clue, look at the other "corrections." Lincoln repeated "We are met" from the preceding sentence, and had to cross it out to put in the proper new opening: "We have come." This is a simple case of dittography. An even plainer case is "gave gave the last full measure of devotion." Another copying error, especially common when dealing with one's own words, is that the mind supplies different pronouns or prepositions while moving ahead of the eye—"the" becomes "a," "for" becomes "of," "that" becomes "the." Then the eye, catching up, makes the copyist go back to the original (almost interchangeable) minor word. These three examples all occur in the Hay text.

That accounts for all the misnamed "variants" in the Hay copy except one, which has received a great deal of attention. Lincoln at first omits, and then supplies above a caret, the word "poor" in "our [∧ poor] power." Since that is one of the discrepancies between the Nicolay copy and the newspaper accounts, it has naturally been asked if the Hay copy came *after* the Nicolay copy but *before* delivery. But there is no reason, given the parallel omissions, to treat this as an error different in kind from omission of "work" and "in." In this case, unlike those two, the phrase from which the word is omitted makes sense without it; so reinsertion can *look* like emendation rather than restoration. But it *can* be the latter, and its proximity to all the other lapses of that kind lead to a presumption in favor of inadvertent omission.

That Lincoln was making a rather hasty copy is seen in the handwriting of the Hay copy. It begins in a small neat hand—there are over fifty characters in the second line. By the end the hand has spread and become more cursive—the number of characters drops by roughly 20 percent (down from about fifty to about forty).

All these points confirm the Hay family tradition, that this was a personal souvenir copied out as a private favor, treasured as such. Thus Hay had no reason to volunteer his copy as evidence for the formation of Lincoln's text—as Nicolay had used his own copy in the biography.

Hay knew the alterations in the text were not an author's variants but a copyist's slips of a pen moving too rapidly. Lincoln was copying, probably, from a clean text. The result does nothing to return us to anything prior to that exemplar (whatever it was). The popular name for this text—"Second Draft"—is no more justifiable than the Nicolay text's title of "First Draft."

5. THE SPRINGFIELD TEXT ("EVERETT COPY")
In his letter presenting the Little, Brown edition of the speeches to the President, Everett wrote:

> I have promised to give the manuscript of my address to Mrs. Governor Fish of New York, who is at the head of the ladies' committee of the Metropolitan Fair. It would add very greatly to its value, if I could bind up with it the manuscript of your dedicatory Remarks, if you happen to have preserved them.

Why would Everett ask for a manuscript of the speech if he had already received one from David Wills? Why would he ask if Lincoln happened to have preserved it? There are several possibilities:

1. The Wills copy could have been—manifestly—just that: a copy. In asking for "the manuscript," Everett may have wanted the actual delivery text. But against this is the fact that (a) Lincoln did not send him the delivery text (it is not done on Executive Mansion letterhead); (b) all that was desired was a text in the President's own hand; and (c) it seems unlikely that Everett enclosed in the Fair's volume his *own* composition or delivery text.

2. A more likely explanation is that Lincoln's text, sent to the printer at Little, Brown, was too marked or damaged, or of the wrong size or format, for an ambitious presentation volume being put up for public auction (or that the text may simply have been consumed in the printer's operations). If it is objected that Everett could not have been so cavalier about the Wills copy sent him, we should remember that this was sent to the printer with a number of other texts—those of the

ministers, the dirge, etc.—that were not cared for or sent back to Wills, so far as we know. Mrs. Fish's request for Everett's own speech came in, presumably, after the texts went immediately to Little, Brown, where they were held up while a decision was made about Seward's speech. Everett was convinced, still, that his speech was the centerpiece of the occasion at Gettysburg.[16] So far as we can tell, Mrs. Fish did not herself ask that Lincoln's be included. Everett was being generous in initiating that proposal himself.

The volume, carefully prepared by Everett, prints his manuscript facing the printed version as it appeared in the Little, Brown edition. There are discrepancies between the two, which he explains in the handwritten introduction to the volume as if this manuscript were his composition draft—though it is clearly not.[17] There are illustrations, cut from publications, interspersed at the appropriate places. Even cannibalizing two copies of the Little, Brown book, cutting and pasting them to correspond with the text on the righthand side, and arranging the illustrations to match the text, would have been time-consuming.[18] If Everett actually copied out his whole long text once again, then preparation of the book would have taken much of his still-precious time. This may explain why the book was not auctioned at the Fair, after all. Everett may well have been unable to finish it in time.

The Lincoln holograph included as pages 57 and 58 of the auction book (Everett's numbering is still visible on the pages exhibited at the Old State Capitol in Springfield) differs from the text Everett published with Little, Brown—for one thing, "under God" has been put in the position it now holds in the familiar version.

6. THE BALTIMORE FAIR TEXTS
("BANCROFT COPY" AND "BLISS COPY")

The historian George Bancroft asked Lincoln for a holograph of the Address to be lithographed for sale at the Baltimore Sanitary Fair of February 1864. When the first text sent did not fit the format of other texts being lithographed, a Colonel Bliss sent Lincoln paper of the proper size for him to use. The copy made on this paper is the last known one in Lincoln's hand. Its neat lines, with the margins required by the lithographic format, make it the text most inviting in appearance. As the final one Lincoln authorized, it has become the one most generally printed. I treat it as the basic text in this book (see Appendix III D 2). It is stylistically preferable to others in one significant way: Lincoln removed "here" from "that cause for which they [here] gave . . ." This seventh "here" is in all other versions of the speech. Lincoln obviously felt that six uses of the word were enough in so short a speech.[19] That he was still making such improvements suggests that he was more concerned with a perfected text than with an "original" one (however that is understood). The hunt for composition drafts, or a delivery text, or the Wills copy, might have amused him; but who can believe it would seriously have concerned him?

APPENDIX

$$\left(\text{II} \right)$$

Where He Said It: The Site

Tourists, arriving at the military cemetery in Gettysburg, almost always ask where Lincoln was standing as he gave the Address. National Park Service markers have for years indicated the obvious place, where the tall column of the Soldiers' National Monument now stands. This is the place of honor in William Saunders's original plan, the center of the circle indicated by the hemispherical rows of graves. It was always meant to be the focus of the layout. Since the monument had not been placed there, yet, when Lincoln spoke, it seemed the logical spot for the speaker's platform.

That spot, besides, was the focus of community attention in the years following the Address. Agents from the Northern states charged with responsibility for the cemetery met in June of 1864 to consider designs for the monument. Progress on the monument was watched with interest as people anticipated its placement—which occurred on July 1, 1869, before a crowd said to exceed the one at the dedication ceremony itself. To the base of the classical column (modeled on that

devoted to Columbus in Genoa) the conclusion of Lincoln's Address was later added. So the honored place was crowned. Where else would one look for the site of the Address?

But a note pasted into one copy of the 1865 committee report on the cemetery claimed that the obvious spot was not the authentic spot. This was not just any copy of the report, but an autographed copy given by the President of the committee, David Wills, to its elected secretary, W. Y. Selleck, the agent for Wisconsin. Selleck signed his own copy, and a note in the same handwriting is pasted into the booklet.

> The stand on which President Lincoln stood in the National Cemetery at Gettysburg on Nov. 19th 1863 when he delivered his ever to be remembered address, was 12 ft. wide and 20 ft. long, and facing to the North West. It was located 40 ft. North East of the outer circle of Soldiers Graves as shown by pencil mark on the Cemetery Maps in the book to which the memorandum is attached.

No one knows when or under what circumstances Selleck pasted this note into his copy, but testimony from such a source has to be taken seriously. If Selleck is right, the platform stood outside the hemisphere of graves, roughly at two on the clock as seen from the Soldiers' Monument. It was on the town side of the cemetery, and the platform faced more toward the town than toward the site of "Pickett's Charge" (so called). It was easily reached from the town, and the crowd in front of the speaker would have had open ground to stand on. The graves would have been behind the speakers as they sat lined up on the platform.

Louis A. Warren defended the Selleck site in his 1964 book, *Lincoln's Gettysburg Declaration: "A New Birth of Freedom."* He used two supporting arguments, from the line of march and from the state of the graves. The published route of the procession to the grounds does not take a natural course if the platform was where the monument now stands. The road from the Gettysburg town square forks, just outside of town, the branch on the left going direct to the old cemetery gate, through and around which most of the crowd would normally move if seeking the monument site. But the official route took the branch on the right, which involves a further turn, left onto the Taneytown Road, and then a second left to reach the monument area. If the platform were placed *below* the fan-shaped area of graves, it would be very near (almost on) the Taneytown Road, and this would have been the obvious route to it. Besides, Warren adds, this site would have the advantage of "protecting the burial area from trespassers during the exercises"—not a negligible consideration if we remember that the hemispherical rows contained over a thousand fresh graves, filled irregularly over the last few weeks, and other ground marked out for burials still to come.

The Selleck site gained considerable support between 1964, when Warren's book appeared, and 1973, when Frederick Tilberg published a strenuous refutation of it. Tilberg, the longtime park historian at Gettysburg, had retired when he wrote his article in *Pennsylvania History*.

Tilberg's strongest argument came from the many press accounts that emphasized the *rise* upon which the platform stood in 1863, the wide *view* afforded in all directions, and the spread of graves *below* the platform. None of these points apply to the Selleck site. Since the graves are on ground falling away from the site of the future monument, the Selleck site, lying farther down the slope and outside the fan-shaped rows of graves, was *not* on a rise but down an incline; it did *not* command a good view in all directions; and the graves spread upward, *above* and behind the platform. This platform would have been placed on ground twenty-five feet lower than that on which the monument now stands.

Tilberg was less successful in addressing Warren's two supporting arguments. On the route, he claimed that the right-fork approach would not be implausibly roundabout, but appropriate, if the procession came *through* the graves, up the central approach to the monument site. But that runs up against Warren's claim that the graves should not be disturbed in their fresh and scattered state. Tilberg's reply is that most of those buried so far were in the "unknown" plots off to the side of the line of march as he reconstructed it. But even a few graves in the path of such a large procession—and it is hard to see how it could have been only a few (the spaces were one-third filled)—would have been a deterrent to such an approach. One does not honor graves by trampling on them.

So, at this stage, only the word of one qualified man—Selleck—was given for the alternate site; and Tilberg could cite equally definite testimony from an equally qualified witness, Whitelaw Reid of the Cincinnati *Daily Gazette,* whose dispatch from the scene, published on November 23, said unequivocally that the platform "was erected on the spot where the monument is to be built, *in front of which* are two semicircular sections with portions set aside for each state" (italics added). The Selleck claim seemed to have had its day, and the monument site was again secure, as the National Park Service markers, literature, and movie had all along been saying.

But then, in 1982, a *third* site was championed by one of Tilberg's successors as park historian, Kathleen Georg (now Kathleen Georg Harrison). Since she has not published her own case for the site, there has not been a debate that would give it a name. I will call it the Harrison site, since other designations (e.g., "near the Brown vault") are clumsy. Harrison took the two key photographs of the crowd in the cemetery—one taken facing the Evergreen Cemetery gateway, the other taken from the second story of that gatehouse—and tried to align every identifiable feature in the pictures with remaining features.[1] This had been attempted before, in publications containing the photographs, but the identification had been made on the basis of a presupposition—that the platform was raised where the monument now stands. The thing to be *proved,* in her search, could not be taken as a *given.* Once one removes that preconception, scales fall from one's eyes, as it were. Harrison went out with an associate (now her husband) to photograph the scene on a late-November day, with atmospheric conditions and foliage roughly the same as in the original photographs. These show nothing, of course, that the naked eye cannot see as one traverses the grounds with the original photos in hand—an exercise she generously took me through.

There was initial reluctance to accept her site, since it lies outside the federal cemetery, separated from it now by a fence. The Harrison site is in Gettysburg's local cemetery, Evergreen, the one presided over in the 1860s by David McConaughy, David Wills's rival in the effort to become Governor Curtin's agent for the military burials. The Harrison site is on or near a Brown family vault erected in the 1950s. Over the years, Harrison has convinced skeptics at the National Park Service, and a new marker has been authorized to indicate, from the Park Service side of the fence, that the stand was raised on the Evergreen side. Funding problems have stalled this plan, but most Park Service guides correct the current markers' information.

According to Harrison's reading of the photos, a flagpole had been erected at what is now the monument site. In the photo taken facing the gateway, the pole is seen to the left of the gate, with bits of Cemetery Hill visible beyond it. Most of the graves lie outside the picture to the left. To the *right* of the gateway—even farther up a slope than the flagpole—is the platform and the tent raised for Everett, with Culp's Hill seen beyond (out to the right of) them. In the picture taken *from* the gateway, these positions are naturally reversed—platform on the left, flagpole almost in the center, grave area to the right.

This site makes sense. The later fences between the cemeteries did not exist. The crowd was bound to treat the two as one general area. The Harrison site had no graves on or around it at the time, nor any between the platform and the flagpole. Once the stand was moved up the slope, a space was created above the graves, looking down on them, in which the crowd could be fitted without impinging on the burial area. In the photo facing the gateway, the crowd ends in a generally straight line just at the flat side of the hemispherical scheme.

The results fit those newspaper accounts that emphasized the height of the position and the view commanded from it. On both counts, the Harrison site is actually better than the monument site, in better accord with the Associated Press report that "the stand . . . was located at the highest point of ground on which [the section of] the battle was fought."

But what is one to make of Whitelaw Reid's claim that the stand was where the monument would be? First, one can put against it an equally definite report in another Cincinnati paper (the *Daily Commercial* of November 23) that the converging lines of the fan-shaped burial area form "the radii of a common center, *where a flag pole is now raised,* but where it is proposed to erect a national monument" [italics added].

It is not hard to see how Reid could take the platform as the future site of a monument. He does not use the precise geometrical language of his journalistic colleague (of radii meeting in their common center at the flagpole) but speaks more generally of the platform's position "in *front* of" the semicircular rows. (Technically, of course, the monument is not in front of the extreme ends of the arcs.) A platform at the Harrison site would have a commanding central position for the whole grave area, above the slope of graves, not disconnected from it by any dip in the land as a natural barrier. There was no reason for an outsider to know the precise boundary between the old cemetery and the new one—a low "open fence" would not be raised till later (the high iron fence seen now was raised in 1934). Besides, Reid saw the scene segmented by lines of troops, by horses led on and off, by crowds shifting all about the area. Most of the crowd came to the scene through or along the gateway to the old cemetery.

Which brings us to the route. Since it could be anticipated that most of the crowd would take, and clog, the more direct approach, a pathway for the procession could more easily be kept open along the indirect way, approaching the platform by going around the fresh graves and coming at the grandstand *away* from the crowd's obvious path of access. This *is* roundabout, but the dignitaries were on horseback. (In fact, a route of less than a mile may have made all the horses seem more a nuisance than an ornament to the occasion.) The parade had more pomp if it wound its way past more of the battle scenery (which lay on the Taneytown Road site).

The Harrison site seems securely established. The author of the best book on Gettysburg's photographs, William A. Frassanito, has been convinced, and says he will alter the next edition of his book to accept Harrison's reading of the pictures. At least one small battle of Gettysburg has, finally, been won.

APPENDIX

III

Four Funeral Orations

Students of Renaissance art realize that artifacts planned for a certain site should be judged in terms of that site. Titian's *Assumption of the Virgin* was done to a scale intended to be visible from the far end of the shadowy Church of the Frari in Venice. Bernini's statue of St. Theresa in ecstasy was designed for a side chapel in Rome where light hit it from secret windows, and where its pious writhing was counterpointed against the calm stares of her carved petitioners. Its frame, in the larger sense, is the whole Church of Saint Mary Victorious.

Lincoln's masterpiece had a setting, too—the event that gave it a context of nineteenth-century oratory, funerary conventions, and the poetry of death. Other works of art are taken into account when a master puts a new altarpiece into the Frari. Lincoln's remarks must be "situated" in their historical moment and generic frame. We linger over Everett much as we walk through the rest of the Frari toward Titian. His speech may no longer be of interest to us on its own merits. But it will live, now, as the foil to that better thing that followed. If

Everett, with his great drawing power, had not created the huge crowd at Gettysburg, Lincoln would have lacked the occasion and the audience for his surprising triumph.

And even Everett's speech has a larger contextual setting. Around the Titian is the Frari; but around the Frari is Venice. So Lincoln plays against the background of Everett; but Everett spoke out of a background of Greek Revival references to Athens, the Kerameikos, and Pericles. The cult of democratic patriotism was felt to be especially meaningful in the nineteenth century, and especially in the vicinity of Everett, America's first truly professional Hellenist. Besides, the Pericles speech, combining (or trying to) Attic democracy and imperialism, has had surprising durability in this country. It was presented as a model of élite patriotism to the students of Eastern prep schools.[1] In World War II, comparison of Lincoln to Pericles seemed to herald an innocent world empire for the young democracy of the West.[2] After the war, the Kennedy family was especially taken with the Hellenism of Edith Hamilton and Huntington Cairns.[3] This made it especially fitting that John Kennedy's most famous speech should echo the rhetorical devices inherited from Greek Funeral Orations, like that of Gorgias.

Ask anyone who heard or read the piece at the time of delivery to recall as much as he can of John F. Kennedy's inaugural address, and he is likely to come up with two outrageous Gorgianisms:

> *Let us never negotiate from fear,*
> *but let us never fear to negotiate.*
>
> *Ask not what your country can do for you,*
> *but what you can do for your country.*[4]

I include the short Gorgias Funeral Oration because Western rhetoric is so marked by the Gorgias tradition, and because Lincoln's love of antithesis is said to resemble that of Gorgias.[5]

A. By Everett

THE ATHENIAN EXAMPLE[7]

1. Standing beneath this serene sky, overlooking these broad fields now reposing from the labors of the waning year, the mighty Alleghenies dimly towering before us, the graves of our brethren beneath our feet, it is with hesitation that I raise my poor voice to break the eloquent silence of God and Nature. But the duty to which you have called me must be performed;—grant me, I pray you, your indulgence and your sympathy.

2. It was appointed by law in Athens, that the obsequies of the citizens who fell in battle should be performed at the public expense, and in the most honorable manner. Their bones were carefully gathered up from the funeral pyre, where their bodies were consumed, and brought home to the city. There, for three days before the interment, they lay in state, beneath tents of honor, to receive the votive offerings of friends and relatives,—flowers, weapons, precious ornaments, painted vases, (wonders of art, which after two thousand years adorn the museums of modern Europe,)—the last tributes of surviving affection. Ten coffins of funeral cypress received the honorable deposit, one for each of the tribes of the city, and an eleventh in memory of the unrecognized, but not therefore unhonored, dead, and of those whose remains could not be recovered.[8] On the fourth day the mournful procession was formed; mothers, wives, sisters, daughters led the way, and to them it was permitted by the simplicity of ancient manners to utter aloud their lamentations for the beloved and the lost; the male relatives and friends of the deceased followed; citizens and strangers closed the train. Thus marshalled, they moved to the place of interment in that famous Ceramicus, the most beautiful suburb of Athens, which had been adorned by Cimon, the son of Miltiades, with walks and

fountains and columns,—whose groves were filled with altars, shrines, and temples,—whose gardens were kept forever green by the streams from the neighboring hills, and shaded with the trees sacred to Minerva and coeval with the foundation of the city,—whose circuit enclosed

> *the olive Grove of Academe,*
> *Plato's retirement, where the Attic bird*
> *Trilled his thick-warbled note the summer long;*[9]

whose pathways gleamed with the monuments of the illustrious dead, the work of the most consummate masters that ever gave life to marble. There, beneath the over-arching plane-trees, upon a lofty stage erected for the purpose, it was ordained that a funeral oration should be pronounced by some citizen of Athens, in the presence of the assembled multitude.

3. Such were the tokens of respect required to be paid at Athens to the memory of those who had fallen in the cause of their country. For those alone who fell at Marathon a special honor was reserved. As the battle fought upon that immortal field was distinguished from all others in Grecian history for its influence over the fortunes of Hellas,—as it depended upon the event of that day whether Greece should live, a glory and a light to all coming time, or should expire like the meteor of a moment; so the honors awarded to its martyr-heroes were such as were bestowed by Athens on no other occasion. They alone of all her sons were entombed upon the spot which they had forever rendered famous.[10] Their names were inscribed upon ten pillars, erected upon the monumental tumulus which covered their ashes, (where after six hundred years, they were read by the traveler Pausanias,) and although the columns beneath the hand of time and barbaric violence, have long since disappeared, the venerable mound still marks the spot where they fought and fell,—

> *That battle-field where Persia's victim horde*
> *First bowed beneath the brunt of Hellas' sword.*

4. And shall I, fellow citizens, who, after an interval of twenty-three centuries, a youthful pilgrim from the world unknown to ancient Greece, have wandered over that illustrious plain, ready to put off the shoes from off my feet, as one that stands on holy ground,—who have gazed with respectful emotion on the mound which still protects the dust of those who rolled back the tide of Persian invasion, and rescued the land of popular liberty, of letters, and of arts, from the ruthless foe,—stand unmoved over the graves of our dear brethren, who so lately, on three of those all-important days which decide a nation's history,—days on whose issue it depended whether this august republican Union, founded by some of the wisest statesmen that ever lived, cemented with the blood of some of the purest patriots that ever died, should perish or endure,—rolled back the tide of an invasion, not less unprovoked, not less ruthless, than that which came to plant the dark banner of Asiatic despotism and slavery on the free soil of Greece?[11] Heaven forbid! And could I prove so insensible to every prompting of patriotic duty and affection, not only would you, fellow citizens, gathered, many of you from distant States, who have come to take part in these pious offices of gratitude—you, respected fathers, brethren, matrons, sisters, who surround me—cry out for shame, but the forms of brave and patriotic men who fill these honored graves would heave with indignation beneath the sod.

5. We have assembled, friends, fellow citizens, at the invitation of the Executive of the great central State of Pennsylvania, seconded by the Governors of seventeen other loyal States of the Union, to pay the last tribute of respect to the brave men, who, in the hard fought battles of the first, second and third days of July last, laid down their lives for the country on these hill sides and the plains before us, and whose remains have been gathered into the Cemetery which we consecrate this day. As my eye ranges over the fields whose sods were so lately moistened by the blood of gallant and loyal men, I feel, as never before, how truly it was said of old, that it is sweet and becoming to die for one's country.[12] I feel as never before, how justly, from the dawn of history to the present time, men have paid the homage of their gratitude and

admiration to the memory of those who nobly sacrificed their lives, that their fellow men may live in safety and in honor. And if this tribute were ever due, when, to whom, could it be more justly paid than to those whose last resting place we this day commend to the blessing of Heaven and of men?

SOUTHERN AGGRESSION

6. For consider, my friends, what would have been the consequences to the country, to yourselves, and to all you hold dear, if those who sleep beneath our feet, and their gallant comrades who survive to serve their country on other fields of danger, had failed in their duty on those memorable days. Consider what, at this moment, would be the condition of the United States, if that noble Army of the Potomac, instead of gallantly and for the second time beating back the tide of invasion from Maryland and Pennsylvania, had been itself driven from these well contested heights, thrown back in confusion on Baltimore, or trampled down, discomfited, scattered to the four winds.[13] What, in that sad event, would have been the fate of the Monumental city, of Harrisburg, of Philadelphia, of Washington, the capital of the Union, each and every one of which would have lain at the mercy of the enemy, accordingly as it might have pleased him, spurred by passion, flushed with victory, and confident of continued success, to direct his course?[14]

7. For this we must bear in mind, it is one of the great lessons of the war, indeed of every war, that it is impossible for a people without military organization, inhabiting the cities, towns, and villages of an open country, including, of course, the natural proportion of noncombatants of either sex, and of every age, to withstand the inroad of a veteran army. What defence can be made by the inhabitants of villages mostly built of wood, of cities unprotected by walls, nay, by a population of men, however high-toned and resolute, whose aged parents demand their care, whose wives and children are clustering about them, against the charge of the war-horse whose neck is clothed with thunder—against flying artillery and batteries of rifled cannon planted on every commanding eminence—against the onset of trained veterans led by skilful chiefs?[15] No, my friends, army must be met by army, battery

by battery, squadron by squadron; and the shock of organized thousands must be encountered by the firm breasts and valiant arms of other thousands, as well organized and as skilfully led. It is no reproach, therefore, to the unarmed population of the country to say, that we owe it to the brave men who sleep in their beds of honor before us, and to their gallant surviving associates, not merely that your fertile fields, my friends of Pennsylvania and Maryland, were redeemed from the presence of the invader, but that your capitals were not given up to threatened plunder, perhaps laid in ashes, Washington seized by the enemy, and a blow struck at the heart of the nation.

8. Who that hears me has forgotten the thrill of joy that ran through the country on the 4th of July—auspicious day for the glorious tidings, and rendered still more so by the simultaneous fall of Vicksburg—when the telegraph flashed through the land the assurance from the President of the United States that the army of the Potomac, under General Meade, had again smitten the invader?[16] Sure I am, that with the ascriptions of praise that rose to Heaven from twenty millions of freemen, with the acknowledgments that breathed from patriotic lips throughout the length and breadth of America, to the surviving officers and men who had rendered the country this inestimable service, there beat in every loyal bosom a throb of tender and sorrowful gratitude to the martyrs who had fallen on the sternly contested field. Let a nation's fervent thanks make some amends for the toils and sufferings of those who survive. Would that the heartfelt tribute could penetrate these honored graves!

9. In order that we may comprehend, to their full extent, our obligations to the martyrs and surviving heroes of the army of the Potomac, let us contemplate for a few moments the train of events, which culminated in the battles of the first days of July. Of this stupendous rebellion, planned as its originators boast, more than thirty years ago, matured and prepared for during an entire generation, finally commenced because, for the first time since the adoption of the Constitution, an election of President had been effected without the votes of the South, (which retained, however, the control of the two other branches of the government,) the occupation of the national capital,

with the seizure of the public archives and of the treaties with foreign powers, was an essential feature.[17] This was, in substance, within my personal knowledge, admitted in the winter of 1860–61, by one of the most influential leaders of the rebellion; and it was fondly thought that this object could be effected by a bold and sudden movement on the 4th of March, 1861. There is abundant proof, also, that a darker project was contemplated, if not by the responsible chiefs of the rebellion, yet by nameless ruffians, willing to play a subsidiary and murderous part in the treasonable drama. It was accordingly maintained by the Rebel emissaries in England, in the circles to which they found access, that the new American Minister ought not, when he arrived, to be received as the envoy of the United States, inasmuch as before that time Washington would be captured, and the capital of the nation and the archives and muniments of the government would be in the possession of the Confederates. In full accordance also with this threat, it was declared, by the Rebel Secretary of War, at Montgomery, in the presence of his Chiefs and of his colleagues, and of five thousand hearers, while the tidings of the assault on Sumter were traveling over the wires on that fatal 12th of April, 1861, that before the end of May 'the flag which then flaunted the breeze,' as he expressed it, 'would float over the dome of the Capitol at Washington.'[18]

10. At the time this threat was made, the rebellion was confined to the cotton-growing States, and it was well understood by them, that the only hope of drawing any of the other slaveholding States into the conspiracy, was in bringing about a conflict of arms, and 'firing the heart of the South' by the effusion of blood. This was declared by the Charleston press, to be the object for which Sumter was to be assaulted; and the emissaries sent from Richmond, to urge on the unhallowed work, gave the promise, that, with the first drop of blood that should be shed, Virginia would place herself by the side of South Carolina.

11. In pursuance of this original plan of the leaders of the rebellion, the capture of Washington has been continually in view, not merely for the sake of its public buildings, as the capital of the Confederacy, but as the necessary preliminary to the absorption of the border

States, and for the moral effect in the eyes of Europe of possessing the metropolis of the Union.

12. I allude to these facts, not perhaps enough borne in mind, as a sufficient refutation of the pretence, on the part of the Rebels, that the war is one of self-defence, waged for the right of self-government. It is in reality, a war originally levied by ambitious men in the cotton-growing States, for the purpose of drawing the slaveholding border States into the vortex of the conspiracy, first by sympathy—which, in the case of South-Eastern Virginia, North Carolina, part of Tennessee and Arkansas, succeeded—and then by force and for the purpose of subjugating Maryland, Western Virginia, Kentucky, Eastern Tennessee and Missouri; and it is a most extraordinary fact, considering the clamors of the Rebel chiefs on the subject of invasion, that not a soldier of the United States has entered the States last named, except to defend their Union-loving inhabitants from the armies and guerillas of the Rebels.

13. In conformity with these designs on the city of Washington, and notwithstanding the disastrous results of the invasion of 1862, it was determined by the Rebel Government last summer to resume the offensive in that direction. Unable to force the passage of the Rappahannock, where General Hooker, notwithstanding the reverse at Chancellorsville, in May, was strongly posted, the Confederate general resorted to strategy. He had two objects in view. The first was by a rapid movement northward, and by manoeuvring with a portion of his army on the east side of the Blue Ridge, to tempt Hooker from his base of operations, thus leading him to uncover the approaches to Washington, to throw it open to a raid by Stuart's cavalry, and to enable Lee himself to cross the Potomac in the Neighborhood of Poolesville and thus fall upon the capital. This plan of operations was wholly frustrated. The design of the Rebel general was promptly discovered by General Hooker, and, moving with great rapidity from Fredericksburg, he preserved unbroken the inner line, and stationed the various corps of his army at all the points protecting the approach to Washington, from Centreville up to Leesburg. From this vantage-ground the Rebel general in vain attempted to draw him. In the mean time, by the vigorous

operations of Pleasanton's cavalry, the cavalry of Stuart, though greatly superior in numbers, was so crippled as to be disabled from performing the part assigned it in the campaign. In this manner, General Lee's first object, namely, the defeat of Hooker's army on the south of the Potomac and a direct march on Washington, was baffled.

14. The second part of the Confederate plan, which is supposed to have been undertaken in opposition to the views of General Lee, was to turn the demonstration northward into a real invasion of Maryland and Pennsylvania, in the hope, that, in this way, General Hooker would be drawn to a distance from the capital, and that some opportunity would occur of taking him at disadvantage, and, after defeating his army, of making a descent upon Baltimore and Washington.[19] This part of General Lee's plan, which was substantially the repetition of that of 1862, was not less signally defeated, with what honor to the arms of the Union the heights on which we are this day assembled will forever attest.

15. Much time had been uselessly consumed by the Rebel general in his unavailing attempts to out-manoeuvre General Hooker. Although General Lee broke up from Fredericksburg on the 3d of June, it was not till the 24th that the main body of his army entered Maryland. Instead of crossing the Potomac, as he had intended, east of the Blue Ridge, he was compelled to do it at Shepherdstown and Williamsport, thus materially deranging his entire plan of campaign north of the river. Stuart, who had been sent with his cavalry to the east of the Blue Ridge, to guard the passes of the mountains, to mask the movements of Lee, and to harass the Union general in crossing the river, having been severely handled by Pleasanton at Beverly Ford, Aldie, and Upperville, instead of being able to retard General Hooker's advance, was driven himself away from his connection with the army of Lee, and cut off for a fortnight from all communication with it—a circumstance to which General Lee, in his report, alludes more than once, with evident displeasure. Let us now rapidly glance at the incidents of the eventful campaign.

16. A detachment from Ewell's corps, under Jenkins, had penetrated, on the 15th of June, as far as Chambersburg. This movement

was intended at first merely as a demonstration, and as a marauding expedition for supplies. It had, however, the salutary effect of alarming the country; and vigorous preparations were made, not only by the General Government, but here in Pennsylvania and in the sister States, to repel the inroad. After two days passed at Chambersburg, Jenkins, anxious for his communications with Ewell, fell back with his plunder to Hagerstown. Here he remained for several days, and then having swept the recesses of the Cumberland valley, came down upon the eastern flank of the South mountain, and pushed his marauding parties as far as Waynesboro. On the 22nd, the remainder of Ewell's corps crossed the river and moved up the valley. They were followed on the 24th by Longstreet and Hill, who crossed at Williamsport and Shepherdstown, and pushing up the valley, encamped at Chambersburg on the 27th. In this way the whole rebel army, estimated at 90,000 infantry, upwards of 10,000 cavalry, and 4,000 or 5,000 artillery, making a total of 105,000 of all arms, was concentrated in Pennsylvania.[20]

17. Up to this time no report of Hooker's movements had been received by General Lee, who, having been deprived of his cavalry, had no means of obtaining information. Rightly judging, however, that no time would be lost by the Union army in pursuit, in order to detain it on the eastern side of the mountains in Maryland and Pennsylvania, and thus preserve his communications by the way of Williamsport, he had, before his own arrival at Chambersburg, directed Ewell to send detachments from his corps to Carlisle and York. The latter detachment, under Early, passed through this place on the 26th of June. You need not, fellow citizens of Gettysburg, that I should recall to you those moments of alarm and distress, precursors as they were of the more trying scenes which were so soon to follow.

NORTHERN RESPONSE

18. As soon as Gen. Hooker perceived that the advance of the Confederates into Cumberland valley was not a mere feint to draw him away from Washington, he moved rapidly in pursuit. Attempts, as we have seen, were made to harass and retard his passage across the Potomac. These attempts were not only altogether unsuccessful, but were so

unskillfully made as to place the entire Federal army between the cavalry of Stuart and the army of Lee. While the latter was massed in the Cumberland valley, Stuart was east of the mountains, with Hooker's army between, and Gregg's cavalry in close pursuit. Stuart was accordingly compelled to force a march northward, which was destitute of strategical character, and which deprived his chief of all means of obtaining intelligence.[21]

19. Not a moment had been lost by General Hooker in the pursuit of Lee. The day after the Rebel army entered Maryland, the Union army crossed the Potomac at Edward's Ferry, and by the 28th of June lay between Harper's Ferry and Frederick. The force of the enemy on that day was partly at Chambersburg, and partly moving on the Cashtown road in the direction of Gettysburg, while the detachments from Ewell's corps, of which mention has been made, had reached the Susquehanna opposite Harrisburg and Columbia. That a great battle must soon be fought, no one could doubt; but in the apparent and perhaps real absence of plan on the part of Lee, it was impossible to foretell the precise scene of the encounter.[22] Wherever fought, consequences the most momentous hung upon the result.

20. In this critical and anxious state of affairs, General Hooker was relieved, and General Meade was summoned to the chief command of the army. It appears to my unmilitary judgment to reflect the highest credit upon him, upon his predecessor, and upon the corps commanders of the army of the Potomac, that a change could take place in the chief command of so large a force on the eve of a general battle—the various corps necessarily moving on lines somewhat divergent, and all in ignorance of the enemy's intended point of concentration—and that not an hour's hesitation should ensue in the advance of any portion of the entire army.

21. Having assumed the chief command on the 28th, General Meade directed his left wing, under Reynolds, upon Emmitsburg, and his right upon New Windsor, leaving General French with 11,000 men to protect the Baltimore and Ohio railroad, and convoy the public property from Harper's Ferry to Washington. Buford's cavalry was then at this place, and Kilpatrick's at Hanover, where he encountered

and defeated the rear of Stuart's cavalry, who was roving the country in search of the main army of Lee. On the Rebel side, Hill had reached Fayetteville on the Cashtown road on the 28th, and was followed on the same road by Longstreet on the 29th. The eastern side of the mountain, as seen from Gettysburg, was lighted up at night by the camp-fires of the enemy's advance, and the country swarmed with his foraging parties. It was now too evident to be questioned, that the thunder-cloud, so long gathering blackness, would soon burst on some part of the devoted vicinity of Gettysburg.[23]

22. The 30th of June was a day of important preparation. At half-past eleven o'clock in the morning, General Buford passed through Gettysburg, upon a reconnaissance in force, with his cavalry, upon the Chambersburg road. The information obtained by him was immediately communicated to General Reynolds, who was, in consequence, directed to occupy Gettysburg. That gallant officer accordingly, with the First Corps, marched from Emmitsburg to within six or seven miles of this place, and encamped on the right bank of Marsh's creek. Our right wing, meantime, was moved to Manchester. On the same day the corps of Hill and Longstreet were pushed still further forward on the Chambersburg road, and distributed in the vicinity of Marsh's creek, while a reconnaissance was made by the Confederate General Pettigrew up to a very short distance from this place.—Thus at nightfall, on the 30th of June, the greater part of the Rebel force was concentrated in the immediate vicinity of two corps of the Union army, the former refreshed by two days passed in comparative repose and deliberate preparation for the encounter, the latter separated by a march of one or two days from their supporting corps, and doubtful at what precise point they were to expect an attack.

FIRST DAY (JULY 1)

23. And now the momentous day, a day to be forever remembered in the annals of the country, arrived.[24] Early in the morning, on the 1st of July, the conflict began. I need not say that it would be impossible for me to comprise, within the limits of the hour, such a narrative as would do anything like full justice to the all-important events of these

three great days, or to the merit of the brave officers and men, of every rank, of every arm of the service, and of every loyal State, who bore their part in the tremendous struggle—alike those who nobly sacrificed their lives for their country, and those who survive, many of them scarred with honorable wounds, the objects of our admiration and gratitude. The astonishingly minute, accurate, and graphic accounts contained in the journals of the day, prepared from personal observation by reporters who witnessed the scenes, and often shared the perils which they describe, and the highly valuable "notes" of Professor Jacobs, of the University in this place, to which I am greatly indebted, will abundantly supply the deficiency of my necessarily too condensed statement.[25]

24. General Reynolds, on arriving at Gettysburg, in the morning of the 1st, found Buford with his cavalry warmly engaged with the enemy, whom he held most gallantly in check. Hastening himself to the front, General Reynolds directed his men to be moved over the fields from the Emmitsburg road, in front of M'Millan's and Dr. Schmucker's, under cover of the Seminary Ridge. Without a moment's hesitation, he attacked the enemy, at the same time sending orders to the Eleventh Corps (General Howard's) to advance as promptly as possible. General Reynolds immediately found himself engaged with a force which greatly outnumbered his own, and had scarcely made his dispositions for the action when he fell, mortally wounded, at the head of his advance. The command of the First Corps devolved on General Doubleday, and that of the field on General Howard, who arrived at 11:30, with Schurz's and Barlow's divisions of the Eleventh Corps, the latter of whom received a severe wound. Thus strengthened, the advantage of the battle was for some time on our side. The attacks of the Rebels were vigorously repulsed by Wadsworth's division of the First Corps, and a large number of prisoners, including General Archer, were captured. At length, however, the continued reinforcement of the Confederates from the main body in the neighborhood, and by the divisions of Rodes and Early, coming down by separate lines from Heidlersberg and taking post on our extreme right, turned the fortunes of the day. Our army, after contesting the ground for five hours, was

obliged to yield to the enemy, whose force outnumbered them two to one; and toward the close of the afternoon General Howard deemed it prudent to withdraw the two corps to the heights where we are now assembled. The great part of the First Corps passed through the outskirts of the town, and reached the hill without serious loss or molestation. The Eleventh Corps and portions of the First, not being aware that the enemy had already entered the town from the north, attempted to force their way through Washington and Baltimore streets, which, in the crowd and confusion of the scene, they did with a heavy loss in prisoners.

25. General Howard was not unprepared for this turn in the fortunes of the day. He had, in the course of the morning, caused Cemetery Hill to be occupied by General Steinwehr, with the second division of the Eleventh Corps. About the time of the withdrawal of our troops to the hill, General Hancock arrived, having been sent by General Meade, on hearing of the death of Reynolds, to assume the command of the field till he himself could reach the front. In conjunction with General Howard, General Hancock immediately proceeded to post troops and to repel an attack on our right flank. This attack was feebly made and promptly repulsed. At nightfall, our troops on the hill, who had so gallantly sustained themselves during the toil and peril of the day, were cheered by the arrival of General Slocum with the Twelfth Corps and of General Sickles with a part of the Third.

26. Such was the fortune of the first day, commencing with decided success to our arms, followed by a check, but ending in the occupation of this all-important position. To you, fellow citizens of Gettysburg, I need not attempt to portray the anxieties of the ensuing night. Witnessing, as you had done with sorrow, the withdrawal of our army through your streets, with a considerable loss of prisoners— mourning as you did over the brave men who had fallen—shocked with the wide-spread desolation around you, of which the wanton burning of the Harman House had given the signal—ignorant of the near approach of General Meade, you passed the weary hours of the night in painful expectation.

SECOND DAY (JULY 2)

27. Long before the dawn of the 2d of July, the new Commander-in-Chief had reached the ever-memorable field of service and glory. Having received intelligence of the events in progress, and informed by the reports of Generals Hancock and Howard of the favorable character of the positions, he determined to give battle to the enemy at this point. He accordingly directed the remaining corps of the army to concentrate at Gettysburg with all possible expedition, and breaking up his head-quarters at Taneytown at ten p.m., he arrived at the front at one o'clock in the morning of the 2d of July. Few were the moments given to sleep, during the rapid watches of that brief midsummer's night, by officers or men, though half of our troops were exhausted by the conflict of the day and the residue wearied by the forced marches which had brought them to the rescue. The full moon, veiled by thin clouds, shone down that night on a strangely unwonted scene. The silence of the grave-yard was broken by the heavy tramp of armed men, by the neigh of the war-horse, the harsh rattle of the wheels of artillery hurrying to their stations, and all the indescribable tumult of preparation. The various corps of the army, as they arrived, were moved to their positions, on the spot where we are assembled and the ridges that extend south-east and south-west; batteries were planted and breastworks thrown up. The Second and Fifth Corps, with the rest of the Third, had reached the ground by seven o'clock, a.m.; but it was not till two o'clock in the afternoon that Sedgwick arrived with the Sixth Corps. He had marched thirty-four miles since nine o'clock on the evening before. It was only on his arrival that the Union army approached in equality of numbers with that of the Rebels, who were posted upon the opposite and parallel ridge, distant from a mile to a mile and a half, overlapping our position on either wing, and probably exceeding by ten thousand the army of General Meade.[26]

28. And here I cannot but remark on the providential inaction of the Rebel army.[27] Had the contest been renewed by it at daylight on the 2d of July, with the First and Eleventh Corps exhausted by the battle

and the retreat, the Third and Twelfth weary from their forced march, and the Second, Fifth and Sixth not yet arrived, nothing but a miracle could have saved the army from a great disaster. Instead of this, the day dawned, the sun rose, the cool hours of the morning passed, the forenoon and a considerable part of the afternoon wore away, without the slightest aggressive movement on the part of the enemy. Thus time was given for half of our forces to arrive and take their places in the lines, while the rest of the army enjoyed a much needed half day's repose.

29. At length, between three and four o'clock in the afternoon, the work of death began. A signal gun from the hostile batteries was followed by a tremendous cannonade along the Rebel lines, and this by a heavy advance of infantry, brigade after brigade, commencing on the enemy's right against the left of our army, and so onward to the left center. A forward movement of General Sickles, to gain a commanding position from which to repel the Rebel attack, drew upon him a destructive fire from the enemy's batteries, and a furious assault from Longstreet's and Hill's advancing troops. After a brave resistance on the part of his corps, he was forced back, himself falling severely wounded.[28] This was the critical moment of the second day, but the Fifth and part of the Sixth Corps, with portions of the First and Second, were promptly brought to the support of the Third. The struggle was fierce and murderous, but by sunset our success was decisive, and the enemy was driven back in confusion. The most important service was rendered towards the close of the day, in the memorable advance between Round Top and Little Round Top, by General Crawford's division of the Fifth Corps, consisting of two brigades of the Pennsylvania Reserves, of which one company was from this town and neighborhood. The Rebel force was driven back with great loss in killed and prisoners. At eight o'clock in the evening a desperate attempt was made by the enemy to storm the position of the Eleventh Corps on Cemetery Hill; but here, too, after a terrible conflict, he was repulsed with immense loss. Ewell, on our extreme right, which had been weakened by the withdrawal of the troops sent over to support our left, had succeeded in gaining a foothold within a portion of our lines, near Span-

gler's spring. This was the only advantage obtained by the rebels to compensate them for the disasters of the day, and of this, as we shall see, they were soon deprived.

30. Such was the result of the second act of this eventful drama,—a day hard fought, and at one moment anxious, but, with the exception of the slight reverse just named, crowned with dearly earned but uniform success to our arms, auspicious of a glorious termination of the final struggle. On these good omens the night fell.

THIRD DAY (JULY 3)

31. In the course of the night, General Geary returned to his position on the right, from which he had hastened the day before to strengthen the Third Corps. He immediately engaged the enemy, and after a sharp and decisive action, drove them out of our lines, recovering the ground which had been lost on the preceding day. A spirited contest was kept up all the morning on this part of the line; but General Geary, reinforced by Wheaton's brigade of the Sixth Corps, maintained his position, and inflicted very severe losses on the Rebels.

32. Such was the cheering commencement of the third day's work, and with it ended all serious attempts of the enemy on our right. As on the preceding day, his efforts were now mainly directed against our left centre and left wing. From eleven till half-past one o'clock, all was still—a solemn pause of preparation, as if both armies were nerving themselves for the supreme effort. At length the awful silence, more terrible than the wildest tumult of battle, was broken by the roar of two hundred and fifty pieces of artillery from the opposite ridges, joining in a cannonade of unsurpassed violence—the Rebel batteries along two thirds of their line pouring their fire upon Cemetery Hill, and the centre and left wing of our army. Having attempted in this way for two hours, but without success, to shake the steadiness of our lines, the enemy rallied his forces for a last grand assault. Their attack was principally directed against the position of our Second Corps. Successive lines of Rebel infantry moved forward with equal spirit and steadiness from their cover on the wooded crest of Seminary Ridge, crossing the intervening plain, and, supported right and left by their choicest

brigades, charged furiously up to our batteries. Our own brave troops of the Second Corps, supported by Doubleday's division and Stannard's brigade of the First, received the shock with firmness; the ground on both sides was long and fiercely contested, and was covered with the killed and the wounded; the tide of battle flowed and ebbed across the plain, till, after 'a determined and gallant struggle,' as it is pronounced by General Lee, the Rebel advance, consisting of two-thirds of Hill's corps and the whole of Longstreet's—including Pickett's division, the élite of his corps, which had not yet been under fire, and was now depended upon to decide the fortune of this last eventful day—was driven back with prodigious slaughter, discomfited and broken. While these events were in progress at our left centre, the enemy was driven, with a considerable loss of prisoners, from a strong position on our extreme left, from which he was annoying our force on Little Round Top. In the terrific assault on our centre, Generals Hancock and Gibbon were wounded. In the Rebel army, Generals Armistead, Kemper, Pettigrew and Trimble were wounded, the first named mortally, the latter also made prisoner, General Garnett was killed, and thirty-five hundred officers and men made prisoners.

33. These were the expiring agonies of the three days' conflict, and with them the battle ceased. It was fought by the Union army with courage and skill, from the first cavalry skirmish on Wednesday morning to the fearful rout of the enemy on Friday afternoon, by every arm and every rank of service, by officers and men, by cavalry, artillery, and infantry. The superiority of numbers was with the enemy, who were led by the ablest commanders in their service; and if the Union force had the advantage of a strong position, the Confederates had that of choosing time and place, the prestige of former victories over the army of the Potomac, and of the success of the first day. Victory does not always fall to the lot of those who deserve it; but that so decisive a triumph, under circumstances like these, was gained by our troops, I would ascribe, under Providence, to the spirit of exalted patriotism that animated them, and the consciousness that they were fighting in a righteous cause.[29]

AFTERMATH

34. All hope of defeating our army, and securing what General Lee calls 'the valuable results' of such an achievement, having vanished, he thought only of rescuing from destruction the remains of his shattered forces. In killed, wounded and missing, he had, as far as can be ascertained, suffered a loss of about 37,000 men—rather more than a third of the army with which he is supposed to have marched into Pennsylvania. Perceiving that his only safety was in rapid retreat, he commenced withdrawing his troops at daybreak on the 4th, throwing up field works in front of our left, which, assuming the appearance of a new position, were intended probably to protect the rear of his army in retreat. That day—sad celebration of the 4th of July for an army of Americans—was passed by him in hurrying off his trains. By nightfall, the main army was in full retreat upon the Cashtown and Fairfield roads, and it moved with such precipitation, that, short as the nights were, by day-light the following morning, notwithstanding a heavy rain, the rear guard had left its position. The struggle of the last two days resembled, in many respects, the battle of Waterloo; and if, in the evening of the third day, General Meade, like the Duke of Wellington, had had the assistance of a powerful auxiliary army to take up the pursuit, the rout of the Rebels would have been as complete as that of Napoleon.

35. Owing to the circumstances just named, the intentions of the enemy were not apparent on the 4th. The moment his retreat was discovered, the following morning, he was pursued by our cavalry on the Cashtown road and through the Emmitsburg and Monterey passes, and by Sedgwick's corps on the Fairfield road. His rear guard was briskly attacked at Fairfield; a great number of wagons and ambulances were captured in the passes of the mountains; the country swarmed with his stragglers, and his wounded were literally emptied from the vehicles containing them into the farm houses on the road. General Lee, in his report, makes repeated mention of the Union prisoners whom he conveyed into Virginia, somewhat overstating their number. He states, also, that 'such of his wounded as were in a condition to be removed'

were forwarded to Williamsport. He does not mention that the number of his wounded *not* removed, and left to the Christian care of the victors, was 7,540, not one of whom failed of any attention which it was possible, under the circumstances of the case, to afford them, not one of whom, certainly, has been put upon Libby prison fare—lingering death by starvation.[30] Heaven forbid, however, that we should claim any merit for the exercise of common humanity.

36. Under the protection of the mountain ridge, whose narrow passes are easily held even by a retreating army, General Lee reached Williamsport in safety, and took up a strong position opposite to that place. General Meade necessarily pursued with the main army by a flank movement through Middletown, Turner's Pass having been secured by General French. Passing through the South mountain, the Union army came up with that of the Rebels on the 12th, and found it securely posted on the heights of Marsh run. The position was reconnoitred, and preparations made for an attack on the 13th. The depth of the river, swollen by the recent rains, authorized the expectation that the enemy would be brought to a general engagement the following day. An advance was accordingly made by General Meade on the morning of the 14th; but it was soon found that the Rebels had escaped in the night, with such haste that Ewell's corps forded the river where the water was breast-high.[31] The cavalry, which had rendered the most important services during the three days, and in harassing the enemy's retreat, was now sent in pursuit, and captured two guns and a large number of prisoners. In an action which took place at Falling Waters, General Pettigrew was mortally wounded. General Meade, in further pursuit of the Rebels, crossed the Potomac at Berlin. Thus again covering the approaches to Washington, he compelled the enemy to pass the Blue Ridge at one of the upper gaps; and in about six weeks from the commencement of the campaign, General Lee found himself on the south side of the Rappahannock, with the probable loss of about a third part of his army.

37. Such, most inadequately recounted, is the history of the ever-memorable three days, and of the events immediately preceding and following. It has been pretended, in order to diminish the magnitude

of this disaster to the Rebel cause, that it was merely the repulse of an attack on a strongly defended position. The tremendous losses on both sides are a sufficient answer to this misrepresentation, and attest the courage and obstinacy with which the three days' battle was waged. Few of the great conflicts of modern times have cost victors and vanquished so great a sacrifice. On the Union side there fell, in the whole campaign, of generals killed, Reynolds, Weed and Zook, and wounded, Barlow, Barnes, Butterfield, Doubleday, Gibbon, Graham, Hancock, Sickles and Warren; while of officers below the rank of General, and men, there were 2,834 killed, 13,709 wounded, and 6,643 missing. On the Confederate side, there were killed on the field or mortally wounded, Generals Armistead, Barksdale, Garnett, Pender, Pettigrew and Semmes, and wounded, Heth, Hood, Johnson, Kemper, Kimball and Trimble. Of officers below the rank of general, and men, there were taken prisoners, including the wounded, 13,621, an amount ascertained officially. Of the wounded in a condition to be removed, of the killed and the missing, the enemy has made no report. They are estimated, from the best data which the nature of the case admits, at 23,000. General Meade also captured 3 cannon, and 41 standards; and 24,978 small arms were collected on the battle-field.

38. I must leave to others, who can do it from personal observation, to describe the mournful spectacle presented by these hill-sides and plains at the close of the terrible conflict. It was a saying of the Duke of Wellington, that next to a defeat, the saddest thing was a victory. The horrors of the battlefield, after the contest is over, the sights and sounds of woe,—let me throw a pall over the scene, which no words can adequately depict to those who have not witnessed it, on which no one who has witnessed it, and who has a heart in his bosom, can bear to dwell. One drop of balm alone, one drop of heavenly, life-giving balm, mingles in this bitter cup of misery. Scarcely has the cannon ceased to roar, when the brethren and sisters of Christian benevolence, ministers of compassion, angels of pity, hasten to the field and the hospital, to moisten the parched tongue, to bind the ghastly wounds, to soothe the parting agonies alike of friend and foe, and to catch the last whispered messages of love from dying lips. 'Carry this

miniature back to my dear wife, but do not take it from my bosom till I am gone.' 'Tell my little sister not to grieve for me; I am willing to die for my country.' 'Oh, that my mother were here!' When, since Aaron stood between the living and the dead, was there ever so gracious a ministry as this? It has been said that it is characteristic of Americans to treat women with a deference not paid to them in any other country. I will not undertake to say whether this is so; but I will say, that, since this terrible war has been waged, the women of the loyal States, if never before, have entitled themselves to our highest admiration and gratitude,—alike those who at home, often with fingers unused to the toil, often bowed beneath their own domestic cares, have performed an amount of daily labor not exceeded by those who work for their daily bread, and those who, in the hospital and the tents of the Sanitary and Christian Commissions, have rendered services which millions could not buy. Happily, the labor and the service are their own reward. Thousands of matrons and thousands of maidens have experienced a delight in these homely toils and services, compared with which the pleasures of the ball room and the opera house are tame and unsatisfactory.[32] This, on earth, is reward enough, but a richer is in store for them. Yes, brothers, sisters of charity, while you bind up the wounds of the poor sufferers—the humblest, perhaps, that have shed their blood for the country,—forget not Who it is that will hereafter say to you, 'Inasmuch as ye have done it unto one of the least of these my brethren, ye have done it unto me.'

CRIME OF REBELLION

39. And now, friends, fellow citizens, as we stand among these honored graves, the momentous question presents itself: Which of the two parties to the war is responsible for all this suffering, for this dreadful sacrifice of life, the lawful and constitutional government of the United States, or the ambitious men who have rebelled against it? I say 'rebelled' against it, although Earl Russell, the British Secretary of State for Foreign Affairs, in his recent temperate and conciliatory speech in Scotland, seems to intimate that no prejudice ought to attach to that word, inasmuch as our English forefathers rebelled against Charles I.

and James II., and our American fathers rebelled against George III. These, certainly, are venerable precedents, but they prove only that it is just and proper to rebel against oppressive governments. They do not prove that it was just and proper for the son of James II. to rebel against George I., or his grandson Charles Edward to rebel against George II.; nor, as it seems to me, ought these dynastic struggles, little better than family quarrels, to be compared with this monstrous conspiracy against the American Union. These precedents do not prove that it was just and proper for the 'disappointed great men' of the cotton-growing States to rebel against 'the most beneficent government of which history gives us any account,' as the Vice President of the Confederacy, in November, 1860, charged them with doing. They do not create a presumption even in favor of the disloyal slaveholders of the South, who, living under a government of which Mr. Jefferson Davis, in the session of 1860–61, said that it 'was the best government ever instituted by man, unexceptionably administered, and under which the people have been prosperous beyond comparison with any other people whose career has been recorded in history,' rebelled against it because their aspiring politicians, himself among the rest, were in danger of losing their monopoly of its offices.—What would have been thought by an impartial posterity of the American rebellion against George III., if the colonists had at all times been more than equally represented in parliament, and James Otis, and Patrick Henry, and Washington, and Franklin, and the Adamses, and Hancock, and Jefferson, and men of their stamp, had for two generations enjoyed the confidence of the sovereign and administered the government of the empire? What would have been thought of the rebellion against Charles I., if Cromwell, and the men of his school, had been the responsible advisers of that prince from his accession to the throne, and then, on account of a partial change in the ministry, had brought his head to the block, and involved the country in a desolating war, for the sake of dismembering it and establishing a new government south of the Trent? What would have been thought of the Whigs of 1688, if they had themselves composed the cabinet of James II., and been the advisers of the measures and the promoters of the policy which

drove him into exile? The Puritans of 1640, and the Whigs of 1688, rebelled against arbitrary power in order to establish constitutional liberty. If they had risen against Charles and James because those monarchs favored equal rights, and in order themselves, 'for the first time in the history of the world,' to establish an oligarchy 'founded on the corner-stone of slavery,' they would truly have furnished a precedent for the Rebels of the South, but their cause would not have been sustained by the eloquence of Pym, or of Somers, nor sealed with the blood of Hampden or Russell.[33]

40. I call the war which the Confederates are waging against the Union a 'rebellion,' because it is one, and in grave matters it is best to call things by their right names. I speak of it as a crime, because the Constitution of the United States so regards it, and puts 'rebellion' on a par with 'invasion.' The Constitution and law not only of England, but of every civilized country, regard them in the same light; or rather they consider the rebel in arms as far worse than the alien enemy. To levy war against the United States is the constitutional definition of treason, and that crime is by every civilized government regarded as the highest which citizen or subject can commit. Not content with the sanctions of human justice, of all the crimes against the law of the land it is singled out for the denunciations of religion. The litanies of every church in Christendom whose ritual embraces that office, as far as I am aware, from the metropolitan cathedrals of Europe to the humblest missionary chapel in the islands of the sea, concur with the Church of England in imploring the Sovereign of the Universe, by the most awful adjurations which the heart of man can conceive or his tongue utter, to deliver us from 'sedition, privy conspiracy and rebellion.' And reason good; for while a rebellion against tyranny—a rebellion designed, after prostrating arbitrary power, to establish free government on the basis of justice and truth—is an enterprise on which good men and angels may look with complacency, an unprovoked rebellion of ambitious men against a beneficent government, for the purpose—the avowed purpose—of establishing, extending and perpetuating any form of injustice and wrong, is an imitation on earth of that first foul revolt of 'the

Infernal Serpent,' against which the Supreme Majesty sent forth the armed myriads of his angels, and clothed the right arm of his Son with the three-bolted thunders of omnipotence.

41. Lord Bacon, in 'the true marshalling of the sovereign degrees of honor,' assigns the first place to 'the *Conditores Imperiorum*, founders of States and Commonwealths;' and, truly, to build up from the discordant elements of our nature, the passions, the interests and the opinions of the individual man, the rivalries of family, clan and tribe, the influences of climate and geographical position, the accidents of peace and war accumulated for ages—to build up from these oftentimes warring elements a well-compacted, prosperous and powerful State, if it were to be accomplished by one effort or in one generation, would require a more than mortal skill.[34] To contribute in some notable degree to this, the greatest work of man, by wise and patriotic counsel in peace and loyal heroism in war, is as high as human merit can well rise, and far more than to any of those to whom Bacon assigns this highest place of honor, whose names can hardly be repeated without a wondering smile—Romulus, Cyrus, Caesar, Ottoman, Ismael—is it due to our Washington, as the founder of the American Union. But if to achieve or help to achieve this greatest work of man's wisdom and virtue gives title to a place among the chief benefactors, rightful heirs of the benedictions, of mankind, by equal reason shall the bold, bad men who seek to undo the noble work, *Eversores Imperiorum*, destroyers of States, who for base and selfish ends rebel against beneficent governments, seek to overturn wise constitutions, to lay powerful republican Unions at the foot of foreign thrones, to bring on civil and foreign war, anarchy at home, dictation abroad, desolation, ruin—by equal reason, I say, yes, a thousandfold stronger shall they inherit the execrations of the ages.

42. But to hide the deformity of the crime under the cloak of that sophistry which strives to make the worse appear the better reason, we are told by the leaders of the Rebellion that in our complex system of government the separate States are 'sovereigns,' and that the central power is only an 'agency' established by these sovereigns to manage certain little affairs—such, forsooth, as Peace, War, Army, Navy, Fi-

nance, Territory, and Relations with the native tribes—which they could not so conveniently administer themselves. It happens, unfortunately for this theory, that the Federal Constitution (which has been adopted by the people of every State of the Union as much as their own State constitutions have been adopted, and is declared to be paramount to them) nowhere recognizes the States as 'sovereigns'—in fact, that, by their names, it does not recognize them at all; while the authority established by that instrument is recognized, in its text, not as an 'agency,' but as 'the Government of the United States.' By that Constitution, moreover, which purports in its preamble to be ordained and established by 'the People of the United States,' it is expressly provided, that 'the members of the State legislatures, and all executive and judicial officers, shall be bound by oath or affirmation to support the Constitution.' Now it is a common thing, under all governments, for an agent to be bound by oath to be faithful to his sovereign; but I never heard before of sovereigns being bound by oath to be faithful to their agency.[35]

43. Certainly I do not deny that the separate States are clothed with sovereign powers for the administration of local affairs. It is one of the most beautiful features of our mixed system of government; but it is equally true, that, in adopting the Federal Constitution, the States abdicated, by express renunciation, all the most important functions of national sovereignty, and, by one comprehensive, self-denying clause, gave up all right to contravene the Constitution of the United States. Specifically, and by enumeration, they renounced all the most important prerogatives of independent States for peace and for war,—the right to keep troops or ships of war in time of peace, or to engage in war unless actually invaded; to enter into compact with another State or a foreign power; to lay any duty on tonnage, or any impost on exports or imports, without the consent of Congress; to enter into any treaty, alliance, or confederation; to grant letters of marque and reprisal, and to emit bills of credit—while all these powers and many others are expressly vested in the General Government. To ascribe to political communities, thus limited in their jurisdiction—who cannot even establish a post office on their own soil—the character of independent

sovereignty, and to reduce a national organization, clothed with all the transcendent powers of government, to the name and condition of an 'agency' of the States, proves nothing but that the logic of secession is on a par with its loyalty and patriotism.

44. Oh, but 'the reserved rights!' and what of the reserved rights? The tenth amendment of the Constitution, supposed to provide for 'reserved rights,' is constantly misquoted. By that amendment, 'the *powers* not delegated to the United States by the Constitution, nor prohibited by it to the States, are reserved to the States respectively, or to the people.' The 'powers' reserved must of course be such as could have been, but were not delegated to the United States,—could have been, but were not prohibited to the States; but to speak of the *right* of an *individual* State to secede, as a *power* that could have been, though it was not delegated to the *United States,* is simple nonsense.

45. But waiving this obvious absurdity, can it need a serious argument to prove that there can be no State right to enter into a new confederation reserved under a constitution which expressly prohibits a State to 'enter into any treaty, alliance, or confederation,' or any 'agreement or compact with another State or a foreign power?' To say that the State may, by enacting the preliminary farce of secession, acquire the right to do the prohibited things—to say, for instance, that though the States, in forming the Constitution, delegated to the United States and prohibited to themselves the power of declaring war, there was by implication reserved to each State the right of seceding and then declaring war; that, though they expressly prohibited to the States and delegated to the United States the entire treaty-making power, they reserved by implication (for an express reservation is not pretended) to the individual States, to Florida, for instance, the right to secede, and then to make a treaty with Spain retroceding that Spanish colony, and thus surrendering to a foreign power the key to the Gulf of Mexico,—to maintain propositions like these, with whatever affected seriousness it is done, appears to me egregious trifling.

46. Pardon me, my friends, for dwelling on these wretched sophistries. But it is these which conducted the armed hosts of rebellion to your doors on the terrible and glorious days of July, and which have

brought upon the whole land the scourge of an aggressive and wicked war—a war which can have no other termination compatible with the permanent safety and welfare of the country but the complete destruction of the military power of the enemy. I have, on other occasions, attempted to show that to yield to his demands and acknowledge his independence, thus resolving the Union at once into two hostile governments, with a certainty of further disintegration, would annihilate the strength and the influence of the country as a member of the family of nations; afford to foreign powers the opportunity and the temptation for humiliating and disastrous interference in our affairs; wrest from the Middle and Western States some of their great natural outlets to the sea and of their most important lines of internal communication; deprive the commerce and navigation of the country of two-thirds of our sea coast and of the fortresses which protect it; not only so, but would enable each individual State—some of them with a white population equal to a good sized Northern county—or rather the dominant party in each State, to cede its territory, its harbors, its fortresses, the mouths of its rivers to any foreign power. It cannot be that the people of the loyal States—that, twenty-two millions of brave and prosperous freemen—will, for the temptation of a brief truce in an eternal border war, consent to this hideous national suicide.

47. Do not think that I exaggerate the consequences of yielding to the demands of the leaders of the rebellion. I understate them. They require of us not only all the sacrifices I have named, not only the cession to them, a foreign and hostile power, of all the territory of the United States at present occupied by the Rebel forces, but the abandonment to them of the vast regions we have rescued from their grasp—of Maryland, of a part of Eastern Virginia and the whole of Western Virginia; the sea coast of North and South Carolina, Georgia, and Florida; Kentucky, Tennessee, and Missouri; Arkansas, and the larger portion of Mississippi, Louisiana, and Texas—in most of which, with the exception of lawless guerillas, there is not a Rebel in arms, in all of which the great majority of the people are loyal to the Union. We must give back, too, the helpless colored population, thousands of whom are perilling their lives in the ranks of our armies, to a bondage rendered

ten-fold more bitter by the momentary enjoyment of freedom. Finally
we must surrender every man in the Southern country, white or black,
who has moved a finger or spoken a word for the restoration of the
Union, to a reign of terror as remorseless as that of Robespierre, which
has been the chief instrument by which the Rebellion has been organized and sustained, and which has already filled the prisons of the
South with noble men, whose only crime is that they are not the worst
of criminals. The South is full of such men. I do not believe there has
been a day since the election of President Lincoln, when, if an ordinance of secession could have been fairly submitted, after a free discussion, to the mass of the people in any single Southern State, a majority
of ballots would have been given in its favor. No, not in South Carolina.
It is not possible that the majority of the people, even of that State, if
permitted, without fear or favor, to give a ballot on the question, would
have abandoned a leader like [James L.] Petigru, and all the memories
of the Gadsdens, the Rutledges, and the Cotesworth Pinckneys of the
revolutionary and constitutional age, to follow the agitators of the
present day.[36]

RECONCILIATION
48. Nor must we be deterred from the vigorous prosecution of the war
by the suggestion, continually thown out by the Rebels and those who
sympathize with them, that, however it might have been at an earlier
stage, there has been engendered by the operations of the war a state
of exasperation and bitterness which, independent of all reference to
the original nature of the matters in controversy, will forever prevent
the restoration of the Union, and the return of harmony between the
two great sections of the country. This opinion I take to be entirely
without foundation.

49. No man can deplore more than I do the miseries of every kind
unavoidably incident to war. Who could stand on this spot and call to
mind the scenes of the first days of July with any other feeling? A sad
foreboding of what would ensue, if war should break out between North
and South, has haunted me through life, and led me, perhaps too long,
to tread in the path of hopeless compromise, in the fond endeavor to

conciliate those who were predetermined not to be conciliated.[37] But it is not true, as is pretended by the Rebels and their sympathizers, that the war has been carried on by the United States without entire regard to those temperaments which are enjoined by the law of nations, by our modern civilization, and by the spirit of Christianity. It would be quite easy to point out, in the recent military history of the leading European powers, acts of violence and cruelty, in the prosecution of their wars, to which no parallel can be found among us. In fact, when we consider the peculiar bitterness with which civil wars are almost invariably waged, we may justly boast of the manner in which the United States have carried on the contest. It is of course impossible to prevent the lawless acts of stragglers and deserters, or the occasional unwarrantable proceedings of subordinates on distant stations; but I do not believe there is, in all history, the record of a civil war of such gigantic dimensions where so little has been done in the spirit of vindictiveness as in this war, by the Government and commanders of the United States; and this notwithstanding the provocation given by the Rebel Government by assuming the responsibility of wretches like Quantrell [sic], refusing to quarter colored troops and scourging and selling into slavery free colored men from the North who fall into their hands, by covering the sea with pirates, refusing a just exchange of prisoners, while they crowd their armies with paroled prisoners not exchanged, and starving prisoners of war to death.[38]

50. In the next place, if there are any present who believe that, in addition to the effect of the military operations of the war, the confiscation acts and emancipation proclamations have embittered the Rebels beyond the possibility of reconciliation, I would request them to reflect that the tone of the Rebel leaders and Rebel press was just as bitter in the first months of the war, nay, before a gun was fired, as it is now. There were speeches made in Congress in the very last session before the outbreak of the Rebellion, so ferocious as to show that their authors were under the influence of a real frenzy. At the present day, if there is any discrimination made by the Confederate press in the affected scorn, hatred and contumely with which every shade of opinion and sentiment in the loyal States is treated, the bitterest contempt is be-

stowed upon those at the North who still speak the language of compromise, and who condemn those measures of the administration which are alleged to have rendered the return of peace hopeless.

51. No, my friends, that gracious Providence which over-rules all things for the best 'from seeming evil still educing good,' has so constituted our natures, that the violent excitement of the passions in one direction is generally followed by a reaction in an opposite direction, and the sooner for the violence. If it were not so—if injuries inflicted and retaliated of necessity led to new retaliations, with forever accumulating compound interest of revenge, then the world, thousands of years ago, would have been turned into an earthly hell, and the nations of the earth would have been resolved into clans of furies and demons, each forever warring with his neighbor. But it is not so; all history teaches a different lesson. The Wars of the Roses in England lasted an entire generation, from the battle of St. Albans in 1455 to that of Bosworth Field in 1485. Speaking of the former, Hume says; 'This was the first blood spilt in that fatal quarrel, which was not finished in less than a course of thirty years; which was signalized by twelve pitched battles; which opened a scene of extraordinary fierceness and cruelty; is computed to have cost the lives of eighty princes of the blood; and almost entirely annihilated the ancient nobility of England. The strong attachments which, at that time, men of the same kindred bore to each other, and the vindictive spirit which was considered a point of honor, rendered the great families implacable in their resentment, and widened every moment the breach between the parties.' Such was the state of things in England under which an entire generation grew up; but when Henry VII., in whom the titles of the two Houses were united, went up to London after the battle of Bosworth Field, to mount the throne, he was everywhere received with joyous acclamations, 'as one ordained and sent from heaven to put an end to the dissensions' which had so long afflicted the country.

52. The great rebellion of England of the seventeenth century, after long and angry premonitions, may be said to have begun with the calling of the Long Parliament in 1640—and to have ended with the return of Charles II., in 1660—twenty years of discord, conflict and

civil war; of confiscation, plunder, havoc; a proud hereditary peerage trampled in the dust; a national church overturned, its clergy beggared, its most eminent prelate put to death; a military despotism established on the ruins of a monarchy which had subsisted seven hundred years, and the legitimate sovereign brought to the block; the great families which adhered to the king proscribed, impoverished, ruined; prisoners of war—a fate worse than starvation in Libby—sold to slavery in the West Indies; in a word, everything that can embitter and madden contending factions.[39] Such was the state of things for twenty years; and yet, by no gentle transition, but suddenly, and 'when the restoration of affairs appeared most hopeless,' the son of the beheaded sovereign was brought back to his father's blood-stained throne, with such 'unexpressible and universal joy' as led the merry monarch to exclaim 'he doubted it had been his own fault he had been absent so long, for he saw nobody who did not protest he had ever wished for his return.' 'In this wonderful manner,' says Clarendon, 'and with this incredible expedition did God put an end to a rebellion that had raged near twenty years, and had been carried on with all the horrid circumstances of murder, devastation and parricide that fire and sword, in the hands of the most wicked men in the world,' (it is a royalist that is speaking,) 'could be instruments of, almost to the desolation of two kingdoms, and the exceeding defacing and deforming of the third. . . . By these remarkable steps did the merciful hand of God, in this short space of time, not only bind up and heal all those wounds, but even made the scar as undiscernable as, in respect of the deepness, was possible, which was a glorious addition to the deliverance.'

53. In Germany, the wars of the Reformation and of Charles V., in the sixteenth century, the Thirty Years' war in the seventeenth century, the Seven Years' war in the eighteenth century, not to speak of other less celebrated contests, entailed upon that country all the miseries of intestine strife for more than three centuries. At the close of the last named war—which was the shortest of all, and waged in the most civilized age—'an officer,' says Archenholz, 'rode through seven villages in Hesse, and found in them but one human being.' More than three hundred principalities, comprehended in the Empire, fermented

with the fierce passions of proud and petty States; at the commencement of this period the castles of robber counts frowned upon every
hilltop; a dreadful secret tribunal, whose seat no one knew, whose
power none could escape, froze the hearts of men with terror throughout the land; religious hatred mingled its bitter poison in the seething
caldron of provincial animosity; but of all these deadly enmities between the States of Germany scarcely the memory remains. There are
controversies in that country, at the present day, but they grow mainly
out of the rivalry of the two leading powers. There is no country in the
world in which the sentiment of national brotherhood is stronger.

54. In Italy, on the breaking up of the Roman Empire, society
might be said to be resolved into its original elements—into hostile
atoms, whose only movement was that of mutual repulsion. Ruthless
barbarians had destroyed the old organizations, and covered the land
with a merciless feudalism. As the new civilization grew up, under the
wing of the church, the noble families and the walled towns fell madly
into conflict with each other; the secular feud of Pope and Emperor
scourged the land; province against province, city against city, street
against street, waged remorseless war with each other from father to
son, till Dante was able to fill his imaginary hell with the real demons
of Italian history. So ferocious had the factions become, that the great
poet-exile himself, the glory of his native city and of his native language, was, by a decree of the municipality, condemned to be burned
alive if found in the city of Florence. But these deadly feuds and hatred
yielded to political influences, as the hostile cities were grouped into
States under stable governments; the lingering traditions of the ancient
animosities gradually died away, and now Tuscan and Lombard, Sar-
dinian and Neapolitan, as if to shame the degenerate sons of America,
are joining in one cry for a united Italy.

55. In France, not to go back to the civil wars of the League, in
the sixteenth century, and of the Fronde, in the seventeenth; not to
speak of the dreadful scenes throughout the kingdom, which followed
the revocation of the edict of Nantes; we have, in the great revolution
which commenced at the close of the last century, seen the blood-
hounds of civil strife let loose as rarely before in the history of the

world. The reign of terror established at Paris stretched its bloody Briarean arms to every city and village in the land, and if the most deadly feuds which ever divided a people had the power to cause permanent alienation and hatred, this surely was the occasion. But far otherwise the fact. In seven years from the fall of Robespierre, the strong arm of the youthful conqueror brought order out of this chaos of crime and woe; Jacobins whose hands were scarcely cleansed from the best blood of France met the returning emigrants, whose estates they had confiscated and whose kindred they had dragged to the guillotine, in the Imperial antechambers; and when, after another turn of the wheel of fortune, Louis XVIII. was restored to his throne, he took the regicide Fouche, who had voted for his brother's death, to his cabinet and confidence.

56. The people of loyal America will never ask you, sir, to take to your confidence or admit again to a share in the government the hard-hearted men whose cruel lust of power has brought this desolating war upon the land, but there is no personal bitterness felt even against them. They may live, if they can bear to live after wantonly causing the death of so many thousands of their fellow-men; they may live in safe obscurity beneath the shelter of the government they have sought to overthrow, or they may fly to the protection of the governments of Europe—some of them are already there, seeking, happily in vain, to obtain the aid of foreign powers in furtherance of their own treason. There let them stay. The humblest dead soldier, that lies cold and stiff in his grave before us, is an object of envy beneath the clods that cover him, in comparison with the living man, I care not with what trumpery credentials he may be furnished, who is willing to grovel at the foot of a foreign throne for assistance in compassing the ruin of his country.

57. But the hour is coming and now is, when the power of the leaders of the Rebellion to delude and inflame must cease.[40] There is no bitterness on the part of the masses. The people of the South are not going to wage an eternal war, for the wretched pretext by which this Rebellion is sought to be justified. The bonds that unite us as one people—a substantial community of origin, language, belief, and law, (the four great ties that hold the societies of men together;) common

national and political interests; a common history; a common pride in a glorious ancestry; a common interest in this great heritage of blessings; the very geographical features of the country; the mighty rivers that cross the lines of climate and thus facilitate the interchange of natural and industrial products, while the wonder-working arm of the engineer has leveled the mountain-walls which separate the East and West, compelling your own Alleghenies, my Maryland and Pennsylvania friends, to open wide their everlasting doors to the chariot-wheels of traffic and travel; these bonds of union are of perennial force and energy, while the causes of alienation are imaginary, factitious and transient.[41] The heart of the people, North and South, is for the Union. Indications, too plain to be mistaken, announce the fact, both in the East and the West of the States in rebellion. In North Carolina and Arkansas the fatal charm at length is broken. At Raleigh and Little Rock the lips of honest and brave men are unsealed, and an independent press is unlimbering its artillery. When its rifled cannon shall begin to roar, the hosts of treasonable sophistry—the mad delusions of the day—will fly like the Rebel army through the passes of yonder mountain. The weary masses of the people are yearning to see the dear old flag again floating upon their capitols, and they sigh for the return of the peace, prosperity, and happiness, which they enjoyed under a government whose power was felt only in its blessings.[42]

58. And now, friends, fellow citizens of Gettysburg and Pennsylvania, and you from remoter States, let me again, as we part, invoke your benediction on these honored graves. You feel, though the occasion is mournful, that it is good to be here.[43] You feel that it was greatly auspicious for the cause of the country, that the men of the East and men of the West, the men of nineteen sister States, stood side by side, on the perilous ridges of the battle. You now feel it a new bond of union, that they shall lie side by side, till the clarion, louder than that which marshalled them to the combat, shall awake their slumbers. God bless the Union; it is dearer to us for the blood of brave men which has been shed in its defence. The spots on which they stood and fell; these pleasant heights; the fertile plain beneath them; the thriving village whose streets so lately rang with the strange din of war; the fields

beyond the ridge, where the noble Reynolds held the advancing foe at bay, and, while he gave up his own life, assured by his forethought and self-sacrifice the triumph of the two succeeding days; the little streams which wind through the hills, on whose banks in aftertimes the wondering ploughman will turn up, with the rude weapons of savage warfare, the fearful missiles of modern artillery; Seminary Ridge, the Peach Orchard, Cemetery, Culp, and Wolf Hill, Round Top, Little Round Top, humble names, henceforward dear and famous—no lapse of time, no distance of space, shall cause you to be forgotten.[44] 'The whole earth,' said Pericles, as he stood over the remains of his fellow citizens, who had fallen in the first year of the Peloponnesian war, 'the whole earth is the sepulchre of illustrious men.'[45] All time, he might have added, is the millennium of their glory. Surely I would do no injustice to the other noble achievements of the war, which have reflected such honor on both arms of the service, and have entitled the armies and the navy of the United States, their officers and men, to the warmest thanks and the richest rewards which a grateful people can pay. But they, I am sure, will join us in saying, as we bid farewell to the dust of these martyr-heroes, that wheresoever throughout the civilized world the accounts of this great warfare are read, and down to the latest period of recorded time, in the glorious annals of our common country, there will be no brighter page than that which relates The Battles of Gettysburg.[46]

B. By Pericles[47]

Many are those who have praised, here, the man 35
who added a speech to this rite, as if it were a fine
thing to orate over men buried from our wars. But
here is one who holds that, for men made heroes by
their actions, enacted honors are sufficient, public
honors like those you have just witnessed, rather than
to risk on one man's eloquence, or lack of it, the
logos/ergon   credibility of so many men's bravery. It is, in fact,
hard to fit words exactly to events whose verisimilitude is in question, since the informed and well-disposed man may want more than the speaker makes
him feel, or know more than he brings to mind, while
the uninformed man resents as overstatement any
praise that goes beyond what he feels capable of.
(Praise of others can only be borne so long as it describes what any hearer feels he might do himself,
while resentment leads to disbelief of anything beyond
that.) Yet, since our elders have decreed this as appropriate, I, in observance of the form, must try to strike
what balance I can with your information and your
disposition.[48]

EPAINESIS
progonoi   I make the ancestors my opening theme, since it 36
dikaion   is right, it is appropriate here, to pay them memory's
autochthones   tribute.[49] They, who dwelt nowhere but here, passed
this land down to us, generation by generation, kept

249

free by their valor. Yet, worthy as they were, the immediately preceding generation [of Marathon] was even more so: entrusted with this realm, by no little labors of their own they extended it to its current borders.[50] But the greatest contributions we ourselves have made, we the living, most of us not yet beyond our prime, who strengthened the realm by making it need no other for purposes of war or peace.[51] The wars waged to bring this about, those of our fathers or ourselves, our spirited repulse of Persian or of Greek invaders, I have no need to recall at length—you know them well. But what lay behind those outward deeds, what really made us great—our training, our frame of government, our natural bent—I shall expound, primarily in praise of these men, but also as a fitting thing to be said on this occasion and proper for this audience to hear, the outsiders in it as well as the citizens.[52]

politeia   Our political arrangement cannot be measured in   37
contest with any other city's since we set the pattern for, rather than imitate, them. By title we are a democracy, since the many, not just the few, participate in governing, and citizens are equal in their legal dealings with each other—though the merit of the individual, not just one's turn by lot, is taken into account when skill for public service is required, lest poverty or obscure background bar the person who has anything to contribute to the city.[53] Political life we all join in freely, while private life is not narrowly scrutinized for conformity of individual taste, nor are censorious glances indulged that cause social friction though they lack legal force. Yet this tolerant approach to private life does not lead to laxity in the observance of public duty—whoever is charged with public office is obeyed, along with the laws themselves, especially those that protect the wronged or

express agreed-on social values (which need no spe-
cific legislation).

In the frequent intervals of our duties, we in-   38
dulge a preference for contests and seasonal festivals,
distributed throughout the year and supplemented by
tasteful private entertainments, whose enjoyment
breaks up monotony. We can afford such pleasures
because imports come in, through our empire, from
everywhere on earth, making others' property belong
to us as much as does our own.[54]

Yet we do not share the anxiety for our posses-   39
sions shown by our enemies—we keep our city open,
not expelling foreigners to prevent their seeing or
hearing things whose exposure could be useful to an
enemy. We rely not so much on secret plans or feints
as on the spirit of the moment. As for military train-
paideia   ing, where others insist on early drill of the harshest
sort to instill manhood, we prove equal to any threat
despite our unstructured regimen. Consider the evidence: Spartans do not come alone but with allies to
invade our land, while we unaccompanied make raids
on other lands, and easily (in most cases) prevail,
though in combat with people desperate for their
homes.[55] No enemy, besides, has ever met our total
force, since our navy is out on patrol and our land
troops are scattered on their several missions. Yet
after each engagement with a part of our forces, the
enemy boasts that he either beat or was beaten by our
entire power. If we recruit ourselves with rest instead
of strenuous drill, relying less on system than on our
natural gift for valor, the result is that we are not
fatigued by facing hardships before they arrive; yet we
are no less hardy than those who drill exhaustively—
points that, along with others, should dumbfound ob-
servers of our city.[56]

We seek an economical refinement, train our   40
minds without softening our bodies.[57] If wealth comes
our way, we turn it to productive deeds, not ostenta-
tious words; if poverty comes, that is no shame to
admit, the shame is in submitting to it. Some citizens
are concerned equally with public and with private
matters, and even those engaged in business keep
informed about politics—we alone count the unpoliti-
cal man not "leisured" but useless. When not making
policy ourselves, we are shrewd judges of it, since we
do not consider discussion an enemy of dispatch; our
fear is to adopt policy without prior debate. In sharp
contrast with others, we are ready to take risks *and* to
calculate the risk. Others are brave in the dark; thinking would just slow them. But the truly brave are
those who face danger undeterred by full recognition
of life's terrors *and* its delights.

Our moral code is also different—we win allies by
favors done and not received. The doer of favors is
more consistent, since he tries to retain the gratitude
he has earned, while the receiver is more grudging,
feeling he repays a debt rather than does a worthy
thing. We alone act not from narrow calculation of our
interest but with the largesse born of security in ourselves.[58]

In short, our city is itself a schooling for Hellas—   41
none of its citizens depends, in my view, on others to
meet every contingency with an easy poise.[59] These
are not just words to ornament this occasion but facts
proved by the measure of the city's power—how else
did she become great but by this genius in her citizens?[60] Only she, put to the test, exceeds repute. Only
to her can foes succumb without cause for shame, or
friends submit without humiliation, considering the
quality of her leadership.[61] By the magnitude of the

evidence, she gives proof of her power to dumbfound the world, now and hereafter, so that no Homer will be needed to praise her in seducing words, which only distract, where hard assessment is needed to do justice to the facts. Every place on land and sea has been compelled to give entry to our enterprise, and we have left behind lasting tokens of our power to help or to harm.[62]

arete   Such was the city these men fought for, rather   42 than lose to others; and shall we, their survivors, not take up the labor? I have prolonged my description of the city to establish that we do not have the same stake in this struggle as those with less to lose, and to make the praises I speak as clear as the evidence will sustain. Most of my task is accomplished. I have sung a hymn to the city, but the valor of these men and their peers gave the city her beauty. No other Hellenes supply, as these do, deeds weighty enough to equal any praises. The death of these, in my judgment, revealed the courage of some at their first encounter, or confirmed the others' established record, so that no prior fault can detract from this offer of their lives for their country, all private harm is canceled by this public benefaction. The rich soldier did not flinch at the thought of losing his possessions, nor did the poor man put off the day of reckoning until he could taste wealth. Our men, yearning to make the enemy pay the price they set, and calculating their own most glorious risk, dismissed other matters to make this exaction; left vague prospects to the future, investing themselves entirely in the project at hand. Seeing the choice was between suffering by defending, on the one hand, or surviving by surrendering, on the other, they escaped what could be said against them by taking the impact of what was done against them on their bodies.[63] So, with the outcome still undecided, at the apex of their glory contending with their fear, they left us.[64]

PARAINESIS

protreptikon

They were such as the city deserves. You, their survivors, may pray for a safer outcome but not adopt a less venturesome attitude. You cannot, after all, prevail with whatever words a speaker may spin out, saying what you already know about the *desirability* of overcoming foes. Your safety is in deeds, in daily devotion to the city's power, in being smitten with that power and seeing how it grew, how brave men, recognizing what was requisite and ashamed not to supply it by their acts (even when some project failed), did not withhold their further sacrifice but made a dearer pledge of it.[65] In a joint offering of their bodies they won their several rewards of ageless praise, and no grave can more attract the eye of mankind—not merely this, in which they lie, but where their glory is laid up imperishable, recallable at any need for remembrance or example. Famous men have all the earth for grave—their epitaph is not inscribed in their land only; it is an unwritten memorial, even in strange lands, not only to their acts but to how they conceived those acts.

Strive, then, with these, convinced that happiness lies in freedom, freedom in bold spirits. Shun not danger from a foe: the unsuccessful man is not the one who should be reckless with his life, *his* lot might improve, but those whose lot could change disastrously by some future reversal—and then how bitter would the disgrace of cowardice seem, looking back on it, when one might have died too strong in the common cause to feel the blow.[66]

43

254

paramythētikon   For such reasons I would console but not pity   44
these men's parents. Raised in a world of varying
chances, they know that this, at least, is gain—to meet
an honorable end (as they now have) and to grieve
honorably (as do you) for those whose lives were cut
off at the fortunate moment. I know this is hard to
convince you of, since you will have memories of past
joy, seeing others happy as you once were. Sorrow is
not for the lack of things one never had, but for the
accustomed thing removed. Yet take strength, you
who can have other children, in anticipation of them.
For you privately, they will lessen the pain over those
lost, and for the city they will provide a double service, swelling both the citizenry and its fighting force.
No one can make sound or fair proposals in our politics who has no children at stake in the outcome. For
those beyond childbearing age, think it gain to have
lived through what joys you had, and, seeing what
little time is left to grieve, bear yourselves up on their
glory. Pride alone perdures, and the one joy in feeble
age is not (as some claim) money, but respect from
others.

You children and brethren of the fallen have a   45
great competition before you—for all speak well of the
dead, and barely will you be granted a similarity to
them, not to mention an equality, no matter how great
your own achievement. The living meet all the resist-
ances of envy, but those who are gone win ungrudging
respect.

I shall mention women's role if I must, out of
consideration to these men's widows, and by way of
sketchy exhortation.[67] Your glory is not to fall below
the level of a woman's nature, and not to be talked of
among men, for good or ill.

I have spoken the best words I could for this   46
occasion, as the law required; and you have done what
was proper for the buried. Henceforth the city will
raise at public expense these men's orphans till they
come of age, as a useful wreath to victors in such
contest. Where valor is rewarded, men serve the city
best. Now, your lamentation done, depart.

C. By Gorgias[68]

EPAINESIS

What did these heroes lack
that becomes a hero?
Or what quality did they display
unbecoming to a hero?

logos/ergon   O for the power to speak
what I desire to say,
and to desire what is fitting,
neither offending the gods
nor inciting human envy.

arete   These men showed godlike valor,
but died the death of men,

paideia   preferring gentle equity
to righteous austerity,
freedom of speech
to niceties of law,

politeia   holding the broadest law,
divine law, to be this:

to speak or not to speak,
to do or leave undone,
the necessary things
at the necessary time,

to show the indispensable virtues,
prudence and firmness,
one for choosing a course,
the other for pursuing it,

supporting those unjustly oppressed,
opposing the unjustly prosperous,
fierce for the required,
flexible on the desired,

by the exercise of reason
checking mindless impulse,
pitting force against the violent,
cooperating with the reasonable,
fearless to those who show no fear,
and terrible in time of terror.

As evidence of these qualities
they have captured these enemy spoils,
set here to honor Zeus
and serve as their memorial.

They were no strangers to natural courage,
nor to licit passions,
to conflict in arms
or to honorable peace—

pious in their practise to the gods,
respectful in the care of their parents,
treating citizens as equals
showing favor to their intimates.

PARAINESIS

paramythētikon   We have a deathless yearning
for these dead,
a yearning immortal
in our mortal bodies
for these mortals.

D. Gettysburg Address
1. Spoken Text (?)*⁹

Fourscore and seven years ago our fathers brought forth upon this continent a new nation, conceived in Liberty, and dedicated to the proposition that all men are created equal. *[Applause]*

Now we are engaged in a great civil war, testing whether that nation, or any nation so conceived and so dedicated, can long endure. We are met on a great battle-field of that war. We are met to dedicate a portion of it as the final-resting place of those who here gave their lives that that nation might live. It is altogether fitting and proper that we should do this.

But in a larger sense we cannot dedicate, we cannot consecrate, we cannot hallow this ground. The brave men, living and dead, who struggled here, have consecrated it far above our power to add or detract. *[Applause]* The world will little note nor long remember what we say here, but it can never forget what they did here. *[Applause]* It is for us, the living, rather to be dedicated here to the unfinished work that they have thus far so nobly carried on. *[Applause]* It is rather for us to be here dedicated to the great task remaining before us,—that from these honored dead we take increased devotion to the cause for which they here gave the last full measure of devotion,—that we here highly resolve that the dead shall not have died in vain *[Applause]*, that the nation shall, under God, have a new birth of freedom, and that the government of the people, by the people, and for the people, shall not perish from the earth. *[Long continued applause]*

2. *Final Text*[70]

Address delivered at the dedication of the cemetery at Gettysburg.

Four score and seven years ago our fathers brought forth on this continent, a new nation, conceived in Liberty, and dedicated to the proposition that all men are created equal.

Now we are engaged in a great civil war, testing whether that nation, or any nation so conceived and so dedicated, can long endure. We are met on a great battle-field of that war. We have come to dedicate a portion of that field, as a final resting place for those who here gave their lives that that nation might live. It is altogether fitting and proper that we should do this.

But, in a larger sense, we can not dedicate—we can not consecrate—we can not hallow—this ground. The brave men, living and dead, who struggled here, have consecrated it, far above our poor power to add or detract. The world will little note, nor long remember what we say here, but it can never forget what they did here. It is for us the living, rather, to be dedicated here to the unfinished work which they who fought here have thus far so nobly advanced. It is rather for us to be here dedicated to the great task remaining before us—that from these honored dead we take increased devotion to that cause for which they gave the last full measure of devotion—that we here highly resolve that these dead shall not have died in vain—that this nation, under God, shall have a new birth of freedom—and that government of the people, by the people, for the people, shall not perish from the earth.

November 19, 1863.   ABRAHAM LINCOLN.

Acknowledgments

My first debt is to the custodians of the archives I visited while working on this book—at the Massachusetts Historical Society, the Pennsylvania State Archives, the National Park Services Library at Gettysburg, the Adams County Historical Society, the Gettysburg College Archives, the Library of Congress Manuscripts Division and Rare Books Division, the Chicago Historical Society, the Illinois State Historical Society, and the Oak Ridge Cemetery Records Office.

For help with the classical background of Everett's speeches, I turned to a former teacher and a former classmate—Bernard M. W. Knox and John P. Peradatto—who responded with their customary generosity and learning.

For nineteenth-century American history, I called on the expertise of George Fredrickson, James Oakes, John Patterson, Thomas F. Schwartz, and Douglas L. Wilson, who read the whole book in draft form and improved it with their comments.

In sorting out the various texts of the Address, I was helped by the advice of James Gilreath and John R. Sellers at the Library of Congress, and of Peter Drummey and Virginia H. Smith at the Massachusetts Historical Society. Mr. Sellers also kindly showed me Lloyd Dunlap's notes and outlines for the book he intended to write about the Address.

For the site of the Address, Park Service historian Kathleen Georg Harrison was a learned guide to all the possible delivery points.

My agent, Anne Sibbald, championed the book, and my editor, Alice Mayhew, gave detailed suggestions for its organization. Katie

265

Melody, who puts in heroic hours at her word processor, typed and retyped. John C. Wills pointed me to sources and books I would not have sought or found without his guidance. With so much help, I surely deserve blame for remaining flaws in the book.

Notes

Prologue

1. Alan T. Nolan, *Lee Considered: General Robert E. Lee and Civil War History* (University of North Carolina Press, 1991), pp. 90–110, 102, 104, 169–70.

2. Edwin B. Coddington, *The Gettysburg Campaign: A Study in Command* (Charles Scribner's Sons, 1984), p. 536.

3. *The War of the Rebellion: A Compilation of the Official Records of the Union and Confederate Armies* (Government Printing Office, 1880–1901), ser. 1, vol. 27, p. 79.

4. Reburial teams found 3,512 Union dead in 1863 and 1864. Southerners turned up 3,320 Confederate dead for transshipment in the early 1880s. It is estimated that 1,500 Confederate bodies escaped the partial later searches. Cf. Gregory A. Coco, *Wasted Valor: The Confederate Dead at Gettysburg* (Thomas Publications, 1990), pp. 41–42. The South left 6,802 wounded at Gettysburg (Coddington, *Gettysburg Campaign*, p. 537). Samuel Weaver, the man in charge of identifying the Union dead, estimated the Southern bodies left in the ground at 7,000.

5. Gregory A. Coco, *A Vast Sea of Misery: A History and Guide to the Union and Confederate Field Hospitals at Gettysburg, July 1–November 20, 1863* (Thomas Publications, 1988), p. 190. Clifton Johnson, *Battlefield Adventures* (Houghton Mifflin, 1915), pp. 195–96.

6. Coco, *Wasted Valor*, pp. 33, 35.

7. David Wills to Governor Curtin, July 24, 1863, Pennsylvania State Archives.

8. Biographical information from the David Wills file in the Adams County Historical Society, especially the obituaries from the *Star and Sentinel* and *Gettysburg Compiler*. Kathleen Georg Harrison, Park Service Historian at Gettysburg, thinks Wills was unjust to the alleged speculator he opposed, David McConaughy. She may be right, though Governor Curtin, with good sources on the two local Republicans, decided for Wills. At any rate, Harrison's important essay, on file in Gettysburg, should be published: "This Grand National Enterprise" (1982).

9. The 1865 *Report of The Select Committee Relative to the Soldiers' National Cemetery* has been reprinted by Thomas Publications in 1988.

10. Wills correspondence with the poets is in the Library of Congress manuscript room.

11. Frank L. Klement, "Ward H. Lamon and the Dedication of the Soldiers' Cemetery at Gettysburg," *Civil War History* 31 (1985), p. 295.

12. Diary of Alexander Ramsey, Minnesota Historical Society.

13. Herndon said Lincoln was "reflective, not spontaneous" (Hertz, p. 95— cf. Herndon-Weik, p. 477). He worked on his House Divided Speech for a year (Don E. Fehrenbacher, *Prelude to Greatness: Lincoln in the 1850s* [Stanford University Press, 1962], pp. 88–94; John S. Nicolay and John Hay, *Abraham Lincoln: A History* [The Century Co., 1890], vol. 2, p. 136). For his First Inaugural he studied Webster's and Clay's speeches and solicited Seward's help (Herndon-Weik, pp. 386–87). For preparation of the Cooper Institute and Second Inaugural speeches, see Benjamin Barondess, *Three Lincoln Masterpieces* (Education Foundation of West Virginia, 1954), pp. 7–8, 62–64; Herndon-Weik, p. 368.

14. Klement, "Ward H. Lamon," pp. 297–98. Cf. Klement, "Lincoln, the Gettysburg Address, and Two Myths" on Lamon's untrustworthy witness, *Blue & Gray* 2 (1984), p. 89.

15. Everett diary in the Massachusetts Historical Society, under date of Nov. 14: "Sent the manuscript of the Address to the office of the Daily Advertiser, in which it fills 6¼ columns and received back proof-sheets of the whole by 5 o'clock in the afternoon." It used to be thought that Everett's speech was in the envelope on the table in Alexander Gardner's photograph of Lincoln. Cf. Charles Hamilton and Lloyd Ostendorf, *Lincoln in Photographs: An Album of Every Known Pose* (University of Oklahoma Press, 1963), pp. 146–49.

16. Saunders's account of this and other notable events in his life was written into an 1898 journal book. A photocopy is in the Library of Congress manuscript room. Saunders had studied his art in Scotland and England (at Kew Garden). In this country, he consulted horticulturists at Yale and was an adviser to important people (like General Grant) who were planning farms or gardens. He created the federal exhibits at the Centennial Exposition in Philadelphia and the Cotton Centennial in New Orleans. Cf. *Yearbook of United States Department of Agriculture*, 1900.

17. The description of events in the Wills house is taken from the copy of a later Wills statement kept in the Library of Congress manuscript room.

18. Everett diary, Nov. 18.

19. The only parallel in the two men's speeches is so slight that Lincoln no doubt overlooked it. The President calls Gettysburg a battle testing whether a nation dedicated to equality "can long endure," so as not to "perish from the earth." Everett spoke of the battle's three "days on whose issue it depended whether this august republican Union . . . should perish or endure" (appendix III A, paragraph 4). Everett also used the phrase "under Providence" (paragraph 33), like Lincoln's "under God."

20. On the site of the platform, see appendix II.

21. Coco, *Wasted Valor*, p. 36. Everett diary, Nov. 17. The anti-Southern sections of Everett's speech came under partisan attack, according to Everett's letter to David Wills on Nov. 28: "There has been some cavil in the semi-disloyal

papers about my choice of topics & manner of treating them, and I have seen nothing of any weight against either" (Massachusetts Historical Society). For the small table Everett placed his manuscript on in speaking, see letter to Wills, Nov. 9, 1863, in Library of Congress manuscript room.

22. Herndon-Weik, p. 386. For Everett's part in recasting the famous conclusion of Webster's speech, see George Ticknor Curtis, *Life of Daniel Webster* (D. Appleton and Company, 1870), pp. 363–64.

23. On Lincoln's *reading* from his delivery text, see appendix I.

24. *Abraham Lincoln: A Press Portrait*, edited by Herbert Mitgang (University of Georgia Press, 1956), p. 355.

25. There is a thorough collection of the evidence about Lincoln's voice in Waldo W. Braden, *Abraham Lincoln: Public Speaker* (Louisiana State University Press, 1988), ch. 8, " 'Penetrating and Far-Reaching': Lincoln's Voice," pp. 96–103.

26. For Lincoln's Shakespearean readings to Hay, to the painter F. B. Carpenter, to parties on the presidential yacht, see Roy P. Basler, *A Touchstone for Greatness: Essays, Addresses, and Occasional Pieces* (Greenwood Press, 1973), pp. 206–77.

27. Klement, *Blue & Gray*, p. 9.

28. "The President at Gettysburg," Chicago *Times*, Nov. 23, 1863 (*Abraham Lincoln: A Press Portrait*, p. 361).

29. Willmoore Kendall, *The Conservative Affirmation* (Henry Regnery, 1963), p. 252: "The caesarism we all need to fear is the contemporary Liberal movement, dedicated like Lincoln to egalitarian reforms sanctioned by mandate emanating from national majorities—a movement which is Lincoln's legitimate offspring." M. E. Bradford, *Remembering Who We Are: Observations of a Southern Conservative* (University of Georgia, 1985), p. 145: "Lincoln, in insisting that the Negro was included in the Declaration of Independence and that the Declaration of Independence bound his countrymen to fulfill a pledge hidden in that document, seemed clearly to point toward a radical transformation of society."

30. Russell Kirk, for instance, prudently does not attack Lincoln but praises, instead, the maxims of his opponent, Calhoun, including the following: "These great and dangerous errors have their origin in the prevalent opinion that all men are born free and equal—than which nothing can be more unfounded and false" (*The Conservative Mind: From Burke to Santayana* [Henry Regnery, 1953], p. 156).

31. James Hurt, "All the Living and the Dead: Lincoln's Imagery," *American Literature* 52 (1980), p. 379.

32. *Willmoore Kendall Contra Mundum*, edited by Nellie D. Kendall (Arlington House, 1971), p. 69.

33. The word count varies by a word or more according to the text one adopts. The text used in this book is the so-called Bliss Copy (appendix III D 2), though the Little, Brown text may be closer to what Lincoln said. For a discussion of the issues, see appendix I.

1. Oratory of the Greek Revival

1. James Hurt, "All the Living and the Dead: Lincoln's Imagery," *American Literature* 52 (1980), p. 377.

2. Ralph Waldo Emerson, "Life and Letters in New England," *Complete Works* (Houghton Mifflin, 1904), vol. 10, p. 331.

3. The standard work on the republican tradition of Rome in the modern world is J. G. A. Pocock's *The Machiavellian Moment: Florentine Political Thought and the Atlantic Republican Tradition* (Princeton University Press, 1975).

4. For Roman symbolism in eighteenth-century America, see Garry Wills, *Cincinnatus: George Washington and the Enlightenment* (Doubleday, 1984).

5. For the importance to romanticism of the shift from Rome to Greece, see Richard Jenkyns, *Victorians and Ancient Greece* (Harvard University Press, 1980); Stephen A. Larrabee, *English Bards and Grecian Marbles* (Kennikat Press, 1943).

6. For the importance of Greece to Hölderlin and his successors, see S. M. Butler, *The Tyranny of Greece over Germany* (Beacon Press, 1935).

7. William H. Pierson, *American Buildings and Their Architects: The Colonial and Neoclassical Styles* (Doubleday, 1976), p. 452.

8. Stephen A. Larrabee, *Hellas Observed: The American Experience of Greece, 1775–1865* (New York University Press, 1957), pp. 28–48. Orie William Long, *Literary Pioneers: Early American Explorers of European Culture* (Harvard University Press, 1935), pp. 27–28, 65, 68–70.

9. At one point Everett considered studying law, and asked Justice Joseph Story, on Harvard's Board of Overseers, to help him escape his commitments to the Greek chair. Cf. Paul Revere Frothingham, *Edward Everett, Orator and Statesman* (Houghton Mifflin, 1925), pp. 71–75.

10. For Lafayette's visit as a culture-shaping event, see Anne C. Loveland, *Emblem of Liberty: The Image of Lafayette in the American Mind* (Louisiana State University Press, 1971); Fred Somkin, *Unquiet Eagle: Memory and Desire in the Idea of American Freedom, 1815–1860* (Cornell University Press, 1967), pp. 131–74. The rallies for Greek independence are treated by Loveland on pp. 113–17.

11. Emerson, "Life and Letters," p. 330.

12. Cf. Frank M. Turner, *The Greek Heritage in Victorian Britain* (Yale University Press, 1981), ch. 4, "The Reading of Homer."

13. Cf. Richard A. Grusin, *Transcendental Hermeneutics: Institutional Authority and the Higher Criticism of the Bible* (Duke University Press, 1991).

14. Cf. Frank M. Turner, "Why the Greeks and Not the Romans in Victorian Britain?," in *Rediscovering Hellenism*, edited by G. W. Clark (Cambridge University Press, 1989), pp. 70–75.

15. Cf. Long, *Literary Pioneers*, pp. 108–58.

16. George Bancroft, *Ancient Greece, Translated from the German of Ar-*

nold H. L. Heeren (Henry G. Bohn, 1847). This is the second edition, revised when it was reprinted in America for Harvard's use in 1842.

17. For the massive switch from Roman to Greek history in nineteenth-century England, see Turner, "Why the Greeks," pp. 61–70, and *Greek Heritage*, pp. 187–263.

18. Arthur M. Schlesinger, Jr., *The Age of Jackson* (Little, Brown, 1953), p. 203.

19. Perry Miller, *The Transcendentalists* (Harvard, 1950), p. 19.

20. Emerson, *Selected Writings*, edited by Brooks Atkinson (Random House, 1940), p. 919.

21. Edward Everett, *Orations and Speeches on Various Occasions* (Little, Brown, 1856–68), vol. 1, pp. 76–77. Even when rereading Thucydides' funeral oration for use at Gettysburg, Everett noted in his diary that the work was over-praised by people like Daniel Webster (entry for Oct. 22).

22. Everett, *Orations and Speeches*, p. 359.

23. Ibid., p. 38. Here is a list of Everett's battlefield orations with references to volume and pages of his published *Orations:*

> 1825: Concord (1.173–200)
> 1833: Bunker Hill (1.354–65)
> 1835: Lexington (1.526–60)
> Bloody Brook (French-Indian War, 1.634–69)
> 1850: Bunker Hill (3.3–40)
> 1857: Bunker Hill (Warren's Statue, 3.526–36)
> 1863: Gettysburg (4.622–59)

24. The six examples of the Attic Epitaphios in surviving literature, with dates (or approximate dates), are:

> 431: Speech of Pericles in the first year of the Peloponnesian War (re-created by Thucydides, c. 400?)
> c. 430: Supposed date for speech of Aspasia recited by Socrates in Plato's *Menexenus* (composed c. 380?)
> c. 400: Model speech of Gorgias, cited in part by Dionysius the rhetorician
> 392: Speech of Lysias during the Corinthian War
> 338: Speech, attributed to Demosthenes, on the Battle of Chaeronea
> 332: Speech of Hyperides during the Lamian War

25. The great scholar Wilamowitz said: "As the ceremonial occasion for a recurrent Memorial Address, the festival of the [military] dead gave birth to Athenian rhetoric, a thing as important to later developments as was the poetry of Athens" (*Griechische Tragoedien* [Weidmann, 1904], vol. 1, p. 205). George Kennedy maintained that Greek respect for formal traditions in oratory came from the authority of the Epitaphios (*The Art of Persuasion in Greece* [Princeton

University Press, 1963], p. 154). A. H. Jones, in *Athenian Democracy* (Oxford, 1957), pp. 43, 60, treats the Epitaphioi as the basic statements of democratic purpose at Athens.

26. Nicole Loraux, *The Invention of Athens: The Funeral Oration in the Classical City*, translated by Alan Sheridan (Harvard University Press, 1986), p. 3.

27. John S. Nicolay and John Hay, *Abraham Lincoln: A History* (The Century Co., 1890), vol. 8, pp. 192–94. Nicolay gave testimony whenever he could to his admiration for Everett. Cf. *Century Magazine* 46 (n.s. 25, 1893–94), p. 602: "For two hours, he held the assembled multitude in rapt attention with his eloquent description and argument, his polished diction, his carefully studied and practised delivery." Cf. Hay's diary, pp. 121, 128.

28. Quoted in Louis A. Warren, *Lincoln's Gettysburg Declaration* (Lincoln National Life Foundation, 1964), p. 101.

29. Alan H. Sommerstein, *Aeschylus: Eumenides* (Cambridge University Press, 1989), p. 11. Cf. Christian Meier, "The *Eumenides* of Aeschylus and the Rise of the Political," in *The Greek Discovery of Politics*, translated by David McLintock (Harvard University Press, 1990), pp. 82–139.

30. For the life-giving aspect of "classic" in this sense, see especially David Tracy, "The Classic," ch. 4 of *The Analogical Imagination: Christian Theology and the Culture of Pluralism* (Crossroads Press, 1981), pp. 99–153.

31. Thucydides 2.36.

32. The Gorgian speech (appendix III C) is truncated, and probably gave basic antitheses for other orators to elaborate. See Thomas Cole, *The Origins of Rhetoric in Ancient Greece* (Johns Hopkins University Press, 1991), pp. 71–81. But the longest surviving Epitaphioi—by Thucydides (appendix III B) and Plato—have literary embellishments that do the work of the larger artifact in which they are embedded. Both contain elements of self-satire. The Attic orators themselves refer to the short time allotted them (Plato *Menexenus* 239b, 246a–b; Lysias 54; Demosthenes 6; Hyperides 4).

33. On the force of the generalizing "we" in the Attic Epitaphioi, see Loraux, *Invention of Athens*, pp. 123–24, 271 ("The *community* of the living, expressing itself *through* the orator"), 273 ("the collective 'we' of the Athenians"); W. Robert Connor, *Thucydides* (Princeton University Press, 1984), p. 65.

34. Hyperides refers to the general Leosthenes, at a time when the Epitaphios was moving toward vaguer praise *(encomium)*. Cf. D. A. Russell and N. G. Wilson, *Menander Rhetor* (Oxford University Press, 1981), pp. 170, 332. See also Loraux, *Invention of Athens*, pp. 254–62 (though she warns against a mechanistic reading of the transition to *encomium*, p. 113). "Demosthenes," unusually, names the Attic tribes—but inclusively, listing them all.

35. On *hoide*, see Loraux, *Invention of Athens*, p. 38.

36. Ibid., p. 277.

37. One funeral speech (by Lysias) has a *thrēnos* contained in it. This used to be thought a survival of the funeral speech's first form; but see John E. Ziolkow-

ski, *Thucydides and the Tradition of Funeral Speeches at Athens* (Arno Press, 1981), pp. 41–52; Loraux, *Invention of Athens*, pp. 44–50.

38. *Menexenus* 239c1.

39. Thucydides 2.46.2.

40. Milton, *Samson Agonistes*, vv. 1721–24.

41. The "right and fitting" formula (*dikaion* and *prepon*, Thucydides 2.36.2) puts individual tragedy in a larger pattern of ordered things. It is not only *dikaion* (*Menexenus* 239d3, Hyperides 14), but fitting (*chrē*, Thucydides 2.46.1; *Menexenus* 239d3), worthwhile (*axion*, Hyperides 3), appointed (*anangkē*, Lysias 81), and fine (*kalon*, Demosthenes 35).

42. Edward Everett, *Orations and Speeches*, vol. 3, p. 536. At another time, speaking in Faneuil Hall, he gestured to a Stuart portrait of Washington and asked the audience to meet its gaze (ibid., vol. 1, p. 361).

43. Edmund Wilson scoffed at this part of Everett's address: "It is amusing to think of the Federal dead heaving with indignation at the failure of the orator to honor their graves" (*Patriotic Gore* [Oxford University Press, 1962], p. 645).

44. Everett, *Orations and Speeches*, vol. 1, p. 518.

45. Ibid., pp. 527–28, 530. Cf. *Henry V*, 4.3.44ff:

> He that shall live this day, and see old age,
> Will yearly on the vigil feast his neighbors. . . .
>   Then shall our names,
> Familiar in his mouth as household words,
> Henry the King, Bedford and Exeter,
> Warwick and Talbot, Salisbury and Gloucester,
> Be in their flowing cups freshly remember'd.
> This story shall the good man teach his son;
> And Crispin Crispian shall ne'er go by,
> From this day to the ending of the world,
> But we in it shall be remembered. . . .

46. Everett, *Orations and Speeches*, vol. 1, p. 560. For similar roll calls of the dead, see ibid., pp. 89, 669.

47. Lane Cooper, *The Rhetoric of Aristotle* (D. Appleton-Century, 1932), p. xxxii, and Charles Smiley, "Lincoln and Gorgias," *Classical Journal* 13 (1917), pp. 124–28.

48. J. D. Denniston, *The Greek Particles*, second edition (Oxford University Press, 1959), pp. 359, 165.

49. Thucydides 2.35.1. Cf. Demosthenes 13–14.

50. The model of the few-for-many sacrifice was Athens' stand against the hordes of Persia, recalled as the type of Athenian heroism in the Epitaphioi (*Menexenus* 239d–241c; Lysias 20–47; Demosthenes 10–11; Hyperides 35–36; cf. Loraux, *Invention of Athens*, pp. 157, 274–75).

51. Demosthenes 24; Hyperides 5. In another Epitaphios, Pericles called the dead heroes the spring of the year (Aristotle *Rhetoric* 1365.34).

52. Thucydides 1.43.2–3. *Menexenus* 247d5–6. Gorgias DK 82 B6, p. 285, line 14, and p. 286, lines 15–17. Lysias 80–81. Demosthenes 32–34. Hyperides 28. Cf. Loraux, *Invention of Athens*, p. 111.

53. Thucydides 2.40–41. *Menexenus* 238c–239b. Gorgias DK 82 B6, p. 285, line 15, to p. 286, line 15. Lysias 17–18. Demosthenes 23. Hyperides 8–9.

54. Thucydides 2.35. *Menexenus* 236d, 246a, 247e. Gorgias DK 82 B6, p. 285, lines 11–13. Lysias 1–2, 19. Demosthenes 1–2, 12, 35. Hyperides 1–2. Cf. Loraux, *Invention of Athens*, pp. 230–41, 246.

55. These passages are intertwined with those cited in note 53 above.

56. Thucydides 2.44–45. *Menexenus* 236c. Gorgias DK 82 B6, p. 286, lines 13–15. Lysias 71–76. Demosthenes 36–37. Hyperides 27–29. Cf. Loraux, *Invention of Athens*, p. 279.

57. Andrew Stewart, *Greek Sculpture: An Exploration* (Yale University Press, 1990), vol. 1, pp. 92–94; vol. 2, plates 517–19.

58. Thucydides 2.36–37. *Menexenus* 237b, 237c, 249a–c. Lysias 17. Demosthenes 4–5. Hyperides 7. Loraux speaks of the way "autochthony [birth from the motherland] may even serve as an etiological myth for this exclusion of women" (p. 284).

59. Thucydides 2.43–44. *Menexenus* 246d–248d. Gorgias DK 82 B6, p. 285, line 7. Lysias 24–26, 77–79. Demosthenes 27–31, 37. Hyperides 3, 40. Cf. Loraux, *Invention of Athens*, pp. 101–2, 107, 115.

60. Thucydides 2.40–41. *Menexenus* 239–45 (ironically framed). Lysias 20. Demosthenes 7–24. Hyperides 3.

61. Plato, as Loraux points out, complains about the *confusion* of life and death that comes from the heady praises of the Epitaphios (*Menexenus* 235a; Loraux, *Invention of Athens*, pp. 268–70).

62. Cooper, *Rhetoric of Aristotle*, p. xxxiii.

63. *Menexenus* 236d3–5.

64. Ziolkowski, *Thucydides*, pp. 74–99 for the *parainesis*, pp. 138–63 for the *epainesis* (which he, departing from Plato, calls more frequently the *paramythia*, "consolation"). On the dangers of a mechanistic rhetoric in works like Ziolkowski's, see Loraux, *Invention of Athens*, p. 246: "Any quantitative examination, based on the drawing up of a frequency table, is a risky business: E. J. [sic] Ziolkowski lists thirty-nine topoi of praise and thirteen of consolation or exhortation and, armed with this result, concludes that Pericles' Epitaphios, which presents all the topoi except eight commonplaces of praise, is ultimately traditional in character."

65. *Menexenus* 240e1–3. Demosthenes 23. Hyperides 28.

66. *Lincoln and the Gettysburg Address*, edited by Allan Nevins (University of Illinois Press, 1964), p. 88.

67. Cooper, *Rhetoric of Aristotle*, p. xxxii.

68. Hurt, "All the Living," p. 379.

2. Gettysburg and the Culture of Death

1. Joseph Story, *An Address Delivered on the Dedication of the Cemetery at Mount Auburn* (Joseph T. Edwin Buckingham, 1831), p. 9. For the relation of Kerameikos to Akademy, cf. Pausanias, *A Tour of Greece* 1.29–30. For the Attic Kerameikos as a model for the rural-cemetery movement, see Blanche Linden-Ward, *Silent City on a Hill: Landscapes of Memory and Boston's Mount Auburn Cemetery* (Ohio State University Press, 1989), pp. 92, 129–30, 192–93.

2. David Charles Sloane, *The Last Great Necessity: Cemeteries in American History* (Johns Hopkins University Press, 1991), p. 55.

3. Philippe Ariès, *L'Homme devant la mort* (Editions du Seuil, 1977), quotes Justice Story's speech anonymously (*"comme on le dit,"* p. 525). The English translation by Helen Weaver adds the name, but inaccurately ("Justice Joseph Stom," p. 532 of *The Hour of Our Death* [Vintage, 1982]). The Père Lachaise Cemetery outside Paris is considered the first burial ground consciously turning from supernatural constraints to the contemplation of nature (1801). The New Burying-Ground in New Haven, opened in 1796 with the backing of Yale professors, has a claim to be the pioneer institution, but it did not win the attention or exert the ideological influence of Père Lachaise or Mount Auburn.

4. Story, *Address*, pp. 11–12.

5. Ibid., p. 14.

6. Ibid., p. 17.

7. Ibid., p. 13.

8. Lady Emmeline Stuart Wortley, *Travels in the United States* (Richard Bently, 1851), pp. 74–75.

9. Linden-Ward, *Silent City*, pp. 309–11.

10. James J. Farrell, *Inventing the American Way of Death, 1830–1920* (Temple University Press, 1980), p. 112.

11. For Rose Hill, see *Dictionary of American Biography*, s.v. Saunders. For Graceland, see Walter L. Creese, *The Crowning of the American Landscape: Eight Great Spaces and Their Buildings* (Princeton University Press, 1985), pp. 205–18. Other important rural cemeteries, after Sleepy Hollow in Concord, were Laurel Hill in Philadelphia, Green-Wood in Brooklyn, and Spring Grove in Cincinnati. Creese sees in these areas the forerunners of national parks (p. 207). Cf. Linden-Ward, *Silent City*, pp. 329–31. Saunders was important in the development of public spaces other than cemeteries. In Washington he landscaped the Capitol grounds, the Department of Agriculture grounds, and an arboretum on the Mall.

12. William Saunders, "Remarks on the Design," in *Report of the Select Committee Relative to the Soldiers' National Cemetery* (1865), p. 148. For the Burkean sublime in the cemetery movement, see Linden-Ward, *Silent City*, ch. 5. Some would distinguish later cemeteries of the mid-century from Mount Auburn in terms of lawn space and density of monuments, but this seems the result not of ideology but of geography, or of the demand for more monuments as families

crowded into the grounds. None of the relevant cemeteries wanted the landscape blocked by monuments. All aspired, as Saunders put it, to provide "a pleasing landscape and pleasure ground effect." At Rose Hill and Graceland, on level terrain lacking the geological drama of Mount Auburn, this led to more open vistas. The specifically military nature of Gettysburg made Saunders exclude all but the central monument in the hemisphere of original graves, but he returned to Gettysburg to help site the earliest state and unit monuments at visually appropriate places in the adjoining grounds. His Rose Hill became as clogged with monuments as did Mount Auburn.

13. Everett, Letter of Nov. 28, 1863, Massachusetts Historical Society.

14. Mark Twain, *The Adventures of Huckleberry Finn*, ch. 17 (*Mississippi Writings* [Library of America, 1982], p. 726).

15. For the sentimental poetry of death, written by Lydia Sigourney, Julia Moore, Phoebe and Alice Carey, and others, see Lewis O. Saum, "Death in the Popular Mind of Pre–Civil War America," in *Death in America,* edited by David E. Stannard (University of Pennsylvania Press, 1975), pp. 30–48; Ann Douglas, *The Feminization of American Culture* (Alfred A. Knopf, 1977), p. 220; Michael Patrick Hern, *The Annotated 'Huckleberry Finn'* (Clarkson N. Potter, 1981), pp. 168–72.

16. Justin Kaplan, *Mr. Clemens and Mark Twain* (Pocket Books, 1968), p. 400: "In their house of mourning, which Clemens and Livy intended to keep so until they themselves were dead, the holidays and anniversaries passed and were marked only in sorrow. Susy's two sisters became priestesses at her shrine."

17. Emerson had earlier exhumed his wife's body (John McAleer, *Ralph Waldo Emerson: Days of Encounter* [Little, Brown, 1984], pp. 109–382). Emerson's youth was strongly influenced by an aunt who wore her own shroud while alive and slept in a coffin-bed. Emerson was initiated early into the culture of death. For the necrophiliac aspect of Transcendentalism in general see Richard A. Grusin, *Transcendentalist Hermeneutics* (Duke University Press, 1991), pp. 36–39.

18. Linden-Ward, *Silent City*, p. 194.

19. J. Hillis Miller, *Victorian Subjects* (Duke University Press, 1991), pp. 43–44.

20. John Cooley, *Mark Twain's Aquarium: The Samuel Clemens 'Angelfish' Correspondence, 1905–1910* (University of Georgia Press, 1991).

21. Garry Wills, "The Angels and Devils of Dickens," *New York Review of Books*, May 16, 1991, pp. 8–11. For the cult of wise innocence, see Emerson, *Selected Writings*, edited by Brooks Atkinson (Random House, 1946), p. 6: "The sun illuminates only the eye of the man, but shines into the eye and the heart of the child."

22. Emerson, "Nature," in *Selected Writings*, p. 408.

23. Ibid., p. 410. Cf. p. 7: "In the tranquil landscape, and especially in the distant line of the *horizon*, man beholds somewhat as beautiful as his own nature." And pp. 5–6: "There is a property in the *horizon* which no man has but he whose eye can integrate all the parts, that is, the poet." Italics added.

24. In the Second Walk, Rousseau is knocked unconscious by a Great Dane and the moment of recovery is a "new birth," making his life *come* to life.

25. The autosuggestive techniques are described in the Fifth Walk.

26. Albrecht Dürer's famous engraving of *Melencolia* (1514), as a companion piece to the *St. Jerome in His Study*, shows the *disordered* intellect contrasted with pious learning (Erwin Panofsky, *The Life and Art of Albrecht Dürer* [Princeton, 1943], pp. 156ff). Richard Burton, for all his fascination with melancholy, warned in orthodox ways that it was a favorite tool of the devil, leading people to suicide, hatred, or resort to the occult. "Melancholy persons are most subject to diabolical temptations and illusions, and most apt to entertain them, and the Devil best able to work upon them" (*The Anatomy of Melancholy* 1.2.i.ii [Tudor, 1927], p. 175). As the rural-cemetery movement took burial out of the churchyard care of theologians, so the romantics freed melancholy from its treatment as a sin or the occasion of sin.

27. John Ruskin, *Modern Painters* 1.2.iii, "Of Truth of Chiaroscuro," and 5.9.xi, "The Hesperid Aeglé." For the painters' inspiration by the Transcendentalists, see *American Light: The Luminist Movement*, edited by John Wilmerding (Harper & Row, 1980), pp. 98–99, 300–302.

28. Story, *Address*, p. 18.

29. Ibid., p. 11.

30. Ibid., p. 7.

31. Emerson, *Complete Works* (Houghton Mifflin, 1904), vol. 2, p. 436.

32. Ibid., vol. 8, p. 324.

33. Herndon-Weik, p. 473.

34. The best treatment of Lincoln's poems is now Douglas L. Wilson, "Abraham Lincoln's Indiana and the Spirit of Mortal," *Indiana Magazine of History* 87 (June 1991), pp. 155–70, though Wilson finds more merit in the poetry than I can perceive.

35. F. B. Carpenter, *Six Months at the White House* (Hurd and Houghton, 1877), pp. 115–16.

36. Jean H. Baker, *Mary Todd Lincoln* (W. W. Norton, 1987), pp. 218–22. Cf. Kaplan, *Mr. Clemens*, pp. 397–400, for Twain and the seances.

37. Herndon-Weik, p. 352. Hertz, pp. 110–11, 409–10.

38. For the claim of religions to be underived, except from God, see Jonathan Z. Smith, *Map Is Not Territory: Studies in the History of Religion* (E. J. Brill, 1978), pp. 242–43.

39. Theodore Parker, "Hildreth's United States," in Centenary edition 8.270–71.

40. George Bancroft, *The History of the United States* (Little, Brown), vol. 2 (1837), p. 35.

41. See, for instance, the personified "woods of Maine" at *A Half-Century of Conflict*, ch. 3, in *France and England in North America* (Library of America, 1893), vol. 2, p. 360.

42. Parker, "Hildreth's United States," p. 282.

43. Ibid., p. 281.

44. Don E. Fehrenbacher, *Lincoln in Text and Context* (Stanford University Press, 1987), p. 283.

45. Story, *Address*, p. 27. Cf. Farrell, *American Way of Death*, p. 106, for other lines at burial.

> 'Tis in love we bear thee thither
> To thy mourning Mother's breast.

46. Mothers seem entirely eliminated in formulae like that of Lysias 17, "Their mother was their fatherland." Cf. Nicole Loraux, *The Invention of Athens* (Harvard University Press, 1986), p. 284.

47. For Lincoln as misogynist, see Robert Wiebe, "Lincoln's Fraternal Democracy," in *Abraham Lincoln and Political Tradition*, edited by John L. Thomas (University of Massachusetts Press, 1986). The case for the other side is made by Roy P. Basler, "Lincoln, Blacks, and Women," in *Public and Private Lincoln*, edited by Cullom Davis (Southern Illinois University Press, 1979), pp. 38–53. Lincoln was an early advocate of women's suffrage (SW 1.5; Herndon-Weik, pp. 133–34).

48. See, for instance, SW 1.514–15, 603, 604, 608, 765, 800, 802, 808.

49. E.g., James Hurt, "All the Living and the Dead: Lincoln's Imagery," *American Literature* 52 (1980), pp. 351–79.

50. Wilson advanced his thesis in a 1954 *New Yorker* article republished in *Eight Essays* (Doubleday, 1959) and incorporated into *Patriotic Gore* (Oxford, 1962).

51. Harry V. Jaffa, *Crisis of the House Divided* (Doubleday, 1959), pp. 182–83. Jaffa's long treatment of this speech signaled the importance it would assume over the next two decades. Previously, it had been treated mainly as an indirect rebuke to those who lynched the abolitionist Elijah P. Lovejoy in 1837 (see Roy P. Basler's note at CW 2.111).

52. George B. Forgie, *Patricide in the House Divided: A Psychological Interpretation of Lincoln and His Age* (W. W. Norton, 1979), pp. 83–86, 249–70. James Hurt, "All the Living," drew on Wilson, Jaffa, and Forgie to discuss "the combination of homage and hostility in Lincoln's treatment of the Fathers," and then added Erik Erikson's categories.

53. Dwight G. Anderson, *Abraham Lincoln: The Quest for Immortality* (Alfred A. Knopf, 1982). See, for instance, p. 190: "The Gettysburg Address illustrates the extent of Lincoln's triumph over Washington."

54. Charles B. Strozier, *Lincoln's Quest for Union: Public and Private Meanings* (Basic Books, 1982). Cf. p. 61 on "the oedipal implications of the speech" to the Lyceum and Lincoln's "identification with the towering genius" of destruction.

55. Dwight S. Anderson, "Quest for Immortality," in *The Historian's Lincoln*, edited by Gabor S. Boritt and Norman O. Forness (University of Illinois Press, 1988), p. 254.

56. Thomas F. Schwartz, "The Springfield Lyceum and Lincoln's 1838 Speech," *Illinois Historical Journal* 83 (1990), p. 49. Since the earlier denunciation of mobocracy preceded Elijah Lovejoy's lynching (see note 51 above), it is now less certain that Lincoln was responding to that episode.

57. Ibid., p. 48.

58. The anti-Jacksonian implications of Lincoln's speech are developed by George Fredrickson, "The Search for Order and Community," in *Public and Private Lincoln*, edited by Cullom Davis et al. (Southern Illinois University Press, 1979), pp. 92–93, and Don E. Fehrenbacher, "The Words of Lincoln," a 1984 essay included in the author's *Lincoln's Text and Context* (Stanford University Press, 1987), p. 282. Fredrickson concludes that "Lincoln was thus giving eloquent expression to the ideology of his [legal] profession as it confronted the challenge of romantic democracy [the Young America he satirized in his speech on inventions], and not making a unique personal statement."

59. One of the most important expressions of this view came from Lincoln's own model for oratory, Daniel Webster, in his famous speech at Bunker Hill (1825):

> We can win no laurels in a war for independence. Earlier and worthier hands have gathered them all. Nor are there places for us by the side of Solon, and Alfred, and other founders of states. Our fathers have filled them. But there remains to us the great duty of defense and preservation.

(The Great Speeches of Daniel Webster [Little, Brown, 1879], p. 135.)

60. John Jay Chapman, "Emerson," in *The Shock of Recognition*, edited by Edmund Wilson (Random House, 1943), p. 604.

61. Marcus Cunliffe, "Commentary on 'Quest for Immortality,'" in *The Historian's Lincoln*, p. 282.

62. Herndon-Weik, p. 353.

63. Anderson, *Abraham Lincoln*, p. 190.

64. Emerson, *Complete Works*, vol. 11, p. 436.

3. The Transcendental Declaration

1. Parker to Herndon, Sept. 9, 1858, in Joseph Fort Newton, *Lincoln and Herndon* (The Torch Press, 1910), p. 208.

2. Ibid., p. 239 (Parker to Herndon, Nov. 13, 1858): "I look for an anti-slavery administration in 1861—I hope with Seward at its head." Parker had been predicting and hoping for a Seward presidency since 1851 (Cobbe edition 4.276–77).

3. Eugene H. Berwanger, *The Frontier Against Slavery: Western Anti-Negro Prejudice and the Slavery Extension Controversy* (University of Chicago Press, 1967), pp. 48–51.

4. Richard Allen Heckman, *Lincoln vs. Douglas: The Great Debates Campaign* (Public Affairs Press, 1967), p. 104.

5. Richard Hofstadter, *The American Political Tradition and the Men Who Made It* (Vintage, 1948), p. 116.

6. The passage is shaped by the pattern of anaphora—not only the three major launchings of the thought—

I will say
and I will say
I say—

but the subsidiary returns to his pronouncing language:

that I am not, nor ever have been
that I am not, nor ever have been

I do not perceive
I do not understand

7. William L. King, *Lincoln's Manager: David Davis* (Harvard University Press, 1960), p. 123.

8. Herndon-Weik, pp. 269–70.

9. George Fredrickson, "Lincoln and Racial Equality," *Journal of Southern History* 41 (1975), p. 45.

10. Mark Twain, *The Adventures of Huckleberry Finn*, ch. 23 (*Mississippi Writings* [Library of America, 1982], p. 777).

11. Ibid., p. 777.

12. Ibid., p. 784.

13. François-Jean Chastellux, *De la félicité publique* (1772). Cf. Garry Wills, *Inventing America: Jefferson's Declaration of Independence* (Doubleday, 1978), pp. xiv–xxiv, 158–62, 357, 368. Of course, Lincoln refers always to the Declaration as Congress passed it, not to Jefferson's own (more empirically grounded) draft (Wills, *Inventing America*, p. 309).

14. Ralph Waldo Emerson, "Nature" (1844), in *Selected Writings*, edited by Brooks Atkinson (Random House, 1940), p. 421.

15. John McAleer, *Ralph Waldo Emerson: Days of Encounter* (Little, Brown, 1984), pp. 569–72.

16. Emerson, "The Emancipation Proclamation" (1862), in *Selected Writings*, p. 886.

17. On the Transcendentalism of the *History*, see Russell B. Nye, *George Bancroft, Brahmin Rebel* (Alfred A. Knopf, 1944), pp. 100–102, 122–23, 138–39, 196–97; Perry Miller, *The Transcendentalists: An Anthology* (Harvard University Press, 1950), pp. 422–29.

18. For Lincoln's meeting with Bancroft, see Nye, *George Bancroft*, p. 194. Bancroft's lecture on progress is in his *Literary and Historical Miscellanies* (Harper & Brothers, 1855), pp. 481–517. Lincoln's lecture on inventions is discussed in ch. 5 below.

19. Bancroft, *Miscellanies*, p. 486. For Bancroft and Schleiermacher, see Orie William Long, *Literary Pioneers: Early American Explorers of European Culture* (Harvard University Press, 1935), pp. 132–33; Nye, *George Bancroft*, pp. 46–48. Like his patron and model, Everett, Bancroft sought out Byron and Goethe while in Europe (Long, pp. 117–19, 139–40).

20. Miller, *Transcendentalists*, p. 502.

21. Herndon to Parker, Feb. 1857, in Newton, *Lincoln and Herndon*, p. 108.

22. Theodore Parker, *Additional Speeches*, vol. 1, pp. 13–15.

23. Parker, "Transcendentalism," in Centenary edition 6.30.

24. Herndon-Weik, p. 323. Cf. Parker, Cobbe edition 8.138: "self-government over all the people"; Cobbe edition 5.105: "a government of all the people, by all the people, for all the people"; Centenary edition 6.27: "government over all the people, by all the people and for the sake of all." The frequency of Parker's use is treated by John White Chadwick, *Theodore Parker: Preacher and Reformer* (Houghton Mifflin, 1900), pp. 322–23.

25. Herndon-Weik, p. 359.

26. Hertz, p. 409.

27. This is the central distinction in what Perry Miller calls Parker's critical statement of belief, the 1841 "Discourse of the Transient and Permanent in Christianity" (Miller, *Transcendentalists*, pp. 259–83).

28. Parker, "The Present Crisis" (1856), in Cobbe edition 6.245. "The Nebraska Question" (1854), in Cobbe edition 5.260–61.

29. Ibid., p. 273.

30. Herndon-Weik, pp. 353–54.

31. Parker, "The Aspect of Freedom in America" (July 5, 1852), in Cobbe edition 4.266.

32. Ibid., pp. 268–69.

33. Ibid., p. 95. Cf. Centenary edition 7.167, Cobbe edition 5.131, 260, 299, 612.

34. Chadwick, *Theodore Parker*, p. 240.

35. Speech of May 12, 1854, in Cobbe edition 5.312.

36. Parker criticized nineteenth-century narrative history for accumulating facts rather than studying their dialectical interplay with ideas. See especially his attacks on William Prescott (Centenary edition 8.172–267). He sought out historical works for his long analytical reviews (ibid., 268–418).

37. Cf. Cobbe edition, 5.274–76, 287–89, 6.142–53, 173, 181–86, 240–41, 270–88, 305–13.

38. J. G. Randall, *Lincoln the President*, vol. 1 (Dodd, Mead, 1945), p. 108.

39. Allan Nevins, *The Emergence of Lincoln*, vol. 1 (Charles Scribner's Sons, 1950), p. 362.

40. David Zarefsky, *Lincoln, Douglas, and Slavery* (University of Chicago Press, 1990), pp. 83–84.

41. Parker, Address of May 12, 1854, in Cobbe edition 6.173.

42. Parker, Speech of June 29, 1858, in Cobbe edition 6.312.

43. Ibid., p. 312.

44. Taney, *Dred Scott* v. *John F. A. Sandford*, 19 Howard 393 (1857), pp. 451–52:

> The right of property in a slave is distinctly and expressly affirmed in the Constitution. The right to traffic in it, like an ordinary article of merchandise and property, was guaranteed to the citizens of the United States, in every State that might desire it, for twenty years. And the Government in express terms is pledged to protect it in all future time, if the slave escapes his owner. This is done in plain words—too plain to be misunderstood. And no word can be found in the Constitution which gives Congress a greater power over slave property, or which entitles property of that kind to less protection than property of any other description.

Over in England, Karl Marx was just as convinced as Parker and Lincoln that there was a conspiracy of interests abetting the Slave Power and planning to extend it. He wrote from London for *Die Presse* of Oct. 25, 1861:

> The whole movement was and is based, as one sees, on the *slave question.* Not in the sense of whether the slaves in the existing slave states should be emancipated outright or not, but whether the twenty million free men of the North should submit any longer to an oligarchy of three thousand slaveholders, whether the vast Territories of the republic should be nurseries for free states or for slavery; finally, whether the national policy of the Union should take armed spreading of slavery in Mexico, Central and South America as its device. [From *Marx and Engels on the United States* (Progress Publishers, 1979), p. 92.]

45. Parker, Speech of Jan. 29, 1858, in Cobbe edition 6.305.

46. Don E. Fehrenbacher, *The Dred Scott Case: Its Significance in American Law and Politics* (Oxford University Press, 1979), pp. 306–14.

47. Kenneth E. Stampp, *America in 1857: A Nation on the Brink* (Oxford University Press, 1990), p. 92. The justices who were in communication with Buchanan, directly or indirectly, were Catron, Grier, Wayne, and Nelson, who were keeping their tactics secret from the other justices.

48. Ibid., pp. 116, 193–95.

49. For slavery "girt about by a ring of fire," cf. Chadwick, *Theodore Parker*, p. 247.

50. James Oakes, *Slavery and Freedom: An Interpretation of the Old South* (Alfred A. Knopf, 1990), p. 102.

51. Parker, Address of May 12, 1854, in Cobbe edition 5.310–12. Cf. Cobbe edition 6.257–58: "All the repressive power of Christiandom gathers about American slavery."

52. Stampp *(America in 1857)* rightly calls the Lecompton Constitution "Politics as Farce" (ch. 10).

53. Parker, Speech of Jan. 29, 1858, in Cobbe edition 6.312—a speech given over five months before Lincoln's House Divided Speech against Douglas.

54. Robert S. Johanssen, *Stephen A. Douglas* (Oxford University Press, 1973), pp. 590–91. Douglas's words, spoken in the Senate on Dec. 9, 1857, were: "It is none of my business which way the slavery clause is decided. I care not whether it is voted down or voted up."

55. Cf. Stampp, *America in 1857*, p. 117, on the suppression of free speech in the South. For the attempts to spread a "gag rule" to the North, cf. William W. Freehling, *The Road to Disunion, Volume I: Secessionists at Bay, 1776–1854* (Oxford University Press, 1990), pp. 289–352.

56. Parker, Speech of Jan. 29, 1858, in Cobbe edition, p. 302. Mark Twain said of his mother (and her generation): "She had never heard it [slavery] assailed in any pulpit but had heard it defended and sanctified in a thousand; her ears were familiar with Bible texts that approved it but if there were any that disapproved it they had not been quoted by her pastors; as far as her experience went, the wise and the good and the holy were unanimous in the conviction that slavery was right." (*The Autobiography of Mark Twain*, edited by Charles Neider [Harper Collins, 1959], p. 30.)

4. Revolution in Thought

1. At the time when Lincoln was calling Douglas a dead lion (SW 1.433), Parker described him as "a mad dog barking at the wolf that has torn our sheep, but *more dangerous than the wolf*" (John White Chadwick, *Theodore Parker: Preacher and Reformer*, Houghton Mifflin, 1900), p. 334.

2. Parker, Speech of May 7, 1856, in Cobbe edition 6.237. At other times, Parker could be withering on the topic of politicians:

> Mr. Facing-Bothways [from Bunyan] is a popular politician in America just now, sitting on the fence between honesty and dishonesty, and, like the blank leaf between the Old and New Testaments, belonging to neither dispensation. [Parker, "The Political Destination of America," in Cobbe edition 4.93.]

3. Parker, "Daniel Webster," in Centenary edition 7.341. Webster's speech on Plymouth Rock (1820) laid the basis of his oratorical fame and did much to create that site's national fame. It contains a denunciation of slavery whose effect on the ten-year-old Parker is easily imagined:

> If there be, within the extent of our knowledge or influence, any participation in The [Slave] Traffic, let us pledge ourselves here, upon the rock of Plymouth, to extirpate and destroy it. It is not fit that the land of the Pilgrims should bear the shame longer. I hear the sound of the hammer, I see the smoke of the furnaces where manacles and fetters are still forged for

human limbs. I see the visages of those who by stealth and at midnight labor in this work of hell, foul and dark, as may become the artificers of such instruments of misery and torture. Let that spot be purified, or let it cease to be of New England. ["First Settlement of New England," in *The Great Speeches and Orations of Daniel Webster* (Little, Brown, 1879), pp. 49–50.]

The other oration Parker heard as a boy was "The Revolution in Greece," 1824 (*Great Speeches*, pp. 57–76).

4. For Lincoln's reliance on Clay in dealing with the slavery issue, see, especially, George Fredrickson, "A Man but Not a Brother," *Journal of Southern History* 41 (1975), pp. 40–44. For a less sympathetic treatment of Clay's influence, see Richard Hofstadter, *The American Political Tradition* (Vintage, 1948), pp. 99–100.

5. Mark E. Neely, Jr., traces the "mysticism" tradition, about Lincoln's attitude toward the Union, from Alexander Stephens to Edmund Wilson. Neely, *The Fate of Liberty: Abraham Lincoln and Civil Liberties* (Oxford University Press, 1991), pp. 231–32.

6. *Reminiscences of Abraham Lincoln by Distinguished Men of His Time* (North American Press, 1881), p. 475.

7. For Webster's work in the landmark cases, see *The Papers of Daniel Webster, Legal Papers*, vol. 3, *The Federal Practice*, edited by Andrew J. King (Dartmouth, 1989), pp. 17–348. For the number of cases pled, cf. Kenneth E. Shewmaker, *Daniel Webster, "The Completest Man"* (Dartmouth College, 1990), p. x.

8. Parker, "Webster," in Centenary edition 7.290–91.

9. For close argument from Story's commentary, see Lincoln's 1848 speech on internal improvements (SW 1.193–94) and notes to his Cooper Union Speech (CW 3.522). He also recommended Story's work on the law of equity (SW 2.180, CW 3.344). Story was appointed associate justice by James Madison in 1811. He served for twenty-four of John Marshall's thirty-five years as chief justice, and lived on into his own thirty-fourth year on the Court, a close runner-up to Marshall in longevity of tenure as in juridical eminence. Story's stature is described well in *The First One Hundred Justices*, by Albert P. Blaustein and Roy M. Mersky (Archon, 1978), p. 41:

> Many students of the Court consider Story its greatest scholar, a virtuoso who contributed to equity jurisprudence, substantially created American law on copyrights and patents, stamped his mark on property, trusts, partnership and insurance law, and helped formulate America's commercial and maritime law.

10. For the unorthodox collaboration of Story and Webster, over the years, see R. Kent Newmyer, *Supreme Court Justice Joseph Story: Statesman of the Old*

Republic (University of North Carolina Press, 1985), pp. 169–76; Joseph McClellan, *Joseph Story and The American Constitution* (University of Oklahoma Press, 1971), pp. 280–83. Story even sat on the circuit court before which Webster practiced.

11. This is from Lincoln's 1857 speech on the Dred Scott decision. Don E. Fehrenbacher demolished the claim of psychobiographer Dwight Anderson that this passage reflects Lincoln's own sense of inner bafflement. His case could have been even more complete if Fehrenbacher had noticed the relevance of the whole passage to Calhoun. Cf. *Lincoln in Text and Context* (Stanford University Press, 1987), pp. 282–83. For Lincoln's study of Calhoun's oratory, cf. Herndon-Weik, p. 421.

12. Herndon-Weik, pp. 327, 386. Hertz, p. 118.

13. Merrill D. Peterson, *The Great Triumvirate: Webster, Clay and Calhoun* (Oxford University Press, 1987), pp. 179–80.

14. *The Papers of Daniel Webster: Speeches and Formal Writings*, vol. 1, *1800–1833*, edited by Charles M. Wiltse and Alan R. Berolzheimer (Dartmouth, 1986), p. 326.

15. Ibid., p. 325.

16. Ibid., p. 348.

17. Ibid., pp. 330, 339–40.

18. Ibid., pp. 577–78. The Wiltse edition includes some obvious misprints—in this passage, "although" for "as though" and "Yet" for "Yes" and a comma instead of a period after "bond of union." Lincoln knew this speech well enough to echo its phrase about America as "the world's last hope" (p. 611; cf. SW 2.415). Kenneth Stampp thinks Lincoln's First Inaugural "the most persuasive constitutional argument for perpetuity [of the Union] ever devised." He does not notice that every element of that argument was taken from Webster, since he considers only the Reply to Hayne and omits "The Constitution Not a Compact." Stampp believes Lincoln drew on Andrew Jackson's 1832 Proclamation on Nullification—a more distant debt, and less likely, given Lincoln's dislike of Jacksonianism.

19. Ronald Reagan, *An American Life* (Simon and Schuster, 1990), p. 196.

20. Webster, *Papers (Speeches)*, p. 251.

21. Joseph Story, *Commentaries on the Constitution of the United States*, bk. II, ch. 1, "The History of the Revolution" (pp. 154, 157–58 of the fifth edition, Little, Brown, 1891). James Wilson, a signer of the Declaration as well as a framer and ratifier of the Constitution, had the same view of the Declaration:

> The act of independence was made before the articles of confederation. This act declares, that "these *united* colonies" (without enumerating them separately) "are free and independent states." [*The Works of James Wilson*, edited by Robert Green McCloskey (Harvard University Press, 1967), vol. 2, p. 829. See also vol. 1, pp. 239–40, 281–82, along with Wilson's speeches in

Ratification of the Constitution by the States: Pennsylvania (Historical Society of Wisconsin, 1976, pp. 385–86, 472–73).]

For Story's reliance on Wilson, see Newmyer, *Supreme Court Justice,* pp. 187–88. Wilson was the only framer to draw on Rousseau's concept of a unitary popular sovereignty—see Garry Wills, "James Wilson's New Meaning for Sovereignty," in *Conceptual Change and the Constitution,* edited by Terence Bell and J. G. A. Pocock (University Press of Kansas, 1988), pp. 99–106.

22. James M. McPherson, *Abraham Lincoln and the Second American Revolution* (Oxford University Press, 1990), p. 77: "Thus, by 1862, the Lincoln administration had, in effect, conceded that this conflict was a war between belligerent governments."

23. John Hay, *Diaries,* Aug. 9, 1863 (p. 77).

24. By Arthur Schlesinger, for instance, in *The Imperial Presidency* (Houghton Mifflin, 1973), pp. 61ff.

25. Cf. Jonathan T. Davis, *Pardon and Amnesty: The Restoration of the Confederates to Their Rights and Privileges, 1861–1898* (University of North Carolina Press, 1953), ch. 5, "President Lincoln's Clemency."

26. Schlesinger, *Imperial Presidency,* p. 61.

27. Schlesinger regularly uses only the short form of address, as "his" President John Kennedy did, which allows him to quote (p. 62) Samuel P. Huntington with approval:

> As Samuel P. Huntington has pointed out, the Commander in Chief clause was "unique in the Constitution in granting authority in the form of an *office* rather than in the form of a *function*"—that is, instead of giving the President simply the function of commanding the Army and Navy, it gave him the office of Commander in Chief [sic] with functions undefined and therefore expansible. Now Lincoln began to regard the Commander in Chief as the locus, if not the source, of the war power.

Since war power in this passage means war-*making* power, Lincoln's attitude is distorted at many levels. He never thought he was making war, which is done against aliens. Furthermore, to make the President commander-in-chief of the army and navy *is* to define his (nonexpansible) function. Even his power over the militia is severely limited (to actual time of rebellion), proving that his war power over civilians is—by *this* clause, anyway—nonexistent.

28. Richard Hofstadter, *The American Political Tradition* (Vintage, 1948), p. 132.

29. Hay, *Diaries,* July 14, 1863 (p. 67):

> He [Lincoln] has never been easy in his own mind about Gen. Meade since Meade's General Order in which he called on his troops to drive the invader from our soil. The Pres't says, "This is a dreadful reminiscence of McClellan. The same spirit that moved McC. to claim a victory because Pa. & Md.

were safe. The heart of 10 million people sunk within them when McClellan raised that shout last fall. Will our Generals never get that idea out of their heads? The whole country is our soil."

30. J. G. Randall, *Lincoln the President* (Dodd, Mead, 1945), vol. 2, p. 161.

31. Cf. Barbara J. Fields, "Who Freed the Slaves?," in *The Civil War: An Illustrated History* (Alfred A. Knopf, 1990), pp. 178–81.

32. It would be a mistake to think that Lincoln's concern for emancipation was expressed only in his military measures directed at the South. As politician and president, he was engaged in many secret and overt measures for opposing slavery. Lawanda Cox lists eight of these:

1. In 1861, Lincoln secretly helped draft emancipation plans for Delaware.

2. In March of 1862, he submitted to Congress his plan for gradual manumission, after working on it "all by himself, no conference with his cabinet." He told Wendell Phillips this message was meant to lead to slavery's death, as a "drop of the crathur" [creature] leads an Irishman back to drunkenness.

3. In July of 1862, he submitted a bill for compensating states that would emancipate their slaves.

4. In December, his annual message encouraged Congress to draft an amendment to accomplish that end.

5. Early in 1863, he collaborated with those trying to bring Louisiana back into the Union on the basis of emancipation.

6. As part of the Louisiana effort, he issued his Amnesty and Reconstruction Proclamation.

7. Meanwhile, he collaborated with General Frederick Steele to bring Arkansas back by way of emancipation. (These efforts made it harder to strike any deals for reunion without emancipation, in case Lincoln had not been re-elected in 1864.)

8. When Congress stalled its consideration of what became the Thirteenth Amendment to receive a Southern commission, Lincoln indulged in one of his "economies" with the truth, telling Congress that no such commission was coming to Washington. (It was coming to Fortress Monroe, just outside the District.)

See Cox, "Lincoln and Black Freedom," in *The Historians' Lincoln*, edited by Gabor S. Boritt and Norman A. Fornes (University of Illinois Press, 1988), pp. 178–81.

33. Neeley, in *The Fate of Liberty*, makes a fine case that Lincoln's supposedly unconstitutional acts were fewer and less grave than is supposed. The book's only flaw comes from its author's belief that Lincoln, even in the First Inaugural, was "lacking a systematic ideology of nationalism" (p. 3). He leans more to the "mysticism" exploration of Lincoln's devotion to the Union than to Webster's constitutional approach to the Declaration of Independence. His case would be even stronger if he considered Lincoln's efforts to put down insurrection (which

included *all* his war measures) in conjunction with his preservation of the Constitution's slave provisions.

34. McPherson, *Abraham Lincoln*, pp. 23–42.

35. Robert Bork, *The Tempting of America: The Political Seduction of the Law* (Free Press, 1990), p. 37.

36. Willmoore Kendall, *The Basic Symbols of the American Political Tradition* (Louisiana State University Press, 1970), p. 91.

37. Ibid., p. 88.

38. Ibid., p. 84: "We can say that, in one fashion or another, every major presidential candidate in recent times has subscribed to it [the national commitment to equality]." Kendall calls this a "remarkable and frightening success" (p. 137).

5. Revolution in Style

1. Actually, Hemingway derived "all Modern American literature" from Twain's novel, but he seems to have been thinking of novels as coterminous with literature (*Green Hills of Africa* [Charles Scribner's Sons, 1935], p. 22).

2. Hugh Kenner, "Politics of the Plain Style," in *Mazes* (North Point Press, 1989), pp. 261–69.

3. Hay used the "Pike County" dialects that Twain also deployed. Hay regretted the change of his birthplace's original name to the more genteel Warsaw.

4. Hackett, an American who several times took his most famous role to Shakespeare's homeland, was "undoubtedly the best Falstaff of his time both in America and England" by the time Lincoln saw him play the role in the actor's sixties (*Dictionary of American Biography*, s.v. Hackett).

5. Robert V. Bruce, *Lincoln and the Tools of War* (University of Illinois Press, 1989), p. 14. Lincoln told Lewis Gallatin, the Harvard paleontologist, about this lecture during a White House visit, increasing the likelihood that he discussed it with Hay in their philological sessions. Cf. George Bancroft, *Literary and Historical Miscellanies* (Harper & Brothers, 1855), pp. 481–517.

6. Herndon says Lincoln labored to vary the length of his sentences, using Calhoun's speeches as models (Herndon-Weik, p. 421).

7. For Seward's role in the drafting of the First Inaugural, see Earl W. Wiley, "Abraham Lincoln: His Emergence as the Voice of the People," in William Norwood Brigance, *A History and Criticism of American Public Address* (McGraw-Hill, 1943), vol. 2, pp. 866–69.

8. SW 2.377, letter to General McClellan: "His route is the arc of a circle, while yours is the chord."

9. Hugh Blair, *Lectures on Rhetoric and Belles Lettres* (Edinburgh, 1783), in the facsimile edited by Harold F. Harding (Southern Illinois University Press, 1965), vol. 1, pp. 226, 189. For Blair's importance in nineteenth-century American rhetoric, see Brigance, *American Public Address*, vol. 2, pp. 202–4.

10. Herndon-Weik, p. 421.

11. Don E. Fehrenbacher, *Prelude to Greatness: Lincoln in the 1850s* (Stanford University Press, 1962), p. 180. Lincoln may have taken his Bible verse from Webster as well. Speaking on May 22, 1857, Webster said: "If a house be divided against itself, it will fall, and crush everybody in it." *Writings and Speeches of Daniel Webster* (Little, Brown, 1903), vol. 4, p. 244.

12. *The Papers of Daniel Webster: Speeches and Formal Writings*, vol. 1, *1800–1833*, edited by Charles Wiltse and Alan R. Berolzheimer (University Press of New England, 1986), p. 287.

13. Richard N. Current, "Lincoln and Daniel Webster," in *Speaking of Abraham Lincoln* (University of Illinois Press, 1983), pp. 11–15. Cf. Hertz, p. 118: "Lincoln thought that Webster's great speech in reply to Hayne was the very best speech that was ever delivered."

14. Blair, *Lectures*, pp. 232–36. Especially p. 236:

> But whether we practice inversion or not, and in whatever part of the sentences we dispose of the capital words, it is always a point of great moment that these capital words shall stand clear and disentangled from any other words that would clog them.

15. Twain's attitude toward "crash-words" is Blair's toward "capital words." Hank Morgan criticizes the King's swearing: "the profanity was not good, being awkwardly put together, and with the crash-word almost in the middle instead of at the end, where of course it ought to have been" (*A Connecticut Yankee in King Arthur's Court*, ch. 35).

16. Blair, *Lectures*, pp. 243–44.

17. Ibid., pp. 245–46. This is, of course, the classical view: "Rhetoric plays a counter part [a term from dance moves] to logic" (Aristotle, *Rhetoric* 354 1).

18. Herndon-Weik, p. 248. F. B. Carpenter, *The Inner Life of Abraham Lincoln: Six Months at the White House* (Riverside Press, 1877), pp. 314–15.

19. David C. Mearns, *Three Presidents and Their Books: Fifth Annual Windsor Lectures* (University of Illinois Press, 1955), p. 54. Mark Twain, known like Lincoln for his mastery of the vernacular, was nonetheless a stickler for grammar, and satirized Southern deficiencies in the matter (*Life on the Mississippi*, ch. 44, in *Mississippi Writings*, p. 489).

20. Herndon-Weik, p. 35.

21. Twain, Letter of Oct. 15, 1888.

22. Blair, *Lectures*, pp. 189, 195.

23. Twain, "William Dean Howells," in *Complete Essays*, edited by Charles Neider (Doubleday, 1963), pp. 400–401.

24. Herndon-Weik, pp. 475–77.

25. Attention to the real force of a word like "with" is characteristic of Blair's criticism:

> *With* expresses a more close and immediate connection, *by* a more remote one. We kill a man *with* a sword; he dies *by* violence. The criminal is bound

with ropes *by* the executioners. The proper distinction is elegantly marked
in a passage of Dr. Robertson's history of Scotland. When one of the old
Scottish kings was making an inquiry into the tenure *by* which his nobles
held their lands, they started up and drew their swords: *"By* these," said
they, "we acquired our lands, and *with* them we will defend them." [*Lectures*, p. 201.]

26. Parker, "The Political Destination of America," in Cobbe edition 4.91.
Twain would later rewrite in this spirit the "Battle Hymn of the Republic": "Christ
died to make men holy, He died to make *white* men free" (*Mark Twain's Fables
of Man*, edited by John S. Tuckey [University of California Press, 1972], p. 418).

27. Blair, *Lectures*, p. 186.

28. SW 2.357-58. I print the text as Charles N. Smiley did in *Classical
Journal* 13 (1917), pp. 125–26. Smiley, a classical rhetorician, counted in this letter
"six completely balanced sentences, eight cases of anaphora, six instances of similar
word endings [homoeoteleuton], six antitheses."

29. Bruce, *Tools of War*, pp. 85–88.

30. Samuel F. B. Morse just developed the code to be used on Henry's
transmitter: Robert V. Bruce, *The Launching of Modern American Science,
1846–76* (Alfred A. Knopf, 1987), pp. 141, 150–57, 275–76.

31. See the memoirs of the War Department's telegrapher, David Homer
Bates, *Lincoln in the Telegraph Office* (Century Co., 1907). By setting up telegraphic liaison with his generals, through Henry Halleck, Lincoln created what T.
Harry Williams has called the first "modern system of command for a modern
war," one "superior to anything achieved in Europe until von Moltke forged the
Prussian staff machine of 1865 and 1870" (*Lincoln and His Generals* [Vintage,
1952], pp. 302–3).

32. Lincoln used Haupt to circularize scientists for suggestions on war-
related research (Bruce, *Tools of War*, pp. 215–17). Haupt's reciprocal esteem for
Lincoln is expressed in the *Reminiscences of General Herman Haupt* (Wright and
Joys Co., 1901), pp. 297–301.

33. John Keegan, *The Mask of Command* (Penguin, 1987), p. 202.

34. James M. McPherson, "How Lincoln Won the War with Metaphors," in
Abraham Lincoln and the Second American Revolution (Oxford University Press,
1990), pp. 93–112. Not all the language McPherson adduces is metaphorical, but
it is all clear and most of it is brief.

35. For evidence of that accord, see *The Papers of Ulysses A. Grant*, edited
by John Y. Simon (Southern Illinois University Press), vol. 9 (1982), pp. 196–97;
vol. 10 (1982), p. 381; vol. 11 (1984), pp. 45, 263, 280, 360, 425, 441; vol. 12 (1984),
p. 185.

36. SW 2.620. Horace Potter, *Campaigning with Grant* (1897, reprinted by
Da Capo, 1986), p. 279.

37. Hannibal *Courier-Post*, March 1, 1835.

38. Francis B. Carpenter, *Six Months at the White House* (Riverside Press,
1877), p. 234.

39. Lane Cooper, the classicist, noted Lincoln's striking asyndeton in *The Rhetoric of Aristotle* (Appleton-Century, 1932), p. xxxiii.

40. Lincoln, conscious of the repeated "here," took out a seventh use in the phrase "they [here] gave the last full measure of devotion" (CW 7.23). The frequency of "that" in the speech was criticized by William E. Barton (*Lincoln at Gettysburg* [Bobbs-Merrill, 1930], p. 147).

41. Cf. Barton, *Lincoln at Gettysburg*, p. 148; Louis A. Warren, *Lincoln's Gettysburg Declaration* (Lincoln National Life Foundation, 1964), p. 106. Lincoln's fondness for the word "proposition" is apparent at SW 1.277, 683, 732, 741.

Epilogue: The Other Address

1. Theodore Parker, "The Nebraska Question" (1854), in Cobbe edition 5.276. Cf. ibid., p. 107, on "the Mexican war—a war mean and wicked even amongst wars," and ibid. 4.1–76.

2. Ulysses S. Grant, *Personal Memoirs* (Library of America, 1990), pp. 41, 42.

3. For Lincoln's embarrassing duel, see Herndon-Weik, p. 183.

4. Thucydides 3.82.3. The passage begins: "War, depriving people of their expected resources, is an instructor of violence, hardening men to match the conditions they face" (3.82.2).

5. Cf. Thucydides 3.82.4: "The settled currency of words for deeds was subjected to random bidding. Mindless dash was called 'the courage of comrades.' Prudent reserve was code for 'funk,' and moderation was no more than a cover for 'cowardice.' "

6. Cf. Thucydides 3.83.2: "Counterscheming became the universal resort. Since no solid policy or binding oath could be relied on, each person tried to cope with unpredictable violence by caring for his own safety rather than trusting anyone else."

7. Alan T. Nolan, *Lee Considered* (University of North Carolina Press, 1991), pp. 59–106.

8. Carl von Clausewitz, *On War*, edited and translated by Michael Howard and Peter Paret (Princeton University Press, 1976), 1.4 (p. 77). Cf. 2.2 (p. 138): "Even where there is no national hatred and no animosity to start with, fighting itself will stir up hostile feelings."

9. This is the title of Russell F. Weigley's chapter on Grant in *The American Way of War: A History of United States Military Strategy and Policy* (Indiana University Press, 1973), pp. 128–52. Grant first caught Lincoln's attention as a master of maneuver (at Vicksburg, a campaign the President called "one of the most brilliant in the world" [SW 2.449]). But his later, grinding procedures—what Lincoln called his "chew and choke" doggedness (SW 2.620)—made him "the most influential figure in the shaping of American strategic thought for the next hundred years, not always with fortunate results" (Weigley in *Makers of Modern*

Strategy: From Machiavelli to the Nuclear Age, edited by Peter Paret [Princeton University Press, 1986], p. 430).

10. Thucydides 2.63.

11. Clausewitz, *On War* 1.1.3 (p. 76), 2.2 (p. 138).

12. James McPherson, "Lincoln and the Strategy of Unconditional Surrender," in *Abraham Lincoln and the Second American Revolution* (Oxford University Press, 1990), p. 84: *"We must strike at the heart of the rebellion to inspire the army to strike more vigorous blows.* Here we have in a nutshell the rationale for emancipation as a military strategy of total war."

13. Edmund Wilson, *Patriotic Gore* (Oxford University Press, 1962), pp. xvii–xviii.

14. These words, from an interview with Quakers, resemble Lincoln's other messages to religious leaders, Presbyterians (SW 2.529–30) as well as Quakers (SW 2.627). See also SW 2.359, 586, 589.

15. For a contrast between Howe's and Lincoln's uses of the Bible, see Garry Wills, *Under God* (Simon and Schuster, 1990), pp. 207–21.

16. Cf. SW 2.520–21, 637–38. Some in the past attributed these proclamations to Seward, who was a cosigner of them (Roy Basler, *A Touchstone of Greatness* [Greenwood Press, 1973], pp. 88–89). But the stylistic arguments for this view—the use of doublings and biblical terms—work in favor of Lincoln's authorship. See, for instance, SW 2.319: "This proposal [voluntary emancipation] makes common cause for a common object. It acts not the pharisee. The change it contemplates would come gently as the dews of heaven, not rending or wrecking anything." The last sentence echoes Isaiah 45.8 (and therefore echoes Shakespeare's Portia).

Appendix I

1. For the newspaper accounts, cf. CW 7.18–21, SW 2.748–49. Gilbert's AP account ran in three New York papers *(Tribune, Times,* and *Herald)* and elsewhere. The other two accounts that approach a stenographic record were in the Chicago *Tribune* and Philadelphia *Inquirer.*

2. William E. Barton, *Lincoln at Gettysburg* (Bobbs-Merrill, 1930), pp. 81–82, 85. Barton's account of the various copies is frequently inaccurate.

3. John G. Nicolay, "Lincoln's Gettysburg Address," *Century Magazine,* vol. 47 (n.s. 25, 1893–94), pp. 604–5.

4. Daniel C. Mearns and Lloyd A. Dunlap, Introduction to *Long Remembered: Facsimiles of the Five Versions of the Gettysburg in the Handwriting of Abraham Lincoln* (Library of Congress, 1963). The evidence for the drafts is most compendiously assembled and discussed in this booklet.

5. It is true that Lincoln wrote extraordinarily clean first drafts of his legal

briefs, which were not meant for publication or verbatim delivery. But for important public papers, and especially for presidential statements, there were tentative drafts later corrected—e.g., the House Divided Speech (tried out on friends), the First Inaugural (corrected with Seward's help), the Emancipation Proclamation (too messy to donate to a charity event).

6. Nicolay seems to have understood the difficulty in his claim that Lincoln used this as a delivery text, yet said so many things that departed from it. (I have only mentioned the three major differences, not minor ones like "on this continent" for "upon this continent," which could be transcriptional variants by the copyists.) Nicolay claims to have seen that Lincoln held the paper as a mere prop while he recited the Address *from memory*. He says those not as close to Lincoln as he, Nicolay, was might have received the impression he was reading ("Lincoln's Gettysburg Address," p. 602). But David Wills, sitting even closer than Nicolay, said he was reading (Wills article quoted in *Lincoln Lore* 1437). So did the New York *Tribune* correspondent, most emphatically: "I can say most positively that Mr. Lincoln read from manuscript" (*Tribune*, May 19, 1882). No one but Nicolay claims that Lincoln was not reading, and Nicolay must be *inferring* that from his assumption that the draft he possessed was the delivery text. Yet even this assumption does not solve his own problem, for why would Lincoln not hold the same text he had memorized? Nicolay meets that problem with a further supposition—that Lincoln had not only memorized a text, but memorized one he had substantially revised in his head during the four hours between his exiting Mr. Wills's door and his standing to speak. Nicolay has the air of one bluffing in the careful sentence that tries to slip this by us:

> The changes may have been prompted by the oratorical impulse of the moment; but it is more likely that in the interval of four hours occupied by coming to the grounds, and the delivery of Mr. Everett's oration, he fashioned the phrases anew in his silent thought, and had them ready for use when he rose to speak.

("Lincoln's Gettysburg Address," p. 604.) The desperate nature of Nicolay's case is demonstrated by his claim that Lincoln needed the help of the newspaper to re-create his own short speech!

7. I examined the pencilings under a magnifying glass at the Library of Congress. The other two with me—including John Sellers of the Library of Congress manuscript division—agreed that the pencil used in the underlining (if that is what it is) was of a sharper, harder lead than the rather blunt one used for the deletion stroke right after it in the text. The latter stroke goes with the writing on the second page.

8. Telegram of Nov. 13, 1863, in Curtin's papers at the Harrisburg State Archives building.

9. *Lincoln Lore* 1437.

10. Library of Congress manuscript room.

11. Massachusetts Historical Society.

12. Abraham Lincoln Papers, Library of Congress.

13. Curtin correspondence, Pennsylvania Archives.

14. Everett diary, Nov. 11, 1863: "It is necessary to have it [Everett's own speech] printed before hand to prevent its being mutilated & travestied by the Reporters, who, under pretense of giving what 'Mr. E. said,' put down a good many things he did not say, & omit a great many which he did, after rendering the whole in a dialect of their own." (Massachusetts Historical Society. Cf. entry for Oct. 29.) Everett's attitude is the normal one for politicians—and far more likely to have been Lincoln's attitude than is the claim of Nicolay that he learned what he had said from the reporters.

15. The Little, Brown text resembles the newspaper account on these points:

a. "We are met to dedicate" for "We have come to dedicate"
b. "the final resting place" for "a final resting place"
c. "our power" (in Gilbert and Hale) for "our poor power"

But it differs from Gilbert in printing "government of the people" for "Governments of the people" and "unfinished" for "refinished." It differs even more from Hale in printing "The world will little note" (not "very little") and "the dead shall not have died in vain" (not "these dead"). These last variants are important, in that Everett would probably have used Hale's account if he had relied on newspapers, since Hale's dispatch appeared in the Boston *Daily Advertiser,* to which Everett had entrusted his own speech for setting.

16. The Little, Brown "authorized edition" of the events, paid for by the cemetery committee, and used to raise money for the monument in Saunders's scheme, is given this title, thanks to Everett's supervision of the publication: *Address of Honorable Edward Everett at the Consecration of the National Cemetery at Gettysburg 19th November, 1863, with the Dedication Speech of President Lincoln and the Other Exercises of the Occasion.* (I consulted the copies of this eighty-eight-page book in the Illinois State Library.)

17. The history of Everett's manuscript can be traced in some detail. He wrote in his diary on Nov. 13: "I spent a considerable part of the day in revising my account of the battle, under the light of General Meade's Report." He had to complete these revisions that day because he wrote in the following entry:

Sent the manuscript of the Address to the Office of the Daily Advertiser, in which it fills 6-¼ columns & received back proof-sheets of the whole by 5 o'clock in the afternoon, as well & correctly set up, and the proofs after my corrections as clear as any that ever passed through my hands, I think a little clearer. It is true most of the manuscript,—that of a copyist,—was in the best possible condition of legibility.

Thus there were three versions, at least, of his speech:

1. A first draft, which took no account of General Meade's battle report. (Meade had sent a short private account to him.)

2. A revised version, taking Meade's report into account—either by alterations on the original pages or by new pages for the parts of the text affected.

3. A copyist's clean version of—which? Number 1 above, or Number 2? The whole of a revised text would have been hard to copy in time to get the text to the printer on the next day. Everett says that "most of the manuscript" was done by the copyist. Presumably he had a copyist preparing the manuscript as he completed parts of it—he complains of the tight schedule if he was to get the text printed before he left for Gettysburg. The alterations he made on the day before printing were probably in his own hand—which means that the printer would have been sent parts of Number 1 (in the copyist's hand) *and* Number 2 (still in Everett's hand).

4. At Gettysburg, Everett had galleys of his speech set up for the newspaper, but he also had a text of stacked pages he put on the stand before him, to be ostentatiously ignored. That was probably the copyist's clean text, supplemented by his own revisions of the battle description—a text he could refresh his memory from just before delivery.

5. Last, there is the text he bound up for Mrs. Fish's auction—which seems to be none of the above, though it is the only surviving copy in Everett's hand. It is, as he says in the introduction, a text that existed before his revisions based on the published Meade report—it contains two passages that show up nowhere else. (See appendix III A, notes 21 and 24.) Yet it is not the composition draft. It is clean, its corrections are of the copyist's sort, it gets looser and less careful as it goes along. There are none of the corrections of Number 2 above, yet it is in his own hand, not that of the copyist (Number 3). It is on pages not in any way soiled, crumpled, or fingered, as any prior text must have been. It appears that Everett made a fresh copy of his own first draft (which was messy, as we know, because he used a copyist to prepare the printer's copy). His own first drafts have not survived, which suggests that he might take no greater care of Lincoln's copy sent him by Wills.

18. One can tell that the printed text comes from book pages, not galleys, because loose glue in places reveals text on the other side. The printed text, cut from the Little, Brown book, differs slightly from the text included in Everett's *Collected Orations*. A critical edition of Everett's speech, noting all variants, is much to be desired.

19. There is actually an eighth "here" in the Hay text ("We are met here on a great battle-field").

Appendix II

1. The photographs, in the Library of Congress collection, are by an unknown photographer (or photographers). They are discussed (though fuzzily reproduced) as numbers II-15 and II-16 in William A. Frassanito's *Gettysburg: A Journey in Time* (Charles Scribner's Sons, 1975), pp. 118–21.

Appendix III

1. Nelson W. Aldrich, Jr., *Old Money: The Mythology of America's Upper Class* (Alfred A. Knopf, 1988), p. 154.

2. See for instance, John Finley, who calls the Pericles oration an "analysis of democracy" that "would seem to have no equal unless it be the Gettysburg Address" (*Thucydides* [Harvard University Press, 1942], pp. 144–45). For the interconnectedness of imperialism and democracy in Athens, see Charles W. Fornara and Loren J. Samons II, *Athens from Cleisthenes to Pericles* (University of California Press, 1991).

3. Paul Mellon was a link between Hamilton, Cairns, and the Kennedys. See Arthur M. Schlesinger, Jr., *Robert Kennedy and His Times* (Houghton Mifflin, 1978), pp. 617–19, S38; Eric N. Lindquist, *The Origins of the Center for Hellenic Studies* (Princeton University Press, 1990), pp. 6–13.

4. Thomas Cole, *The Origins of Rhetoric In Ancient Greece* (The Johns Hopkins University, 1991), p. 78.

5. Charles N. Smiley, "Lincoln and Gorgias," *Classical Journal* 13 (1917), pp. 124–28.

6. The text is taken from Everett, *Orations and Speeches on Various Occasions*, vol. 4 (Little, Brown, 1868). Everett corrected his text with later information when he republished it in this form. Since he delivered it from memory at Gettysburg, it is not known how much he departed from his original text, though he says he shortened it drastically to meet his two-hour time limit (Diary, Nov. 19).

7. Subheads are added for the reader's convenience, and the paragraphs are numbered for ease of reference.

8. Everett is making an implicit comparison to the separate burial sites for those from different states at Gettysburg, and to the section for the unknown dead.

9. Milton, *Paradise Regained* 4.244–46. Milton was the poet Everett liked best, cited most, and—according to Emerson—made especially musical whenever he recited any lines from him.

10. Everett is making Marathon, not the Kerameikos, the true classical parallel to Gettysburg, since the Americans, too, are buried where they fell. (Arlington would later become the American Kerameikos for burying the military dead no matter where they died.)

11. For Everett's pilgrimage to Greece during his period of classical studies for the doctorate at Göttingen, see his search for Troy and Thermopylae described in *Orations and Speeches*, vol. 1 (1856), p. 359.

12. Horace, Odes 3.2.13: *"Dulce et decorum est pro patria mori."*

13. The first invasion of the North had ended at the Battle of Antietam in Maryland (Sept. 17, 1862).

14. The monumental city was Baltimore, famed for its monuments to Washington (the first in America) and to the War of 1812.

15. The horse with the thunderous mane is from Job (39.19)—the same horse who says "Ha, ha" (39.25).

16. News of Grant's victory at Vicksburg reached Washington with that of the Gettysburg outcome. The appropriateness of the date made Lincoln remember how both Adams and Jefferson had died on the same Fourth of July. It was just as fitting that "on the 4th the cohorts of those who opposed the declaration that all men are created equal 'turned tail' and run" (SW 2.475–76).

17. "More than thirty years ago"—i.e., at the time of the Nullification controversy of the early 1830s.

18. Leroy P. Walker of Alabama, the Confederate secretary of war, was an unbalanced man who resigned by Sept. of 1861.

19. Respect for Lee makes Everett include him among "the responsible chiefs of the rebellion" of paragraph 9, who mainly execute (rather than create) the design to seize the federal government. See notes 21 and 24 below for the way Everett deleted criticism of Lee from his first draft.

20. Everett overestimates the enemy's strength, in time-honored fashion (cf. Thucydides on the Spartan claims in #39 of appendix II B). See note 26 below.

21. In the copy of Everett's draft contained in the Fish presentation volume (see appendix I), there is an additional passage:

> It is difficult to see, in these vagrant excursions of Ewell's divisions and Stuart's cavalry the Mars of that eminent skill which is claimed for the rebel general. They had the effect, it is true, of spreading alarm through the country and harassing the unarmed population; but they did not deceive the Union Commander, as to what must be his main objects, if he had in reality any well-conceived plan of operations, which is doubtful. The utmost he could expect to accomplish was to attack this separate corps of Hooker's army before they could be concentrated, and then, if seconded by fortune, descend upon Baltimore and Washington. General Lee, however, states that his objects in directing the raids in Carlisle and York were to keep the Union army East of the mountains, and preserve his own communications with Virginia.

22. Even Lee's sympathetic biographer admits Lee's lack of planning at Gettysburg, blaming it on the loss of intelligence incurred by sending Jeb Stuart's cavalry off on its own (Douglas Southall Freeman, *R. E. Lee: A Biography* [Charles Scribner's Sons], vol. 3 [1935], pp. 68, 147–48).

23. "Devoted" means "marked for sacrifice," the classical sense still evident in Lincoln's phrase "the last full measure of devotion." See OED, s.v. "devotion" 4.

24. Another extra paragraph in the Fish volume at Springfield:

> General Lee states, in his report, that he had not intended to fight a general battle so far from his base. But when one considers that Genl.

Meade's army was between him and Baltimore and Washington, the main objects of his campaign, that his base was in Virginia, by the line of the Cumberland Valley, from which he was emerging by the Chambersburg road, it is not very apparent when he could have expected to fight a battle nearer his base, as every day's march carried him farther from it.

25. Everett does not say that he also had the unpublished reports of Meade's staff.

26. Shelby Foote gives the figures on this day as 50,000 effective troops and 272 guns for the South, 80,000 effectives and 354 guns for the North. *The Civil War: A Narrative: Fredericksburg to Meridian* (Vintage, 1986), p. 497.

27. Lee met with reluctance from his generals on the left of his line (Ewell) and on the right (Longstreet), and put up with it. Frustration at this long delay probably contributed to his stubborn *precipitancy* on the next day. (Freeman, *R. E. Lee*, pp. 92–93, 160.)

28. Sickles fell contending for "the peach orchard" under the two Round Tops.

29. It has been argued that Lincoln added "under God" to his Address after hearing the words "under Providence" in this sentence. That argument assumes that "under God" was not in Lincoln's delivery text—but see appendix I.

30. Though not as infamous as Andersonville would become, Libby Prison of Richmond was the earliest subject of complaint about mistreatment of captured Union soldiers. (William B. Hesseltine, *Civil War Prisons* [Ohio State University Press, 1930], pp. 114–32. See the further reference to Southern treatment of prisoners in paragraph 49.)

31. Lincoln had to sit and listen to this favorable treatment of Meade, derived in large part from Meade himself. Meade had voted for Everett's ticket over Lincoln's in 1860. Lincoln's own judgment, expressed in his unsent letter to Meade, was very different:

> You fought and beat the enemy at Gettysburg; and, of course, to say the least, his loss was as great as yours. He retreated; and you did not, as it seemed to me, pressingly pursue him; but a flood in the river detained him, till, by slow degrees, you were again upon him. You had at least twenty thousand veteran troops directly with you, and as many more raw ones within supporting distance, all in addition to those who fought with you at Gettysburg; while it was not possible that he had received a single recruit; and yet you stood and let the flood run down, bridges be built, and the enemy move away at his leisure, without attacking him. [SW 2.478–79]

Lincoln's secretaries reflected his attitude when they described Meade in pursuit after Gettysburg: "with the utmost caution, [he] advanced inch by inch" (John G. Nikolay and John Hay, *Abraham Lincoln: A History* [Century Co.], vol. 7 [1890], p. 275). Actually, Lincoln understated the case against Meade, who had roughly a hundred thousand troops to Lee's fifty thousand at this point, and Lee had run almost out of ammunition and food (Foote, *The Civil War*, p. 594).

32. This is one of two passages in Everett's speech that Lincoln praised: "The tribute to our noble women for their angel-ministering to the suffering soldiers, surpasses, in its way, as do the subjects of it, whatever has gone before" (SW 2.537).

33. Everett singles out one orator and one martyr from each of the British revolutions of the eighteenth century, against Charles I and James II. In the first, John Pym (c. 1583–1643) led in Parliament and John Hampden (1594–1643) died in battle. In the second, William Russell (1639–83) was executed and John Somers (1651–1716) helped complete the Glorious Revolution. Everett was an Anglophile who had been America's minister to the Court of St. James's. Comparing the Confederate rebellion to the British revolutions was as intolerable to him as, for Edmund Burke, was any comparison of those events with the French Revolution.

34. In antiquity, Plutarch had begun his *Parallel Lives* with the biographies of the founders of the Greek and Roman states. It became a commonplace to put such "founders" first in any list of the benefactors of mankind—the origin of the cult of "the fathers" that Everett and Lincoln shared with most of their contemporaries.

35. This is the other passage Lincoln singled out for praise in Everett's address: "The point made against the theory of the general government being only an agency, whose principals are the States, was new to me, and as I think, is one of the best arguments for the national supremacy" (SW 2.537).

36. This appeal to South Carolina's patriots of '76 imitates one of the most eloquent passages in Webster's Second Reply to Hayne, a speech in which Everett collaborated.

37. A reference to Everett's opposition to Lincoln and the Republicans before the firing on Sumter.

38. William C. Quantrill was a Confederate guerrilla raider who terrorized Union sympathizers in Kansas and Missouri. Cf. Foote, *The Civil War*, pp. 704–6, on his "three hour orgy of killing" in Lawrence, Kansas.

39. For starvation in Libby, see note 30 above.

40. "The hour is coming and now is": cf. Gospel of John 16.32, "Behold, the hour cometh, yea, is now come."

41. As an Anglophile, Everett had often closed his orations on Revolutionary War battlefields with a memory of the things America still had in common with the mother country after separating itself from her. Southerners could have appealed to those passages if their rebellion had succeeded. But the bonds on this continent were even closer, as Everett is justified in arguing.

42. Everett again imitates Webster's Second Reply to Hayne. Cf. ch. 4.

43. "It is good to be here" echoes Peter at the spot where Jesus was transfigured—Matthew 17.4: "Lord, it is good for us to be here" (cf. Mark 9.5).

44. John Reynolds, "whom many considered not only the highest ranking but the best general in the army" (Foote, *The Civil War*, p. 468), was directing the defense of McPherson Ridge in the first stages of the battle at Gettysburg when he was shot through the head by a sniper. The reference to "the wondering ploughman" echoes Vergil's *Georgics* 1.493–97:

Then, after length of time, the labouring swains,
Who turn the turfs of those unhappy plains,
Shall rusty piles from the ploughed furrows take,
And over empty helmets pass the rake—
Amazed at antique titles on the stones,
And mighty relics of gigantic bones.
                 —DRYDEN TRANSLATION

This is more apt than most of Everett's classical allusions, since his audience had seen rain and hogs as well as farmers turn up shallowly buried bodies in the months preceding this address, and tourists would still be finding bullets and bits of gear at the site almost a century later.

45. See appendix III B.

46. "Down to the latest period of recorded time" is an echo of Lincoln's favorite play: "To the last syllable of recorded time" (*Macbeth* 5.5.21). Cf. Lincoln's own eulogy to Clay (1852): "His memory will endure to the last syllable of recorded time" (SW 1.260).

47. I translate the text established by J. S. Rusten, *Thucydides: The Peloponnesian War, Book II* (Cambridge University Press, 1989). The endless debate over Thucydides' adherence to what Pericles actually said in 431 B.C.E. has an interesting parallel, for American historians, in the "Liberty or Death" speech of Patrick Henry of 1775 as reported in William Wirt's *Sketches of the Life and Character of Patrick Henry* (1817). Most scholars think Thucydides completed work on the speech of Pericles after the Peloponnesian War ended in 404—almost thirty years after the speech was delivered. Wirt began collecting reports of the Henry speech in 1805—exactly thirty years after *that* speech was delivered. The arguments for both men's fidelity to such a well-remembered speech are remarkably similar. Moses Coit Tyler wrote, in *Patrick Henry* (1898):

> Wirt's version certainly gives the substance of the speech as actually made by Patrick Henry on the occasion named, and, for the form of it, Wirt seems to have gathered testimony from all available living witnesses, and then, from such sentences or snatches of sentences as these witnesses could remember, as well as from his own conception of the orator's method of expression, to have constructed the record which he handed down to us. [Pp. 150–51.]

Compare that with Thucydides' description of his own method:

> As for the words used about the war, in its preliminary stage or as it was fought, it was difficult to recover a verbatim memory of what was said—both for me, when I had heard it, and for those reporting to me from other places; but I judge that each speaker would have said what was generally [*malista*] called for [*deonta*] by the situation (whatever that was), given the policy [*gnōmē*] that was actually being advanced at the time [1.22].

Both men, therefore, balance their knowledge of what is reported with what they know of the speaker and his situation. But both writers were also influenced by their own view of the war they were describing and interpreting. Both are highly didactic writers. They also appear, on the face of it, to be idealizing their speakers (though with Thucydides this may be no more than an appearance). The grounds for trust are similar in each case, as well as for misgiving. But Wirt's text can be compared with other writings of Henry (a thing impossible with Pericles)—and a computer study of the language indicates that much of the vocabulary and syntax of the Henry speech probably comes from Wirt's principal informant on the 1775 event, St. George Tucker. Cf. Stephen T. Olsen, "Patrick Henry's 'Liberty or Death' Speech: A Study in Disputed Authorship," in *American Rhetoric: Context and Criticism*, edited by Thomas W. Benson (Southern Illinois University Press, 1989), pp. 19–66.

48. This opening paragraph is drawn in many directions by clever antitheses.

a. There is a double contrast of the one and the many: Many praise the (one) man who added the speech, but I (Pericles) am *one* who does not; because it makes the credibility of *many* men's acts depend on the eloquence of *one* speech.

b. Ordinance from without *(nomos)* is contrasted with inherent natural traits *(physis)*—i.e., the added rite with the bravery already recognized.

c. Words must not only match the deeds of the heroes (the normal problem alluded to in Epitaphioi) but the expectations of the hearers based on each one's information and disposition.

On this latter point, Pericles is made to suggest endless difficulties. He mentions only two cases, but they obviously stand by synecdoche for many possible permutations:

The informed and well-disposed man can have one or other of his qualifications (information or disposition) offended—satisfying only one will not make the speaker succeed, even with this single hearer.

The uninformed may also be disappointed. Naming only one attribute, in this case, is shorthand. The other (disposition) can also be offended. In fact, there is no reason to think the informed is always well-disposed, or vice versa. There are at least four different categories of hearers implied in this scheme: the informed and well-disposed, the informed but ill-disposed, the uninformed and well-disposed, and the uninformed and ill-disposed. No wonder Pericles says he can only hope to strike a balance of some sort with the audience as a collection of minds with different degrees of information and emotion, with different degrees of support for or opposition to those praised and the one praising. He is addressing not only what each one thinks and wants but what each wants to think or thinks he wants!

What is going on here? Pericles is, after all, delivering a eulogy to heroes in front of patriots. Why should they be disposed to question the men's exploits? Most speakers in such a situation know they are given license to praise without misgiving. Not speaking ill of the dead *(de mortuis nil nisi bonum)* is a rule usually observed at funerals—and certainly at state funerals for defenders of their country.

Some have thought Thucydides is describing his *own* problems as a historian in winning assent to the verisimilitude *(dokēsis tēs alētheias)* of his account, and compare this to his wooing of the reader's assent when he says he tested what happened by challenging the memory and disposition *(eunoia*—cf. *eunous* in the Pericles speech) of his informants (1.22). But why would Thucydides attribute to Pericles' audience the supposed resistance of his own readers? He is writing a long account of a complex part of history (three decades' worth). Pericles is offering praise in a limited situation where everyone can be counted on to be uncritical.

Thucydides makes Pericles create difficulties for himself to signal that he (Pericles) is going to make some outlandish claims in his speech—things that are (and should be) "dumbfounding." Though he claims this is done only as a form of praise for the dead, the conception of power attributed to the city is in fact startling and disturbing. Contrast it with the conventions expressed in Gorgias' fashionable antitheses, which are intended "neither to offend the gods nor to incite human envy" (appendix III C). Thucydides may be agnostic about offending the gods, but what his Pericles says will clearly stir human resentment—especially since Pericles expressly mentions that he speaks to the outsiders present.

49. "I make the ancestors my opening theme": Pericles uses a formula from the poets—as, later, he says he has "hymned" the city.

50. The meiosis of "no little labors" invests the historical generation with mythical "labors" like those of Herakles.

51. The first of several claims to self-sufficiency (see notes 54, 55, 57, 58, 59)—a mockery of all the cities whose tribute Athens relied on. Pericles has omitted the customary praise of mythical forebears to make the audacious claim that the *greatest* Athenians are the contemporary empire builders.

52. By emphasizing the presence of outsiders, Thucydides makes us listen to Athenian boasts as they would receive them.

53. An artful sentence. It does not specify the mechanism for promoting merit (election), but suggests, against the facts of the time, that election benefits principally the deserving poor. Pericles answers critics of democracy who disliked sortition (appointment by lot) by saying the lot is not the only thing used (though he leaves vague the sphere of election as opposed to lot). Plato objected to elections as well as sortition, since he thought only the virtuous know how to choose the virtuous. In his own Epitaphios, he reduces Pericles' claim to absurdity by saying autochthony makes all Athenians equally noble in birth, so the government will be an aristocracy no matter who is promoted. In his jingle, *isogonia* (equality of birth) insures *isonomia* (equality of rule). *(Menexenus* 238d–239a. Cf. Gregory Vlastos, *"Isonomia Politikē,"* in *Platonic Studies* [Princeton University Press, 1973], pp. 188–201.)

54. "Through our empire"—i.e., "because of the greatness of the city."

Pericles calls Athens self-sufficient in that it makes its very own *(oikeioteron)* what belongs to others.

55. "We unaccompanied": It was the policy of Pericles to make dependent cities contribute money, not military manpower, in order to maintain a monopoly on force within the empire. Cf. Plutarch, *Pericles* 12.3, with Thucydides 1.99.

56. The contrast of Spartan system *(nomoi)* with Athenian natural gifts *(tropoi)* is part of a general polarization of the cities in terms of *nomos* versus *physis*. What Pericles praised as a gift for spontaneity and improvising, restive subject-cities called an impulsiveness that "will not let themselves—or any others—stay at rest" (1.70.9). The "dumbfounding" aspect of the city is ridiculed by Plato, who has Socrates confess that Epitaphioi not only make him feel ten feet tall, but dazzle those around him into thinking him bigger and more impressive and— shrewdest touch for Socrates, of all people—"rather handsome" *(kallion)*. (*Menexenus* 235a–b. Cf. Nicole Loraux, *The Invention of Athens: The Funeral Oration in the Classical City*, translated by Alan Sheridan [Harvard University Press, 1986], pp. 311–12.)

57. Pericles' critics did not think his refinements economical, since he paid for them with the dependent cities' tribute (Plutarch, *Pericles* 12), and things like the great gold-and-ivory statue of the Parthenon supposedly tempted his friend Pheidias to embezzlement (Aristophanes, *Peace* 605–6).

58. A fourth claim to self-sufficiency—made possible by the tribute money of the dependent cities.

59. In fact, every Athenian citizen is *individually* self-sufficient. (Pericles' critics claimed he made the citizens *dependent* on paid public service like jury duty.)

60. "Genius": again, the natural *tropoi* that precede all *nomoi*.

61. Repeated emphasis on the unique *(monē)* nature of the city makes some people overlook the effrontery of this claim, before "outsider" members of the empire, that they can (justly) feel no humiliation in submission.

62. "power to help or to harm"—this naked claim of power to do good *or ill* has made Periclean sympathizers over the ages try to alter the text. The boast, at a time when Attica had just been ravaged by Sparta, that *all* other places were open to Athenian incursion (including, presumably, Sparta) is one of the things whose verisimilitude, Pericles admitted, would be hard to establish.

63. This is one of the more strained uses of the *logos-ergon* contrast that runs throughout the speech. Adam Parry counted thirty-two uses of the device in this oration (*Logos and Ergon in Thucydides*, 1957 Harvard dissertation printed by Ayer Company, p. 159; on its use in this sentence, see pp. 167–70).

64. "The rich soldier . . . left us," all one sentence in Greek, is called by Hellmut Flashar "probably the most difficult sentence in Thucydides' history." Some misunderstandings of it can be obviated if one recognizes that the opening stress on rich and poor extends to the commercial imagery implicit in words like *timōreisthai* and *ephiesthai*.

65. Most translators and commentators treat this sentence as if the lovers were "smitten" with the *city*, though "the city's *power*" is the proper antecedent. The language of being "smitten" *(erastēs)* with "the people" is the mark of a demagogue in Aristophanes (*Acharnians* 143; *Knights* 732–34, 1340–44).

66. I omit "not" from "his lot might improve," as Rusten suggests.

67. Since, by his own doctrine, Pericles should not talk much of women, this mention (omitted in other Epitaphioi) is curt. Rusten confutes efforts to soften the sexist reference to women's (inferior) nature.

68. I translate the text given in Hermann Diels and Walther Kranz, *Die Fragmente der Vorsokratiker* (Weidmann, 1960), vol. 2, pp. 285–86. The date could be anytime from 427 B.C.E. (when Gorgias first visited Athens) to 376 (when he died). In the absence of other indicators I suggest c. 400, around the time of the Thucydides Epitaphios, which seems to have been influenced by Gorgias (or to have influenced him). These two put more emphasis than do the other authors of Epitaphioi on human envy, opposition to *nomoi*, response to challenge, menace to foes, and human foibles ("licit passions").

69. This is the text Everett arranged for Little, Brown to print. For reasons to consider it the closest to Lincoln's spoken text, see appendix I. I have added applause notations from the trustworthy Associated Press report of Joseph L. Gilbert.

70. This is the so-called Bliss text, the last from Lincoln's hand, used as the standard text throughout this book.

Indexes

Index to the Gettysburg Address

Index to Other Major Lincoln Texts

Index

PHOTO CREDITS